Watermelon Democracy

Modern Intellectual and Political History of the Middle East
Fred H. Lawson, *Series Editor*

Select Titles in Modern Intellectual and Political History of the Middle East

Emirate, Egyptian, Ethiopian: Colonial Experiences in Late Nineteenth-Century Harar
Avishai Ben-Dror

Hakibbutz Ha'artzi, Mapam, and the Demise of the Israeli Labor Movement
Tal Elmaliach; Haim Watzman, trans.

National Elections in Turkey: People, Politics, and the Party System
F. Michael Wuthrich

National Symbols in Modern Iran: Identity, Ethnicity, and Collective Memory
Menahem Merhavy

Ottoman Rule of Law and the Modern Political Trial: The Yıldız Case
Avi Rubin

The Revolt of the Young: Essays by Tawfīq al-Hakim
Mona Radwan, trans.

Shaykh Yūsuf al-Qaraḍāwī: Spiritual Mentor of Wasaṭī *Salafism*
Sagi Polka

Why Alliances Fail: Islamist and Leftist Coalitions in North Africa
Matt Buehler

For a full list of titles in this series, visit https://press.syr.edu/supressbook-series/modern-intellectual-and-political-history-of-the-middle-east/.

Watermelon Democracy

Egypt's Turbulent Transition

Joshua Stacher

Syracuse University Press

Syracuse, New York 13244-5290

First Edition 2020

20 21 22 23 24 25 6 5 4 3 2 1

∞ The paper used in this publication meets the minimum requirements of the American National Standard for Information Sciences—Permanence of Paper for Printed Library Materials, ANSI Z39.48-1992.

For a listing of books published and distributed by Syracuse University Press, visit https://press.syr.edu.

ISBN: 978-0-8156-3677-9 (hardcover)
978-0-8156-3687-8 (paperback)
978-0-8156-5500-8 (e-book)

Library of Congress Cataloging-in-Publication Data

Names: Stacher, Joshua, 1975– author.
Title: Watermelon democracy : Egypt's turbulent transition / Joshua Stacher.
Description: First edition. | Syracuse, New York : Syracuse University Press, 2020. | Series: Modern intellectual and political history of the Middle East | Includes bibliographical references and index. | Summary: ""Watermelon Democracy" works from the premise that the 2011 uprising in Egypt and subsequent violent repression emerged from deep patterns in that country's modern history. By examining four aspects of the uprising, and juxtaposing actual events with findings in the literature, Stacher aims to explain aspects of the Egyptian case that the theoretical literature cannot"— Provided by publisher.
Identifiers: LCCN 2019058554 (print) | LCCN 2019058555 (ebook) | ISBN 9780815636779 (hardcover) | ISBN 9780815636878 (paperback) | ISBN 9780815655008 (ebook)
Subjects: LCSH: Authoritarianism—Egypt. | Political participation—Egypt. | Political violence—Egypt. | Egypt—Politics and government—2011– | Egypt—History—Protests, 2011–2013.
Classification: LCC DT107.88 .S73 2020 (print) | LCC DT107.88 (ebook) | DDC 962.05/5—dc23
LC record available at https://lccn.loc.gov/2019058554
LC ebook record available at https://lccn.loc.gov/2019058555

Manufactured in the United States of America

To Kimmy, Eli, and Noah
May you always read passionately, think clearly,
and express yourself fearlessly.
May you fight for and win a borderless world,
with equality and dignity for all.

Contents

Illustrations

Preface

A Watermelon Democracy

According to my field notes for December 2, 2005, in the middle of the night Samer Shehata and I are standing in the Nile Delta city of Mansoura. It is cold but Egypt-cold, not Cleveland-cold. Samer and I are researching the third round of the parliamentary elections and have come to Mansoura to follow the campaigns of two Muslim Brotherhood candidates, Yusri Hani and Sabr Zahir. We have been there for a few days. All the Brotherhood members are sleeping in places other than their homes because seventy-four people from the group in the governorate of al-Daqahliyya had been arrested in recent days before the third round began.

In the first two rounds, the Muslim Brotherhood had won 76 of the Parliament's 308 elected seats (24 percent). Another 136 parliamentary seats were to be contested in a third round of voting. The intelligentsia, political onlookers, and media commentators are wondering if the Brotherhood will crack 100 seats in the National Democratic Party–dominated Parliament. Even if they failed to win another seat, they had already far surpassed the 17 seats they won in 2000. The head of the Brotherhood's outgoing parliamentary bloc, a gruff politician named Muhammad Mursi, is running for reelection in Zagazig about sixty-five kilometers away from Mansoura.

Although control of the People's Assembly (Maglis al-Sha'b) is not in doubt, Egyptians and researchers have never seen opposition representation like what the Brotherhood earned in the first two rounds of the 2005 parliamentary elections. For round three, the security and intelligence services change their approach, tightening their grip—a skill they have honed over the years. The Brotherhood will go on to win 12 seats in the third round for a total of 88 seats, or 20 percent of Parliament. The elections feel like a historic breakthrough, but Husni Mubarak's regime remains in firm control. There are clashes and lots of tear gas, but the mobilization never outpaces the regime's security preparations to contain it. The number of Brotherhood members winning parliamentary seats is new, but the atmosphere feels normal. A national uprising or revolutionary push from below seems unimaginable despite the injustices on display.

After all, earlier in September Mubarak (1928–2020) had just won another six-year term in Egypt's first multicandidate presidential election. And few conversations about politics take place without reference to the rumors that Mubarak's son Gamal is eyeing the presidency. Everyone seems to be bracing for a hereditary succession like Syria witnessed in June 2000. While a few regarded the potential presidency of Gamal Mubarak positively, the overwhelming majority are either silenced by embarrassment or incensed at the prospect. Some say, "We are not chattel to be inherited," while others invoke the hopeful logic that "this is a republic, not a monarchy" will prevent it from happening.

This year has also seen weekly protests by a grassroots group called the Egyptian Movement for Change, or Kifaya. Dozens of spin-off groups are appearing and disappearing from the scene. Labor mobilizations are also starting to take off as the social costs of recent economic reforms—reforms made by a cabinet led by Prime Minister Ahmad Nazif but widely regarded as "Gamal's cabinet"—begin to be felt. Gamal Mubarak refuses to say the word "democracy" or deny that he seeks the presidency, which only fuels conspiracy theories (though these theories are supported by an increasing amount of circumstantial evidence).

In Mansoura that night, we are gathered with well over a thousand people waiting for the ballots to be counted and the results to be announced. Everyone knows the opposition cannot win and the regime is rigging the vote. But this does not stop the hearty few from registering their presence. Earlier that day in the village of Talkha, I had watched the Central Security Forces (CSF), or al-Amn al-Markazi, block the entrance to a school serving as polling station. I went around the corner of the school and saw an elderly woman slowly ascend a wobbly ladder to climb through a window to cast her vote. Young boys and men helped her up and through the window like they were helping her onto public transportation. This spectacle does not shock me.

Later that night in Mansoura, it is mostly supporters from the Muslim Brotherhood outside the guarded counting station. The atmosphere is orderly. A part of the street is left open to allow cars carrying state officials traveling to or from the counting station to pass without obstruction. The crowd is segregated, with women on one side of the street and men on the other. The chants are equally orderly. One appeals to the honesty of the country's judges, who oversee the counting—"Ya qudaa, aul bi-gid, al-Masr di mish 'izbat had!" (Oh judges, say for real, this Egypt is not the estate of anyone!)

At 1 a.m., there is still no official announcement, and the CSF looks bored and tired. No reinforcements seem to be coming. Whoever is making decisions about security here is not anticipating a problem. Neither are we, so I tell Samer, "It's late. They are not going to announce the results anytime soon. Let's go eat." We start to walk and a boy, perhaps fifteen years old or so, who is out selling something or playing, beelines to us. Curious, he asks what we're doing there, and when I say, "I've come to see Egyptian democracy," he bursts out laughing. Pointing to the security forces guarding the counting station, he replies, "Democracy? You see this, we live in a watermelon democracy." As Samer joins him in laughter, I give Samer a confused look. "Did he say 'watermelon democracy'?" Samer says he will explain later.

A common joke in Egypt, I learn and later hear reference to all the time, refers to the gamble of buying a watermelon. The skin of every melon at the fruit stand shines a deep, rich green, tantalizing you with the promise of a sweet, juicy treat inside. But you never know what is inside the watermelon until you split it open. Sometimes it is the delectable reddish-pink fruit that you eagerly anticipated; sometimes it is unripe and unsatisfying. Sometimes the watermelon lies. Egyptians thus dub anything a watermelon that turns out to be less than advertised and that raised expectations high but later seems to be nonsense or empty talk. The political transition in Egypt after protests overthrew Husni Mubarak in 2011 is one such watermelon.

When the young man in Mansoura on election night in 2005 said "We live in a watermelon democracy," he was not referring to the surprise of cutting open a watermelon. The result of the wider election was not in doubt. Yet he was referring to the way the election was a spectacle, empty of meaning. He was also questioning if democracy can be real. The problem is people do not get to know for sure unless you slice open the watermelon and find out what is inside.

The political transition Egypt experienced after the revolutionary uprising began in January 2011 seemed empty of what many had hoped for in the early days. In Egyptian politics today, no one is getting what they want. Everyone is unsatisfied. The protesters who made revolutionary demands from 2011 to 2012, nearly overwhelming the state, have been contained and are now ignored. The civil society activists and ordinary citizens who fought for a fairer and more humane social order have become targets of unrelenting state violence, often leading to their incarceration or exile, if not death. Organized groups that won procedurally fair elections fell victim to a military coup cheered on by political rivals. Generals who would likely rather not rule openly have been forced to try to govern a state coming apart at the seams. The great majority of ninety-seven million Egyptians struggle to make ends meet in an economy that no leader wishes to reform and that has once again become subject to the dictates of an International Monetary Fund (IMF) structural adjustment program. International governments that pine for so-called autocratic stability in Egypt routinely lie to cover up the crimes of their ally, the post-2013 military-backed regime-in-formation. Transnational aid networks end up bankrolling Egypt's leadership and propping up a bare minimum standard of living for the masses, with no end to these burdens in sight. Everyone is constantly absorbing shocks from perpetually deteriorating political, economic, and social conditions. The Egyptian state—once one of the more robust in the region—is shedding its basic administrative capacities for the sake of self-preservation. None of these outcomes was envisioned when Egypt's uprising began in January 2011. At the conclusion of the uprising's first eighteen days, indeed, everything but this disheartening tableau seemed possible.

Revolutionary popular uprisings that immobilize the operations of an autocratic regime are rare. As Mark Beissinger's research shows, uprisings that transform the political system into a democracy are rarer still.[1] More common is the return of authoritarianism after a revolutionary uprising. Beissinger speaks of an erosion of the political gains and space as time marches on.[2] When an uprising occurs and leads to a political transition, the evidence suggests an autocracy is more likely than democracy over the long term. What the transitions or regime change literature shows, however, is wedded to an outcome of democracy or autocracy rather than the process that produces one or the other over the years following mass protest upheaval.

This book strives to go beyond outcome-based determinations by showing readers the architecture of forging autocracy after Egypt's revolutionary uprising and a turbulent transition. That the government headed by President 'Abdel Fattah al-Sisi is autocratic is not in doubt. Yet, merely naming Egypt an autocracy conceals the maneuvers and events over disparate fields that assist in building an autocracy or democracy on the site of a previous regime. Outcome-based analysis renders the process, which includes maneuvers and events, invisible. Central to this book's line of inquiry is to show what a new autocracy keeps from the past, what aspects it abandons, what challenges it faces when navigating and establishing a new regime, the new constituent parts it incorporates, and the new practices and routines it strives to develop with the governed society.

This book examines central aspects of Egypt's uprising and transition so as to contribute to these debates by showing the process by which a new authoritarian regime is forged and fashioned on top of the ruins of one that was disrupted by mass political participation.[3] To demonstrate this objective, I examine the central parts used to counter Egypt's revolutionary push: namely, I will explore the relationship between protests, opposition groups, and rulers; the work elections do during a transition; what state violence can and does not achieve; and the continuities and increasing inequalities of Egypt's political economy of crisis spending and social revolt.

I chose these specific areas to comment on because of the lived-experience of being a researcher of politics during this exciting and tumultuous period in Egypt. On periodic trips to Egypt after the uprising and before the coup, each trip yielded a new area of emphasis. Divided linkages among opposition groups and tension among revolutionaries and other opposition groups were part and parcel of what Egypt's uprising inherited. Elections factored in nearly all of my research trips. During some visits, elections were happening, while during other visits, people were preparing for them. Political economy also had moments of exaggerated importance especially when tourism rents dropped, the Egyptian pound started to collapse, and the gap between state revenues and expenditures dramatically increased. State violence became ubiquitous and more deadly as the transition progressed. Driving around the capital, one passes unmarked and sometimes changed landscapes where cascading state violence was unleashed on the bodies of dissenters. Therefore, the product of this labor is a book that shines a light on these areas of inquiry when also trying to understand how these areas were emphasized and de-emphasized at different times throughout the process. By showing the process of how Egypt's leaders are trying to rebuild an authoritarian regime, this book refuses to erase or make invisible key events for the sake of determining an outcome of autocracy. Rather, it shows the contested process of how this state of affairs came to pass. This also leaves open the possibility of more change in the future.

A larger goal is to carve out analytical space between the poles of regime change (democracy/autocracy) and no change at all (autocracy). After all, few could look at Egypt on the brink of an uprising in 2010 and after the coup in 2013 and say it was politically the same place. How, then, do we account for the changes we collectively witnessed? This book argues that an incumbent ejection occurred before the state was overrun in 2011. Beyond Mubarak's ejection, the daily practices of the regime he oversaw also collapsed, leaving a brittle state and political vacuum through which the transition traversed. Even though the state fragmented, and ruling elites lost the grip over Egyptian citizens that they had maintained for decades, greater revolutionary change was postponed.

The 2011 uprising initiated a nearly thirty-month-long political transition led by the country's leading generals, who had no intention of facilitating democratic governance unless they were forced to by ongoing mobilization. Indeed, the generals largely spearheaded the counter-revolutionary response to the social activism, and the transition period culminated in the military orchestrating a coup d'état that ended the experiment in July 2013. This book traces the ebbs and flows of social activity and incumbent responses during the transition by showing how the generals of the Supreme Council of the Armed Forces (SCAF) used existing opposition divisions, elections, state violence, and political economy to stop the mobilization before scrapping the transition in order to create a new regime. Time will tell if they will succeed or fail in this endeavor.

The fact that Egyptians tried to launch a revolution and did not succeed is not exceptional. This is actually the expectation of the scholarly literature. Yet, the uprising changed the internal configurations of Egypt's state, changed an older regime, and after military generals took matters into their own hands, meant that a new regime had to be built. This book navigates this process of refashioning and reconstituting an authoritarian regime after revolutionary moments. By detailing the ways in which the senior generals in Egypt recalibrated the state and began constructing a new regime, I show the continuities and changes of a state that barely survived a national uprising. But, more importantly, we will all see more clearly the continuities and changes that occurred for politics in Egypt over the past decade.

This manuscript is not a chronological narrative of what transpired in Egypt since 2011. Others have reconstructed the twists and turns, and there were far too many contingencies for most authors to render the story fully and fairly. Rather, this study looks at continuity and change in Egyptian politics across the Mubarak period (1981–2011), the tumultuous transition after his ouster (2011–13), and the afterlives of a military coup (2013–present). This happens by examining four key areas: the relationship between popular protests and political incumbency, the role of elections in a transition, the use of state violence after the fall of a dictator, and the dynamics of the political economy before, during, and after a revolutionary episode.

No book is ever a complete or definitive accounting of something as complicated as a revolutionary uprising and its aftermath. This one is no exception. As a researcher, my choices of research and my interests reveal my personal biases and values. These views were reinforced as my friends, acquaintances, and comrades watched and lived through the daily developments in Egypt since 2011. The ecstasy of witnessing from afar and in person people that I am deeply committed to try to change their political situation will forever be a lifetime highlight. I do not miss the activity or speaking invitations or media attention. I miss hearing about political dreams for change and witnessing the social possibilities that magical moment unleashed. Between the 2011 uprising and the 2013 coup, I have never felt so much personal, professional, or research solidarity. I also never learned as much as during those twenty-nine months. But the years I had spent in Egypt between 1998 and 2007 prepared me well to witness the 2011 uprising and the continuing process unfolding there.

The alternative of the ecstasy has been the anguish I felt watching a military coup destroy people's lives and stomp on their hopes. Research about contemporary politics that involves interacting with people there feels impossible now. If I endanger people with their state because they talk to me, I do not want to be party to this dynamic. Yet the research and writing has helped me come to terms with what happened and helped me explain to others what I think transpired. I have incorporated many of the lessons revolutionary Egypt taught me into my own daily praxis. Egyptians have always taught me more than I can ever return. All I can do is collaboratively witness, faithfully document what I learn, and educate others. Commitments to the people you think about and the events, places, and ideas that you research can never, by definition, be a hobby. With this book, I have tried to take Egyptians seriously and represent what they say to me and what I saw accurately.

Acknowledgments

Books take a long time to write. This one took longer than it should to finish. So many people helped me think about Egypt's uprising that it is hard to remember all the contributors, collaborators, funding sources, or institutions that hosted me to hear about and constructively criticize this research. But we would never arrive at this point without the many efforts to build a community of care, friendship, solidarity, love, and scholarship. Of course, I alone am responsible for any flaws that follow.

I began writing this book by coauthoring a paper with Hesham Sallam on opposition relations and incumbents in fall 2011. We jointly decided to not publish that paper, and Hesham graciously gave me our work. I have reworked it in ways to make it mine, but without Hesham, I would not have known where to start. Hesham is one of the absolute best analysts of the politics of Egypt I have ever met. Thank you for sharing your knowledge and experiences with me.

Another part of this book was conceived and written while in residence as a fellow at the Woodrow Wilson Center during the 2012–13 academic year. I am honored that this book will be in the Wilson Center's library. The Project on Middle East Political Science graciously sponsored my participation in panels about Egypt as well as awarded me a Travel, Research, and Engage grant. Furthermore, Kent State's University Research Council provided grant money that facilitated a couple of field research trips. Without this support, this book would be less ambitious and less certain in its arguments.

Other informal support groups improved my arguments. While in Washington, DC, a group of us came up with the idea of the Egyptian Revolution Working Group. We would meet, present papers, and debate them. People that frequently participated or gave me feedback include Elliott Colla, Hesham Sallam, Adel Iskandr, Dina Bishara, Holger Albrecht, Diane Singerman, Paul Sedra, Nathan Brown, Mona Atia, and Samer Shehata. To be around and in conversation with such a diverse collection of scholars made my work better. It was a special moment because of you all. Thank you.

Other universities and places hosted me as I presented different aspects of this book. Some of these institutions include Case Western Reserve University, Cleveland State University, John Carroll University, Ohio State University, Dayton University, the American University of Beirut, University of Texas at Austin, University of Chicago, Georgetown University, George Washington University, Stanford University, University of Ghent, New York University, University of Pennsylvania, Harvard University, University of Michigan, Colgate University, Davidson College, University of Denver, Tulane University, and Washington and Jefferson College. I was also fortunate to share my research at The Carter Center, the National Endowment for Democracy, the Middle East Institute, and the Happy Dog in Cleveland. Of course, I am also indebted to the Middle East Studies Association (MESA) for the opportunity to present my work and hear others share their research each year.

There were a number of people that helped me clarify what I wanted to say, gave me ideas to develop my chapters, debated points with me, suggested further readings, and remained kind throughout the creative process. Some gave direct feedback on this book's arguments. Others offered their solidarity by teaching me things that I ended up writing about. They include the participants of the book workshop that I organized at a crucial moment when I was filled with self-doubt and uncertainty. Thanks to Jillian Schwedler, Vickie Langohr, Steven Brooke, Lisa Bhungalia, and Pete Moore. Without their time, patience, and excellent but necessary criticisms at the workshop, this book would not be what it became. Without the careful editing work of Allison Brown, fewer people would understand what I was trying to say. The exiled Egyptian artist Ganzeer and I discussed the book and the title. In addition to being supportive, he also designed a book cover that makes me smile every time I look at it. Thank you all.

These people blended into a wider network of comrades and friends that I love to be around, organize, or struggle with in spaces like the Middle East Research and Information Project (MERIP) and the MESA. I also want to thank the editors at *Jadaliyya* for the excellent work and excellent voices they include. I learn so much from all of you.

This list is not exhaustive but, in alphabetical order, I would also like to thank these people for walking (and occasionally running) with me in my academic, activist, and personal life. I admire you all more than you will realize. You inspire me to keep asking questions and show me how to grind through the research. If not directly providing me advice, I learn from you all through your example and by emulating your model. Thank you Sharif Abdel Kouddous, Gasser Abdel-Razek, Reem Abou-El-Fadl, Ziad Abu Rish, Amr Adly, Max Ajl, Chris Alexander, Kristen Alff, Amro Ali, Hannah Allam, Issandr El Amrani, Khalil al-Anani, Michele Penner Angrist, Abdullah Al-Arian, Samer Al-Atrush, Lina Attalah, Ara Ayer, Hossam Bahgat, Asli Bâli, Andrew Barnes, Orit Bashkin, Asef Bayat, Joel Beinin, Miriam Beinin, Lisa Bhungalia, Koen Bogaert, Mehrzad Boroujerdi, Casey Boyd-Swan, Laurie Brand, Steven Brooke, Michaelle Browers, Jason Brownlee, Matt Buehler, Michelle Campos, Sheila Carapico, Sarah Carr, John Chalcraft, Laryssa Chomiak, Ryan Claassen, Andy Clarno, Elliott Colla, Basil El-Dabh, Omar Dahi, Leena Dallasheh, Rochelle Davis, Jennifer Derr, Bob Dodge, Vincent Durac, Mohamed Elmenshawy, Mike Ensley, Noura Erakat, Wael Eskandar, Samera Esmeir, Basma Fahoum, the late Kevin Floyd, Patrick Gallagher, Tony Ganzer, Gennaro Gervasio, Pascale Ghazaleh, Mona El-Ghobashy, the late Ellis Goldberg, Amoaba Gooden, Neve Gordon, Maryam Griffin, Bassam Haddad, Sherine Hafez, Lisa Hajjar, Vladimir Hamed-Troyansky, Amr Hamzawy, Kevan Harris, Ian Hartshorn, Farrah Hawana, Waleed Hazbun, Katie Herrold, Jim Heun, Evan Hill, Raymond Hinnebusch, Walt Hixson, Amira Howeidy, Mike Hudson, Asli Igsiz, Stephanie Jansky, Toby Jones, Tim Kaldas, Anjali Kamat, Matan Kaminer, Jenny Kelly, Arang Keshavarzian, Ashraf Khalil, Laleh Khalili, Rami Khouri, Mimi Kirk, Janet Klein, Charles Levinson, Darryl Li, Ursula Linsey, Rob Lisy, Zach Lockman, Miriam Lowi, Alex Lubin, Ellen Lust, Shana Marshall, Vivienne Matthies-Boon, Julie Mazzei, Babacar M'Baye, Una

McGahern, Maya Mikdashi, Isaac Paul Miller, Shane Elizabeth Minkin, Penny Mitchell, Ayman Mohyeldin, Story Monforte, Pete Moore, Ahmed Morsy, Dan Moulthrop, Tamir Moustafa, Dan Murphy, Ashley Nickels, Elizabeth Nugent, Walter (Larry) Orwin, Sumita Pahwa, Chris Parker, Sarah Parkinson, Nicola Perugini, Stacey Philbrick Yadav, Lisa Pollard, Danny Postel, Nicola Pratt, Mezna Qato, Mouin Rabbani, Haggai Ram, Nancy Reynolds, Hugh Roberts, Shira Robinson, Max Rodenbeck, Bruce Rutherford, Curt Ryan, Hesham Sallam, Jillian Schwedler, Sherene Seikaly, the late Anthony Shadid, Emad Shahin, Omar Shakir, Adam Shatz, Samer Shehata, Jack Shenker, Ahmad Shokr, Omar Sirri, Erin Snider, Jeannie Sowers, Rebecca Stein, Lior Sternfeld, Chris Stone, Joe Stork, Ted Swedenburg, Idris Kabir Syed, Sherene Tadros, Andrea Teti, Lloyd Thomas, Chris Toensing, Jim Tyner, Bob Vitalis, Kate Wahl, Max Weiss, Jessica Winegar, Brandon Wolfe-Hunnicutt, Elijah Zarwan, Jailan Zayan, Sami Zemni, and Dave Zirin. Thanks for sharing your ideas, humor, and solidarity. Much love to you all.

I would also like to single out the work of my undergraduate and graduate students at Kent State. They generously work with me and help me proof my work, design charts, format text and footnotes, and offer moral support. Thanks especially to Evan Cerne-Iannone, Joe Kusluch, and Pádraigín O'Flynn. Thank you and I cannot wait to see what research you bring into the world.

My parents, Kim and Marcia Stacher, have been unwavering pillars of support. Not only do they provide unconditional encouragement, they also instill confidence in me every day. Thank you both for being for me such wonderful role models of integrity and empathy. You taught me from the time I was young to use my privilege to help others more vulnerable than me. I love you both more than I will ever be able to put into words. My wife, Jasna, also deserves loving thanks. Thank you for building a life with me and for teaching me to live more simply, value what is really important in life, enjoy the moment as the kids grow, and go on more dates.

This book is dedicated to my kids—Eli, Kimmy, and Noah. Although Kimmy and I remain apart for much of the year, I cannot stop thinking about the life she is making in Egypt. And our conversations during our lunch dates together have gotten more serious as the years pass. Eli and Noah were both born as this book was being written. They vigorously opposed me writing any of this because they wanted me to hold them more, share more meals with them, cuddle with them more, read more to them, and play with them more. I do not know what any of them will remember about what it took for everyone to hold this book today. But without their inspiration, laughter, and love, I doubt I would have finished this book. I love you three more than you ever know, and I promise to keep working for a world filled with equality, justice, and love.

Lastly, in his 1844 notebooks, Karl Marx provided some advice for good living while criticizing greedy vampire capitalists. This is a reminder for all of us to eat more, drink more, buy more books, go to the theater more, dance more, think more, love more, theorize more, sing more, paint more, fence more, and so forth. This is the practice that we all need to win a better world.

Watermelon Democracy

Introduction

What If . . .

> Al-sha'b yurīd isqāṭ al-niẓām! (The people want the fall of the regime!)
> —Protest chant in Egypt and countries around the Arab world, 2011

> "Yasquṭ yasquṭ ḥukm al-'askar!" (Down, down with military rule!)
> —Protest chant in Tahrir Square, Cairo, 2011

Revolutionary Beginnings

What happens on the road between a revolutionary atmosphere and revolution? This question animates the rest of this book, which explores the various ways new leaders, who slide into top positions of a state apparatus disrupted by mass protests, try to forestall, elide, or divert popular demands for democratization, better economic opportunities, and social justice. Because these new leaders were unable to rely on the power of persuasion or an ability to convince the people to let them rule uncontested, a high-stakes contest began in 2011 as to whether democracy or autocracy would prevail in Egypt. The country remains ground zero for explaining how revolutionary protests from below overwhelmed and defeated an entrenched authoritarian regime. Egypt is also a laboratory for showing the ways new leaders pursued strategies that ultimately culminated in a military coup d'état, which ushered in an obsessive attempt to crush dissent and fashion together a new authoritarian regime. During the transition, the military's top generals wanted security and protection within the system. After their coup, they began regime-making from its core.

For these military generals of the Supreme Council of the Armed Forces (SCAF) to achieve their dream of creating a new regime that is predictable, maintains a routine, and is adaptable, they harnessed continuities from the past as well as introduced innovations to establish a new deteriorating normal. That this situation is normal or anywhere near complete remains in doubt. Yet, beyond debate, Egypt's senior generals are the current ruling class. How long SCAF will remain in that role is an open question. Egypt's senior generals are regime-making on the ruins of a political order that has already failed. Yet, how Egypt reached this point of generals trying to establish a new regime requires a close study of four central areas: opposition relations during revolutionary moments, elections, state violence, and political economy. By examining the continuities and changes in these areas, we gain a better understanding of the process of autocratic recalibration and invention after a popular revolutionary uprising.

The uprising in Egypt began on Tuesday, January 25, 2011. While the state commemorated National Police Day, people in Cairo used the holiday to venture into the streets. The overthrow of Tunisia's Zine El Abidine Ben Ali eleven days prior had made Egyptians, who had been left behind by their state elites as well as by the legal opposition groups, begin to have "unthinkable thoughts" about political change.[1] Egyptian protesters wanted to use the momentum Tunisians willed into the world and press their own leaders. The nearly five weeks of protests in Tunisia, which culminated in Ben Ali's dismissal, modeled the gatherings of dissent despite repeated threats from their own Interior Ministry.[2] There is no evidence that anyone involved in the protests believed they were on the brink of toppling Husni Mubarak, much less launching a revolution. Protesters seized the occasion to be heard on a public holiday that praises the despised police. Without any of these antecedents, one could argue that January 25 would have likely just been another ordinary day.

Despite the appearances of political liberalization because of nearly weekly protests as well as presidential and parliamentary elections in 2005, Egypt, in the years prior to the uprising, had been a dangerous environment for expressing political dissent.[3] Since early 2006, the country had been in the midst of a thorough crackdown in which state security arrested hundreds of the Brotherhood leaders and members and increased policing against labor organizers. The government had also restricted press freedoms, after previous years had seen a proliferation of newspapers, blogs, and satellite TV channels. In 2007, the state also introduced new constitutional amendments to protect its flank against all emerging forms of dissent.[4] All indications seemed to suggest that hereditary succession, not revolution, was on the table.[5] Furthermore, in December 2010, Egypt had experienced the most flagrantly rigged election during Mubarak's nearly thirty-year presidency, producing a National Democratic Party (NDP) majority of 93.3 percent.[6]

Circumstances were even worse for activists because of Egypt's biggest foreign patron. US president Barack Obama had been unwilling to put any pressure on Egypt's rulers. Before departing for Cairo in June 2009, Obama had said that he did not regard Mubarak as an authoritarian leader. As he responded in an interview with the BBC, "I tend not to use labels for folks. I haven't met him. I've spoken to him on the phone. He has been a stalwart ally in many respects, to the United States."[7] Days later, the capital's streets were emptied and people were told to not even look out their window as Obama's motorcade travelled to Cairo University for his address.[8] Few Egyptians, whether in the state or in the streets, actually believed the US government's rhetoric about democracy or human rights. Successive US administrations over decades had conditioned this obvious realism by Egyptians.[9]

None of this background, which erected one obstacle to change after another, mattered when Egyptians called for protests in January 2011. In the days leading up to the protests, a twenty-six-year-old activist, Asma' Mahfuz, posted a video to YouTube calling people into the streets. She said, "I, a girl, am going down to Tahrir Square, and I will stand alone. And I'll hold up a banner. Perhaps people will show some honor. Don't think you can be safe anymore. None of us are. Come down with us and demand your rights, my rights, your family's rights. I am going down on January 25th and will say no to corruption, no to this regime."[10] The question was, would anyone show up?

The Interior Ministry issued statements ahead of the protest. The director of security for Cairo Governorate stated, "The security apparatus will deal firmly and decisively with any attempt to break the law." No protest permits were granted. Habib al-'Adli, the interior minister, had orders to "arrest any persons expressing their views illegally."[11] Meanwhile, leaders of the opposition parties and the Muslim Brotherhood issued statements saying that they would not participate in the January 25 demonstration. But the protest organizers persisted in their planning, announcing twenty simultaneous protests at an appointed time. The Ministry of Interior and security forces prepared accordingly. On January 25, an unannounced twenty-first demonstration met in front of al-Hayiss sweet shop in Cairo's Bulaq al-Dakrur district. Strategically, this gathering became important because it caught the security forces off guard. After protesters assembled in Bulaq al-Dakrur, they marched down Gami'at al-Duwal al-'Arabiyya Street in Mohandeseen toward downtown to meet with the other announced protests converging from other parts of Cairo. Even though the activists did not anticipate a revolution, security was prepared for the announced protests. Despite all this, and in addition to the legal or organized opposition not joining the protests, security forces began to lose their control over society.

The uprising spread around the country. People occupied squares in places like Alexandria, Mansoura, and Asyut. Videos from Suez showed crowds storm a police station and burn it to the ground. With each day of clashes with security, the protests grew in size. The state shut off the internet, but the crowds only got bigger. Different opposition groups, including the Muslim Brotherhood, sensed Mubarak's vulnerability and joined the fray. The number of protesters continued to multiply as various leaders of the US administration, including Vice President Joe Biden and Secretary of State Hillary Clinton, placed their support behind Mubarak.

The government tried to get ahead of the uprising. But Mubarak's regime had refused to listen to Egyptians for years, and now it was losing the ability to speak to them as well. Mubarak's cabinet reshuffle was met with popular indifference. His speeches proved incapable of pulling people out of the streets. Others, such as spymaster and new vice president 'Umar Sulayman, tried to meet with opposition figures. Egyptians barely reacted to these incidents in the news. They were too busy exploring new political possibilities about the future and had no time for business as usual or piecemeal concessions.

When budding revolutionaries were not repelling proregime attackers, they were organizing the squares, arranging logistics, making new alliances, treating the wounded, debating the merits and limitations of different political visions, enjoying live music in the square, and pressuring Mubarak to resign. Workers began a national strike. Schools closed. Everyone became obsessed with removing authoritarian managers, whom they called "mini-Mubaraks," from public spaces, work environments, and schools. In an effort to stem the tidal wave, someone ordered the prisons emptied. This maneuver was intended to scare Egyptians back into their homes, seeking safety so the security forces could apprehend the released criminals and regain control of public spaces. The news of the emptied prisons barely fazed people, who instinctively established popular committees to protect and maintain order within their residential neighborhoods and public spaces.

The army came out onto the streets to separate the crowds from the security forces, who were being beaten at every turn as years of anger and frustration at the state security state boiled over. While condemning the security forces, protesters tried to befriend the deployed military officers and soldiers in the hopes that they would defect from the regime. The NDP, which had over two million members, vanished into thin air. The party's headquarters near Tahrir Square was torched for good measure. Politicians fled into exile or disappeared quietly back into society. After only eighteen days of protest, the army forced Mubarak out of office. In the words of Mona El-Ghobashy, "Egypt's momentous uprising did not happen because Egyptians willed it into being. It happened because there was a sudden change in the balance of resources between rulers and ruled."[12]

During the course of the uprising, a revolutionary atmosphere emerged. This atmosphere looked like chaos but was far from it. New horizontal organizing networks proliferated as hierarchy became muted. No one saw a revolution coming—not the protesters, not the government, not the security forces, not the armed forces, not the foreign governments with long-standing interests in the country, and not the academics that had committed themselves and their research agendas to Egyptians. While no one saw the January revolution coming, Rabab El-Mahdi and Philip Marfleet had two years earlier suggested that more attention should be paid to contentious politics from below and noted that radical political change was necessary.[13] Yet, even if no one could have foreseen a revolutionary attempt, it would not have mattered. There was nothing any entity supportive of the crumbling status quo could have done to convince the crowds otherwise. After decades of dividing and ruling opposition groups, anesthetized elections, police brutality, and a deteriorating political economy, state authority melted away like snow on a warm day.

Scholars agree about what constitutes revolution. Theda Skocpol says that revolution is a "rapid, basic transformation of a society's state and class structures; and they are accompanied and in part carried through by class-based revolts from below."[14] Political and social revolutions are special historical events, but they do happen.[15] Egypt's revolutionary uprising in 2011 was hardly the first time that the world had witnessed such an attempt. In fact, some are now comparing the 2011 uprising to the one Egypt experienced in 1919.[16]

Leon Trotsky's account of the beginning of the Russian Revolution describes events and dynamics unmistakably similar to those in Egypt. People in 1917 Russia had not planned a revolution. The state had seeming total control over society. Yet women in factories started a protest. Clashes broke out between the hated police and protesters, who curried favor with the military. The power projection of the elites decreased as the number of protesters multiplied. Everything changed once the protesters grabbed the initiative from the state. Once the revolutionary atmosphere happened, the balance of power between the state and society shifted. The following passage Trotsky wrote about the 1917 Russian Revolution could just as easily have been penned by an Egyptian about the 2011 uprising:

> Everywhere aimless movements, conflicting currents, whirlpools of people, individuals astounded as though suddenly gone deaf, unfastened trench coats, gesticulating students, soldiers without rifles, rifles without soldiers, boys firing into the air, a thousand-voiced tumult, hurricanes of wild rumor, false alarms, false rejoicings. Enough, you would think, to lift a sword over all that chaos, and it would scatter apart and leave never a trace. But that is a crude error of vision. It is only a seeming chaos. Beneath it is proceeding an irresistible crystallization of masses

> around new axes. The innumerable crowds have not yet clearly defined what they want, but they are saturated with an acid hatred of what they do not want. Behind them is an irreparable historic avalanche. There is no way back.[17]

Trotsky, in describing the Russia of February 1917, outlines the atmosphere at work in the Egypt of January and February 2011. Yet few can credibly claim that Egypt's uprising, unlike Russia's, developed into a full-scale revolution, even if both cases witnessed revolutionary atmospheres emerge and processes begin.

A revolutionary atmosphere consumed Egypt in 2011. A process began. The uprising looked, felt, and sounded like the beginning of other revolutions the world has witnessed in places like Iran in the late 1970s. Yet Egypt's process failed to break through. Revolutionary atmospheres do not necessarily culminate in revolution. Therefore, such atmospheres and the beginning of processes cannot be assumed to lead to progressive change.

Despite Trotsky's conflation of atmosphere, process, and revolution, he is correct in that there is no going back. Once a regime's humpty-dumpty falls off the wall, even the most powerful cannot put the old regime back together. Egypt's state was disrupted and began to shed administrative capacities. Mubarak's regime, specifically the daily routinized practices between ruling and ruled, collapsed. The transition began with a collapsed regime, a fragmenting state, and in the transitional vacuum of political uncertainty. The moment became decisive: Will democracy emerge or will a new autocracy be built? Revolution or not, Egypt's process could not be returned to its preuprising political situation. The question, then, becomes why did Egypt fail to realize a revolution like Russia or Iran experienced? Furthermore, why did Egypt's uprising produce a transition that led to the military's regime-making experiment? The answer is not as simple as repression by counterrevolutionary forces or the machinations concocted by the "deep state."[18] These responses are to be expected, as revolution inevitably summons counterrevolutionary responses.

If political revolutions are rare, then revolutions or political transitions that end in a democratic breakthrough are even rarer. As Mark Beissinger shows, there have been forty-two revolutions since 1980, if we agree that a revolution is a mass protest movement that displaces a leader and aims to change the established order of politics and society.[19] Out of these revolutions, twenty-eight of them witnessed protesters demanding more political and civil rights as well as free and fair elections. As Beissinger argues, "Most did in fact result in some degree of fairer electoral competition and broader civil and political freedoms in their immediate wake, though in many cases these achievements subsequently eroded."[20] Therefore, the expectation is not that a revolutionary uprising results in democracy. Rather, such political moments are more likely to produce a new form of autocracy that maintains continuities from the older deceased regime and adds innovations into the new one being forged.

This book is about the popular expansion and elite erosion of political space following a revolutionary protest mobilization in contemporary Egypt. In particular, I examine the process of Egypt's revolutionary uprising and how a new ruling class began building a new autocracy by incrementally corroding gains made by protesters and harnessing viable continuities to govern. I achieve this by exploring the dynamics of opposition relations during a revolutionary mobilization and then examining how newly empowered SCAF generals from the defeated regime try to recapture state authority by diluting the demands from revolutionaries. To achieve this aim, I explore the fields of opposition relations, elections, state violence, and political economy to show the ways that these generals try to regroup by fashioning together old and new figures into government before trying to develop routine practices between those who govern and those who are governed. In short, SCAF's generals are trying to build a new autocratic regime. As a process, the construction of this new regime in Egypt is incomplete.[21]

By examining these areas of opposition relations, elections, state violence, and political economy, this book not only engages important topics connected to political transitions but also shows the intimate ways in which new leaders try to incrementally design a new regime on top of a previously discredited one. Such an approach also details the challenges these new autocrats confront based on their decisions to divide and rule opposition groups, employ elections, unleash state violence, and fail to alter the political economy. Rather than debate whether the revolution succeeded or failed to deliver democracy to Egyptians, this book reveals the process of building a new and different authoritarian regime on the ashes of a collapsed order.

Irony abounds, however. It is practically a given to assume that the military is at its apex in terms of political power in Egypt these days.[22] 'Abdel Fattah al Sisi governs without visible challenges from below and looks to do so for the foreseeable future. Regional and international states enable, finance, and protect al-Sisi's brutal rule and many human rights violations. Some argue that al-Sisi has created a political arena worse than the one Mubarak lorded over.[23] To be able to govern this way, the debilitated state that al-Sisi inherited relies on capacious amounts of movement restrictions, repression, and mass incarceration. Yet, calling how al-Sisi and his apparatchiks govern "a regime" extends too much credit. Such a designation gives away too much because there is no coherence and they remain ad hoc in their strategies. Egypt's ruling generals know that they do not want mass mobilization. Other than this, their aims are ambiguous and conditioned by structural contradictions and challenges they either inherited (economy, opposition relations) or manufactured (elections, state violence) during the transition.

The Egyptian president and the major institution from which he draws his authority to lead are confronted by a more divided and polarized society, a weaker economy, an enfeebled state that has lost some of its administrative capacities, and an inability to integrate society politically. There is no ruling party, no semiautonomous judiciary, no legal or illegal opposition allowed to organize or mediate between the state and society, no quasi-competitive elections, and no way to maintain social welfare benefits for an ever-expanding population. Al-Sisi and the other generals continue to regime-make on the ashes of a state Mubarak ran. He sits atop the throne of a state that is a shadow of itself compared to the Mubarak-led apparatus, and which a revolutionary movement has already collapsed.

This book tells the story of how Egypt's most senior military generals gutted a revolutionary atmosphere and process before deciding that if a new regime was to be built that foreclosed the possibility of future uncontrolled mass mobilizations, they would have to lead from in front of the curtain of state power. Before and after imposing that reality, SCAF's generals engaged in autocratic regime-making by playing on the divided relationships of Egypt's systemic and antisystemic opposition, using elections, deploying state violence, and continuing to crisis spend in Egypt's political economy of social revolt. These dynamics become more focused after the 2013 coup.

Ultimately, and despite grim appearances to the contrary, SCAF's regime-making in Egypt may eventually produce an autocratic juggernaut that is flexible, that is expansive in its tools of manipulation, that penetrates society, and that is adaptable beyond leaders immediately reaching for the iron fist of repression. But, then again, the process might also fail entirely. After all, Egypt's leaders are surrounded by another round of uprisings in Sudan, Algeria, Iraq, Lebanon, and Iran.

Just as revolutionary atmospheres and processes rarely produce democracy, blocking revolutionary outcomes does not simply default to authoritarianism. Blocking a revolution that has taken down a regime leaves a political vacuum. Therefore, like democracy, autocracy requires architects, engineers, and construction workers. This book details Egypt's 2011 revolutionary uprising and the ways that people from surviving institutions of a defeated regime regroup and try to incrementally establish a new autocratic regime. It is unclear if they will succeed in this endeavor as Egyptians are dragged through an oppressive hellscape while they try. Yet, by piecing together wider slices of issues that defined Egypt's transition, we can gain insights into how the dreams of revolutionary movements get transformed into a new, more repressive political order by SCAF, who have appointed themselves the guardians of the state.

How People Talk about Egypt

At this stage, the many books about Egypt's experience in the so-called "Arab Spring" have a dedicated shelf in the library.[24] In addition to books that trace the narrative of Egypt's uprising and the dark turns the transition traveled to produce a military coup,[25] other studies of the uprising look at its different aspects. These books include research that focuses on the role of women[26] or highlights mobilization[27]—be it citizen[28] or labor.[29]

Other books detail the changing relationships of the security forces and military and their use of the revolutionary attempt to integrate themselves more deeply into the political system.[30] Another publication looks at different areas, from factory-shop floors to hip-hop artists, to document the changes from "Mubarak Country" to the events after the January 2011 protests began.[31]

Shifting to more large-scale understandings of the wider narrative, other books present different stories. Early works detailed the revolutionary optimism of the early moments.[32] The optimism turns to criticism of the Muslim Brotherhood as they began to play a larger role because of the transition's elections. In addition to arguing that the Muslim Brotherhood co-opted the revolution, some scholars expressed an affinity for simpler prerepublican days.[33] The Brotherhood's illiberal governing behavior also becomes causal for explaining the military's forced reluctance to conduct a coup d'état.[34] Still other books seek to amplify the paths of characters from representative movements, where readers see the revolutionary moment from different points of view.[35] Others describe how Washington viewed the uprisings' participants as inexperienced protesters who confusedly believed they were participating in a revolution while making one mistake after another.[36] Egypt's military is now a subject of intense study as well.[37]

People that watched Egypt's revolutionary atmosphere enter a turbulent transition remained cautiously optimistic. Some, such as Alfred Stepan and Juan Linz, suggested that where a country was before an uprising likely dictated how far toward democracy it could progress.[38] While they warned that moving toward democracy would be a Herculean task, they shared the assumption that a reentrenchment of authoritarianism was unlikely in states like Egypt.[39] Why, then, did autocracy return to Egypt in the form of military regime-making after a trying transition?

As Nathan Brown notes, there was blame to share among participants, who encouraged bad behavior, participated in an unbalanced playing field, never dismantled the state's infrastructure of authoritarianism, and lived with the overarching legacy of autocracy.[40] While spreading the blame around is not wrong per se, it is also not helpful because there is no larger cause that leads to the military coup or its afterlives. Egypt arrives at that situation in a haphazard but structured way. The situation of returning autocracy is the default because the past has trapped its current subjects, who must make decisions that likely cannot outpace their path-dependency. Yet, if this approach is too sprawling, other scholars pursue this outcome of a failed uprising with equal or greater determinism.

Some scholars eschewed a retelling of events in order to explore the structural limitations Egypt possesses. In this case, they reveal a generalizable pattern by exhuming certain attributes to explain why any revolutionary attempt was doomed from the beginning. For example, the varying processes in Tunisia, Egypt, Yemen, Syria, Libya, Bahrain, Iraq, Algeria, Sudan, and Lebanon—in addition to states like Jordan and Morocco that prevented full-blown uprisings at this time—have provided a host of cases to reflect on autocratic durability, breakdown, and political transitions.

The scholarly consensus is that for whatever excitement the uprisings produced, the returns on the protests were stingy. As Jason Brownlee, Tarek Masoud, and Andrew Reynolds argued, "While the uprisings constituted the most serious challenge to authoritarian regimes in the Middle East and North Africa since the Cold War, when the dust settled, the results were relatively limited: mass protests rocked less than half of the region's dictatorships, and replaced incumbents in only four countries."[41] Brownlee, Masoud, and Reynolds cite two factors as vitally important for the popular overthrow of an autocratic leader in 2011: oil resource wealth and hereditary succession.[42] Thus, Tunisia, Egypt, and Yemen experienced leadership changes because they did not have oil rents to reinforce their rule and had not personalized politics by having a father-to-son leadership succession. In places that had one or both of these factors, no leadership change resulted even if protests began, such as in Syria or Bahrain.[43] The structuralist approach is appealing because it strips the context away from decisions made by protesters or generals as well as from a string of isolated events that become connected into a larger individualized trajectory. The study, however, comes off as overdetermined. For example, while the cases these scholars use prove their hypothesis, the analysis does not explain or apply to the near electoral uprising in Iran in 2009, nor does it hold true for Iran between 1977 and 1979. It also does not hold true for the 2019 resignation of long-time president Abdelaziz Bouteflika in Algeria, which ranks sixteenth in terms of oil world reserves.

Others, such as Robert Springborg, invest in a wider explanation of why Egypt's revolutionary attempt was destined to fail from its beginning. Springborg argues that the uprising failed to rise to the level of an Eastern European colored revolution because Egyptians exist in a traditional, or unmodern, state. While Springborg concedes that analysts can look to the relative power and divisions of the competing forces, such as the young Facebook activists or Muslim Brothers, a more comprehensive approach tells us more about why democracy failed to take root.

Springborg notes that Egypt has underdeveloped "human resources," and of the seven major areas that corroborate a higher chance for democracy, Egypt scores poorly on all those indexes. These areas include median age, the ratio between rural and urban populations, wealth, the size of the middle class, material security, the role of the welfare state, and levels of education. In Springborg's words, "the Egyptian population was just too young, too rural, too poor, too lacking a middle class, too materially insecure, too dependent upon the government and too poorly educated and trained to perform the political organizational tasks required to construct a democracy."[44] Such a dim and reductionist view of Egyptians might constitute social science for some, but it is also inaccurate because from the moment the crowds captured the initiative from the state, a host of counterrevolutionary state institutions, as well as regional and international actors, began to prey on the nascent movement for democracy.

If these arguments are too expansive or overdetermined, other arguments focus on too narrow a group to explain the lack of a democratic breakthrough. A popular interpretation, which some of the research mentioned above also argued, is that a democratic revolution failed to transpire in Egypt because of the chosen strategies and inexperience of the protesters. This argument is victim blaming because it lays a disproportionate amount of responsibility at the feet of protesters, who were, after all, fighting a seasoned authoritarian regime. For example, after the 2013 coup, *Time* magazine published a cover story that said that Egypt had the "world's best protesters" but also the "world's worst democrats."[45] This theme was echoed in subsequent analyses, such as that implied about Jehane Noujaim's documentary *The Square*, which chronicles the downfall of the revolutionaries through the story of three activists with different backgrounds.

In his review of the film, Max Fisher argued that its politics were "dangerous" and criticized the way the documentary "contributes to Egypt's poisonous atmosphere of polarization and distrust by its one-sided and often polemical portrayal of the Muslim Brotherhood."[46] While Noujaim's film does treat revolution as the ideal aspiration, Fisher's review points to the way the film suggests that the inflexible protesters are to blame for the military intervention and the return of the generals.

Similarly and more precisely, conservative pundit Eric Trager diagnosed the failed revolution as the result of the revolutionaries' rejection of formal politics. In his words, "They [the protesters] practically never leave Tahrir Square. They don't venture into the poorer neighborhoods of Cairo. They don't speak with their fellow citizens in the Nile Delta or Upper Egypt. . . . The activists don't really engage anyone who doesn't fit their general profile: young, semi-cosmopolitan, and vaguely leftist."[47] This lack of flexibility, he suggests, was what enabled the military coup. More scholarly and historically grounded research pointed out that the opposition—whether it came from the systemic or antisystemic groups—could agree on little more than that they did not want Mubarak.[48] This disagreement among these opposition groups could be traced back at least a decade.[49]

Criticisms that emphasize the failures of the opposition, however, miss the mark because revolutionaries were not the most influential group in terms of introducing or blocking political change. A focus on the people seemingly pushing the revolutionary situation obscures that in any revolution, only a small fraction of people organize on the ground. The majority of participants in any mass protest are people that come out in support. Many who join protests lack a definitive ideology but have grievances and are open to a range of possibilities.

While everyone might not settle on a pure revolution, they want change, even if it is ambiguously under a banner of "bread, freedom, and social justice." Thus, while it may seem that more leadership from Egypt's revolutionaries would have been beneficial, strong leadership has not defined other revolutionary atmospheres historically. Furthermore, there are other processes, including global ones, that limit the protesters' ability to be in control.

There are also legitimate criticisms of protesters that do not definitively, on their own, cause the eventual military coup. These criticisms also do not fixate on their choices. Egyptian revolutionaries instinctively adopted the approach of horizontal organizing after the January 2011 uprising started. This deeply deliberative grassroots style of organizing is based on a model of direct democracy.[50] It involves a wide process of consultation that is time-consuming and hard in terms of building consensus. Horizontalism exists at odds with institutional or formal politics, which have more anchoring effects on the direction of revolutionary or transitional possibilities.

Not only does horizontal organizing take a long time, but it also comes with certain costs because of its decentralization. In the words of Asef Bayat, horizontalism allows for novelties in organizing but also invites "a precarious operation, uncertain commitment, vague message, blurred strategy, and a quick breakdown of mobilization."[51] While horizontalism is also apparent in Trotsky's account of the Russian Revolution and accounts of the revolution in Iran, there are discernable differences between the cases of Egypt, Iran, and Russia.

While the world was not oblivious to the historical processes unfolding in Iran or Russia, Egypt's revolutionary uprising unfolded in real time in the media and on the internet. The flows of information empowered the activists on the ground to control their narratives, but it also allowed the competing counterrevolutionary forces to respond and try to dilute and contain the revolutionary atmosphere at a much earlier stage than in other cases. From late January 2011, when it was clear that revolution was an option, through the transitional period between February 2011 and June 2013, counterrevolutionary elites tried to drain the prospects of revolution. SCAF attempted to apprehend the revolutionary process by deploying strategies, tactics, and tools that worked in concert over time. SCAF did not know where or what their end point was besides getting the mobilization to stop or change its emphases. The constant barrage of attacks on the revolutionary ethos allowed SCAF to slow the damage of the Mubarak regime's immobilization and ineffectiveness during the initial protests.

In addition to the speed with which a counterrevolutionary could respond as well as the constant news updates on Facebook and Twitter, there is another issue of timing, as Asef Bayat has discussed. Egypt's revolutionary attempt came at a peculiar historical moment, which is defined as the neoliberal stage of advanced capitalism.[52] When Bayat analyzes the process in Egypt and compares it to his lived experience of Iran in the late 1970s, he notices telling differences.[53] For example, he notes how in 2011 Egypt the revolutionaries lacked an intellectual foundation like that provided by the work of ʿAli Shariʿati in Iran. Furthermore, he notes a genuine lack of radicalism in the tradition of the revolutionary protests compared to the 1960s and 1970s. These differences allowed Egypt's military to insert itself as a midwife to a process that never broke definitively with the older order or state.

In Cold War–era revolutionary settings, there had been strong anticolonial sentiments as well as other ideological frames such as Marxism-Leninism or Islamism.[54] Egypt's uprising in 2011 unfolded nearly thirty years into a neoliberal moment that has witnessed the state's relinquishing of social services provision in favor of investment in securitizing society. Thus, when Egyptians used horizontal activism, the state's resources for reading such open organizing had been well-developed. As Bayat argues, "States came to possess far more knowledge about the dissenting movements than movements knew about their states."[55] In addition to its repressive side, neoliberalism has an appropriation mechanism that deradicalizes dissent: "It commercializes activism, human rights, civil society, gender equality, sustainable development and poverty reduction, draining their radical intent."[56] It also turns the demand for social justice into a dissent without a vision.

Egypt's new incumbents after Mubarak's ejection used their ability to police and repress while making preemptive arguments to counter calls for change without a known destination. These twin responses could win over broad segments of the population that viewed the generals as a safer wager than the uncertainty the revolutionaries offered. Thus, while revolutionaries might have lacked a tangible program, they opened space that allowed domestic, regional, and international status quo advocates and counterrevolutionaries an opportunity to make a rebuttal. When given this chance, these forces pounced with antirevolutionary discourses, money, and violence. This book is concerned with protesters but more interested in examining the purveyors of counterrevolution, who were supported by international actors, cash, and weapons, as the leading reason Egypt's revolutionary attempt ended in SCAF trying to build a new autocratic regime.

Certain themes emerge from this literature review on Egypt's uprising. Firstly, some note that the protesters were in control of what they wanted and botched the revolution's execution. If they did not have clear political ideologies or platforms to disseminate their views, then it is their fault. Others show that even if the protesters played it perfectly, there were larger structural factors that would have blocked the emergence of democracy.

Yet, democracy is not even the most likely result when a revolutionary atmosphere and process begin. The anticipation should have been that democracy was a long shot. Rather than drown in the details required to produce a narrative, focus on individuals as representative of the larger groups that they identify with, reflect on whether Egyptians should have waited for a more convenient season to rise up, or blame the outmatched Brotherhood or their narrow-minded policies, there remains another way to explain what transpired in Egypt. Yet, such an approach requires us to relinquish the notion of an outcome of either success or failure.

Most of the scholarly work and reporting on the aftermath of Egypt's uprising focuses on the outcome as a failure. This is not in dispute. If we commit to outcome-based thinking, Egypt's uprising failed. Few people that marched in protests, participated in elections, or hoped for better days would view Egypt's uprising and transition as a success. The idea that the experiment ends in a coup accentuates the point that the revolutionary uprising failed. But, how do we take this statement of fact one step further? I argue that we must understand what happened in Egypt as an ongoing social struggle, which is historically grounded and contingent. Then, one can unmask and show the process by which Egypt witnesses a revolutionary atmosphere, an uncertain transition, a coup, and the military attempts at regime-making.

This book differs from the ones listed above because it compares political life during the late-Mubarak period, the transition, and the aftermath of the coup to reveal the continuities and changes between these periods. Furthermore, by adopting a process-oriented approach with a wide lens on different theories of political transitions, a more nuanced analysis emerges. Rather than engage conventionally in the transitions literature to determine if democracy (success) or autocracy (failure) results, this book seeks to go beyond this designation by showing how new leaders try to block democracy from emerging before investing in a military takeover of the political system where they attempt to orchestrate a new autocratic regime. Showing this process and how it applies to opposition relations, elections, state violence, and political economy helps flesh out the dynamics more precisely and in multiple areas of how Egypt's current reality came to pass.

Outline of the Book

Each subsequent chapter considers what the evidence from Egypt teaches us about different topics and theories, developed across the past several decades, on regime change and political transitions. Yet, rather than submit to the outcome-based thinking in studies about transitions, this book uses these topics to reveal the process of how the military generals that assumed control of Egypt's disrupted state and collapsed regime tried to obstruct, dilute, and prevent the realization of the revolutionaries' demands. When uncontrolled popular protest continued to be an option after over two years of Egypt's transition, the military generals decided to cancel the experiment and build a new autocratic regime with their own people at the helm. Not only does this wider account demonstrate that the military generals had no grand plan other than preventing democracy from happening, but it also shows the incremental steps and pauses on the tools the generals used to manipulate the opposition's divided and distrusted relationships. It also shows how elections, state violence, and the constraints of a political economy of social revolt factored into SCAF's regime-making attempt.

Not only are these interrogations important in terms of intellectually wrestling with what occurred in Egypt, but they also serve as a bridge that helps bring the underrepresented field of Middle East studies into mainstream social science debates. By approaching Egypt's transition through the topics of the relationship between opposition groups and protests, the role of elections, the use of state violence, and political economy, this book aims to make Egypt more legible to those familiar with the case as well as those seeking to learn about it.

Chapter 1 considers the divided relationships between opposition groups during a revolutionary mobilization, which can lead to a result of incumbent ejection. This result represents a middle outcome that is neither democratic nor autocratic. After the uprisings began in 2011, places like Egypt became new locations to think about regime change and political transitions. The central lesson that Egypt taught those that study transitions is that regime durability or breakdown cannot be viewed in absolute terms on a "democracy–authoritarian" continuum. The ejection of long-time incumbent Husni Mubarak was not a case of state collapse, but it also was not an instance of regime continuity either. By focusing on incumbent ejection, we see an event produced neither by limited elite maneuvers nor by popular revolutionary mobilization. This chapter considers other factors that help set the stage for Egypt's transitional purgatory.

The chapter argues that the history of linkages between systemic opposition groups and their antisystemic counterparts is the most important factor influencing whether the protesters can overtake the state during revolutionary moments. While an uprising with divided opposition groups can produce incumbent ejection, it is less likely to be able to sustain wider state collapse. Instead, a disrupted state with regime practices that are a dead letter means that a political vacuum emerges. The subsequent transition unfolded in this vacuum. The divided opposition in Egypt's revolutionary uprising limited the amount of change the population could enforce on elites housed in surviving, if fragmented, state institutions. Once the initial mobilization ebbed after the head incumbent was ejected, the surviving military elites could exploit the divided linkages among the opposition to regain the initiative, even as the state continued to fragment in terms of cohesion and capacity. As part of its examination of the structure of regime and opposition relations, this chapter also looks at the challenges and limitations of horizontal organizing during revolutionary moments.

Chapter 2 considers the political labor that elections do in a transitional setting. Within the literature on authoritarian durability, elections have been a central object of study: whether shown as an opportunity to strengthen patron-client relationships, a mechanism for distributing social services and money, or a moment of unpredictable but temporary change, elections in places like preuprising Egypt have been regarded as having few constructive or empowering effects. This expectation changes, however, when it comes to transitions following the removal of a dictator. Researchers of the politics of the Middle East have hypothesized that the meaningful value of elections would grow if the region's autocratic systems ever changed. This prediction aligns with the last two decades of general political science theorizing about how elections have democratizing effects. In fact, some in the discipline consider elections to be a new mode of transition. Taken at face value, Egypt's elections between 2011 and 2012 do tell the story of a budding transition from autocracy toward democracy. The 2013 military coup aborted this experiment. Elections in postcoup Egypt are proving meaningless again after the 2014 "election" of 'Abdel Fattah al-Sisi, or in the most recently elected Parliament.

While elections might unintentionally produce more inclusive change over the long term, isolating elections as moments of empowerment can yield a misleading interpretation of the character of a political transition. Most troublingly, as this chapter shows, generals used transitional elections to create a new exclusivist political arena that marginalized revolutionary voices in order to contain them and defeat the push for change. This chapter takes the role of transitional elections seriously but argues that rather than unleash emancipation, "free and fair" elections can also be disempowering events that enable the reconstitution of exclusivist practices. To complete the case, this chapter compares elections before the uprising, during the transition, and after the coup. Through detailing the events, participant observation, discourse analysis, and interviews, this chapter argues that a series of elections in a narrow, formal transition period is more about the production of a political order than democratization or autocratization.

Chapter 3 turns to the topic of state violence during a political transition. Since the uprising began, and especially after the 2013 coup, the state's use of violence has escalated and expanded; indeed, Egypt is experiencing the most repressive period in its modern history. Yet whereas state violence and its political effects have been an object of study in other regions such as Latin America, little research exists about the use of state violence in Egypt or in the other countries of the Middle East and North Africa. Consequently, explanations tracking the ways in which state violence in the region changes over time are also missing. At a minimum, state violence is neither random, nor is it all the same. For example, one might ask: Are we witnessing the reactive violence of system preservation, or violence as an elite instrument to engineer new power relationships within a rebellious society?

While isolating types of state violence as variables does not singularly explain Egypt's transition, it can illuminate the relative strength of the state apparatus vis-à-vis a contentious and restive society. This chapter argues that when elites operate in an equilibrium with society, state violence is limited and reactive so as to protect existing inequalities against organized political challenges. As popular mobilization disrupts or attacks the status quo and state elites try to regroup, they increase their use of state violence but in a preservationist and reactive manner. Yet when elites have the upper hand against a rebellious society and wish to engineer a different political field, they use constitutive state violence, which is about creating a new political reality rather than preserving an existing one. Such violence produces a sharp escalation in death tolls. This chapter explores the case of Egypt to show how changes in the elites' deliberate use of patterned corporal state violence reveals an attempt to produce a regressive political order.

Chapter 4 considers the political economy of Egypt's uprising and interrogates the relationship between a state's fiscal health, neoliberal economic policies, and political transitions. After the uprising that dislodged

President Husni Mubarak, SCAF's generals initially pursued policies that excluded popular social forces as they reorganized the economy around the Defense Ministry and the foreign investors partnering with them. The companies connected to the Defense Ministry are what some call "Military Inc."[57] Yet since al-Sisi has become president, the military has shifted from designing the economy around itself toward some profit-losing ventures that create alliances with the Egyptian business community as well as create more jobs for underemployed Egyptians. Military Inc., with help from transnational capital, is now in the expensive business of regime-building. The fundamental dynamic of Egypt's economy remains: governing elites continue to increase the size of the state and maintain large social expenditures, leading to incremental fiscal exhaustion. The pursuit of neoliberal policies also will not work, since they would fundamentally undermine the state erected after 1952. The leaders of Egypt's state are economically cornered.

This chapter argues that rather than understand the uprising as an economic rupture, we should see in the presidency of al-Sisi continuity with the pre-2011 period. Egypt's generals have doubled down on the Mubarak regime's crisis spending to compensate for the state's declining fiscal health. Like their predecessors since the mid-1970s, they rely on foreign aid and other rents. The new ruling class has failed to address the structural fiscal weakness of the state. Such research findings, this chapter argues, expose the tensions within ongoing processes of political continuity and change in Egypt.

The concluding chapter returns to Egypt after the coup ended Egypt's transition. Rather than a cohesive regime reestablishing order and bringing authoritarian "stability," it finds that the politics of Egypt remain unsettled as competing units in the state apparatus battle each other and a worn-down but restive population. As a result, the power of the generals, previously assumed to be unassailable, has been exposed as mere projection, though their precarious position actually means increased repression that surfaces unpredictably for Egyptians. More broadly, this chapter also examines the implications of Egypt's revolutionary attempt, its turbulent transition, and the afterlives of the coup. Specifically, the conclusion contemplates what this means for understanding the process of how new leaders attempt to make a regime on the ruins of one burned down by revolutionary protests.

All of these chapters bring together theories about political transitions with careful field research in Egypt to show how a new authoritarian regime tries to constitute itself in a political vacuum of an undetermined transition. The goal is to understand what we collectively witnessed and the types of dilemmas those of us committed to Egypt confront as the transition process morphs in terrible and terrifying regime-making ways. By drawing on local, transnational, and theoretical lessons, the hope is we can better comprehend what politics in Egypt looks like in a situation where demands for bread, freedom, and social justice have been deferred to another time of reckoning. Few felt that such issues could be put off in 2011. Now, the situation in Egypt is demonstrably more dire. This book offers no grand suggestions for organizing a resistance to these circumstances. Yet, good praxis requires that we understand Egypt's last revolutionary moment so that we might be ready to recognize the origins and context of the next round of revolt.

1

Retiring Mubarak

Protests, Opposition Relations, and Incumbent Ejection

As the 2011 national uprising rocked Egypt's autocracy to its foundation, the activists involved in the revolutionary protests began to believe their ability to summon millions for a street action was a foregone conclusion. As Ahmad Maher, founding member of the April 6 Movement told NPR days after Mubarak's ejection from the presidency, "We can always go back to the street . . . if they don't meet our demands, we'll take to the streets again."[1] This belief was made more credible because the leading incumbents could not convince those they ruled to leave the streets and return home.

Days before some protesters placed all their faith in using protests to change state policy, long-time intelligence chief Omar Sulayman begged the crowds to stop gathering. As he said, "I call upon the young people, the heroes of Egypt: go back to your houses, go back to your work. The homeland needs your work."[2] Watching Egypt's most powerful public figures deflate in real-time is disorienting. Even if you have imagined a better world, nothing clouds the mind more than the rapid collapse of normalized regime norms, which endows the powerless with authority and silences those who control and administer the levers of life. Perhaps it is the unfamiliar territory that causes us to believe our delusions. Or, maybe it is the process of revolution that instinctively cycles through new and different dreams that three weeks earlier would have been impossible.

Institutions and personnel connected to the state and the Mubarak regime did not anticipate the uprising and also did not possess an easy path to stop it. The protesters immobilized Mubarak's regime and disrupted the state's administrative capacities. If the state was to survive, the remnant elites needed to come up with a sleight of hand to demobilize the streets, squares, and factories around the country. Yet, they were powerless and cornered. Only the opposition could partially save them. Given that the rareness of a revolutionary mobilization is only eclipsed by the even more special outcome of an uprising establishing a successful democracy, exploring this central node between the incumbents and opposition helps us understand different possibilities for political change and continuities, which structured Egypt's transition.

While both of the quotes above show the power of protests and the impotence of elites in a moment of upheaval, the protesters and surviving elites interact with a deeper historical structure of societal relations that guides what is politically possible in such moments. These relationships between a state and different kinds of opposition groups, therefore, are a key signifier for understanding democratic or autocratic afterlives of a revolutionary uprising.

This chapter focuses on the initial responses by Egypt's old (Mubarak) and new (SCAF) elites and how they used existing relationships between systemic and antisystemic opposition groups to avoid the state's collapse in 2011. In the end, SCAF collectively sacrificed the president, watched the regime's routinized interactions between state and society fall, and reconfigured the ruling coalition with itself at its center. Yet, not everything connected to the old regime died, and the generals introduced new wrinkles as they slid into the helm of a fragmenting state being challenged from below.

While the actions of SCAF's generals suggest they were not thinking of regime-making at this stage, they—like Mubarak and his allies—tried to forestall any expression of democracy and equality becoming a feature of the political system. This approach would change by 2013 when the military and a state apparatus, which had by then regrouped, used mobilization to launch a coup to cancel Egypt's transition. The coup also marks the beginning of SCAF's regime-making experiment. The generals could not magically cover this distance alone. SCAF needed help, and they found saviors in the systemic Muslim Brotherhood's willingness to aid the military's political ascent.

When we think of revolutionary atmospheres, the analytic dynamic usually defaults to a dichotomy of the regime vs. society.[3] Such a dichotomy did not exist during Egypt's uprising. What appeared as a clean binary of the state and society masked a different reality. This chapter argues that an inherited structure of a three-cornered triangle between Mubarak's military, the systemic Brotherhood, and the antisystemic opposition helped produce an incumbent ejection rather than more expansive state collapse. An incumbent ejection is also not a regime change, but it signals that the predictable interactions between the state and society may no longer hold. Incumbent ejection can end a regime but not replace it immediately. Instead, a political vacuum emerges, but incumbent ejection does not level the playing field between the state, systemic, and antisystemic groups. Instead, incumbent ejection advantages those in the state that survive the purge because it reframes the time horizon and gives new state elites more time to demobilize protesters and end the threat.

Incumbent ejection is when part of an autocracy's elites is replaced. In this scenario, the person who occupies the ultimate position in the governing hierarchy is removed, as are those in his inner circle and some privileged constituents in the ruling coalition. Previously excluded members in society may or may not be incorporated into representative assemblies and elected offices. In cases of incumbent ejection, unlike cases of state collapse, central state institutions such as the military, security forces, intelligence agencies, and bureaucracy survive but are disrupted. These institutions go unreformed as state power redistributes throughout the apparatus. In such cases, elites from these institutions become more empowered or gain greater influence regardless of who eventually occupies elected offices and posts in government. While the ancien régime fades away, continuities in many of the hegemonic practices remain embedded in features of the subsequent political transition. The transition process that follows an incumbent ejection determines whether a democracy or an autocracy is constructed.

Mapping out the relative differences between opposition groups under authoritarian regimes provides nuance beyond a simplistic regime-versus-opposition framing that often is used to understand events when an uprising starts. Appreciating diversity within and delineating the different roles opposition groups play, this chapter argues, are the most critical factors influencing an uprising. Not only did these divisions among the opposition provide SCAF generals with the option of incumbent ejection, which enabled parts of the old regime to survive in modified form, but also the triangular design drifted into the transition process.

Most notable in this respect is the difference between systemic and antisystemic opposition groups. The latter reject the formal politics of an autocratic regime, as they feel entering into politics with an autocratic state that defines what is legal dilutes the ability to push for any measures beyond incremental change. They therefore remain outside of formal politics, such as elections, and instead have a proclivity for street protests. Systemic opposition groups, by contrast, participate in formal politics and mostly adhere to a regime's rules. Scholars that work on the region have noticed this trend of an obedient opposition for decades.[4] The events in Egypt also invite a comparison with the 1998 overthrow of Suharto in Indonesia. The tension between systemic and antisystemic opposition was on full display. In his research on the overthrow of Suharto, Edward Aspinall described the systemic opposition—which he calls the "semiopposition"—as groups that criticize the regime but use its terminology and do not contest its core interests or assumptions.[5] Over the long term, he explains, "the daily compromises required fostered acceptance of regime ideology and gave rise to a mentality of acquiescence to regime norms."[6] Aspinall's description of the "semiopposition" in Suharto's Indonesia has wider applicability to other autocratic regimes. In fact, this design sounds very much like Egypt's legal political parties as well as the outlawed Muslim Brotherhood under Mubarak's presidency. Scholars that focus on Egypt's systemic opposition made such points in the decade before the 2011 uprising.[7]

The transition in Egypt continues to be represented as an outcome of either autocracy or democracy, with many scholars focusing on the role of the military and how it acted as the most essential factor.[8] Given the 2013 military coup d'état in Egypt and the expansion of state violence against those clamoring for freedom, this narrative—in which an uprising overwhelms a state apparatus, defections occur, the regime changes, and a transition begins but in a way that produces a "return to authoritarianism" or "authoritarian transformation"—may seem to make sense.[9] And while this narrative might reflect events in Egypt, it commits important errors. First, writing this history as an instance where Egypt's military defects from the Mubarak regime under popular pressure over-argues SCAF's action. The military's leadership never defected from the Egyptian president.[10] While a longer view could make such a claim look accurate, describing the generals' maneuvers as defection during the first eighteen days extends too much credit. The generals of SCAF were responding in an unprepared ad hoc manner. Their goal during the eighteen-day period, shared with the Mubarak government, was to decrease or stop the exponentially growing protests. Secondly, this argument keeps the analysis fixed in terms of either democracy or autocracy—and prematurely names an outcome before a process begins. An incumbent ejection is a change but not regime change. Incumbent ejection occupies a middle ground between continuity of a regime or regime change. In other words, this middle ground is an undetermined vacuum. Various political possibilities at such a moment exist, including movement toward democracy or autocracy.

Understanding Egypt's uprising in 2011 as resulting in an incumbent ejection clarifies that the forced departure of a long-term autocrat was produced neither by an elite regime breakdown nor by revolutionary mass mobilization. Rather, Mubarak's resignation was a mixture of both phenomena, which were not mutually exclusive and independent from one another. The lens of incumbent ejection allows us to reconcile Mubarak's removal in February 2011 and the election of Muhammad Mursi from the previously outlawed Muslim Brotherhood in June 2012. While these events suggest the regime changed—after all, the former president became a temporary prisoner, and the former prisoner became a temporary president—we know that something short of regime change occurred. The separateness of opposition groups that participated in the uprising serves as an entry point to explain why the changes of personnel in the ruling coalition were never complemented by a regime change, whether in the form of the military's exit from public life, the reform of the security sector, or the fulfillment of the protesters' demands for bread, freedom, and social justice.

Joint protests that included the separate systemic opposition groups and antisystemic opposition groups allowed popular mobilization to rapidly alter the balance of power between the state and social forces. But, ultimately, these divided linkages saved the remnant incumbents. When the mobilization was at its peak, the protesters prevented the incumbents from having the initiative. This frustrated the attempts by both the state elites and systemic opposition to stop the mobilization. But after the protests were partially demobilized after Mubarak's ejection, the formal transition tells a different story: apprehending the amount of change possible, the remnant incumbents used systemic opposition forces such as the Muslim Brotherhood and the legal opposition parties to reinforce the fragmenting state and led a transition that marginalized the voices demanding greater change. The systemic opposition partnered with SCAF to stabilize the unsettled political situation that the uprising introduced. SCAF seemed obsessed with securing and protecting their position within Egypt's state during the transition. Yet, the ongoing demands and protests eventually forced the generals to launch a coup, which began their attempt to fashion together a new regime.

Egypt teaches us the lesson of incumbent ejection through examining the interplay between opposition relations and incumbents during mass protests. This lesson helps us theorize how autocratic regimes structure and often nurture the character of systemic opposition groups as well as how the interactions between split opposition configurations during an uprising condition and affect the subsequent political transition. Examining the events surrounding Egypt's 2011 uprising reveals the dynamics of the undertheorized but frequently occurring phenomenon of incumbent ejection.[11] Such analysis also exposes the limitations of elite-centric analyses by highlighting the role of mobilized protest movements in creating pressure for incumbent ejection that also does not compel incumbents into a credible pact with the antisystemic opposition.

Opposition, Protest Movements, and Popular Pressure

The systematic study of politics bolsters a rich theoretical literature about transitions that includes revolutions, regime change, and political liberalization; such studies should have been helpful for understanding this seismic event and its aftermath in Egypt. However, the patterns of antiregime dissent and resistance that emerged during Egypt's 2011 uprising challenge scholars of transitions to reconsider the role of protest movements and opposition groups in their analyses.

While the early literature on transitions acknowledged the role of mass mobilization as a source of leverage for systemic opposition groups to extract favorable concessions from incumbents through a pact,[12] this model takes the linkages between leaders of the systemic opposition and antisystemic opposition sector for granted.[13]

This analytic assumption of a unified opposition also limits the explanation for cases where mass mobilization plays a role in only changing a leader. This shortcoming becomes evident in the study of transitions in postcommunist Europe. After the fall of the Soviet Union, scholars studying mobilization and regime change rejected the pact-transitions of 1980s Latin America and instead focused on who writes the rules of how a transition will unfold.[14] Michael McFaul suggested that the structures of a previous autocracy have to be dismantled if democracy stands a chance. Failing this, however, McFaul predicts the autocrats are likely to make a return. He also does not believe in pact-making because it leaves a state in an unstable middle category of regimes. As McFaul argues, "A distribution of power clearly favoring democrats at the moment of transition has helped produce liberal democracy ten years later. A distribution of power clearly favoring dictators of the ancien régime has yielded new forms of authoritarian rule a decade later. Both causal paths have resulted in stable regimes."[15] Valerie Bunce is even more explicit about how opposition protests can nudge leaders, but this power does not mean cascading democratization. "Political protests," she claims, "performed a number of valuable functions. They signaled the breakdown of the authoritarian order; created a widespread sense that there were alternatives to that order; pushed authoritarian leaders to the bargaining table; created (and sometimes restored) a large opposition united by its rejection of the incumbent regime; and gave opposition leaders a resource advantage when bargaining with authoritarian elites."[16] This bargaining never develops into a formal pact. For Bunce, like McFaul, the focus is whether there is a break or bridge created from a state's autocratic past. While a national uprising might translate into electoral victories for the opposition forces in the first election after the mobilization, only a longer time horizon can tell if democratization occurs. In both cases, these researchers emphasize the outcome of democracy or autocracy over how the process unfolds.

Bunce's and McFaul's publications appeared around the time that Thomas Carothers critiqued the transitions paradigm in a landmark article in 2002.[17] According to him the central concern is that regimes had adopted the institutional facades of democratizing states or democracies without their substance.[18] As the transitions paradigm waned, the attention of scholars turned to elite-managed processes such as managing multiparty elections and their democratizing (or stabilizing) functions under hybrid or autocratic regimes.[19] Efforts to better situate mass demonstrations and protest movements continued to lag.[20] There are few sustained attempts to explore the relationship between such antisystemic "outside" opposition groups and systemic "inside" opposition groups operating within the realm of elections and parliaments.

While there have been efforts to study the relationship between included and excluded oppositions, and moderate and radical oppositions, the complexities of, and diverse orientations within, opposition politics have largely been muted in theoretical frameworks about transitions.[21] As a result various regime challengers are subsumed under the broad label "opposition" with the assumptions that in authoritarian settings, the opposition's momentum and initiative primarily come from leaders of parties and groups engaged in elections and systemic politics, and, secondly, that groups formally organized as "opposition" are in fact interested in pushing the boundaries of political contestation or pushing autocrats out of office.[22]

As described below, however, the instigators of antiregime mobilization in 2011 Egypt were concentrated within protest movements. They operated beyond the systemic opposition groups that sought office or enjoyed parliamentary representation. Nor was this dynamic exclusive to the uprising; the myriad movements that initiated the call for the demonstrations on January 25 had emerged and developed in clear tension with the systemic opposition across the previous decade,[23] and remained strongly at odds with them during the uprising. Several times during the eighteen days of revolutionary mobilization, regime elites and systemic opposition tried to contain the popular demands and peel off segments of protesters. The aim seemed to be to use elite agency to structure and maintain the existing lines of political hegemony. This strategy failed, which forced elites to repeatedly reconfigure the ruling coalition to try to reduce the number of protesters in the streets. The mobilization limited the ability of the state's political elites, systemic opposition groups, and independent figures to defuse the crisis. Not only did it structure the bargaining weight of state elites and systemic opposition groups during the days of protest, but it also created the vacuum of an uncertain transition after Mubarak's dismissal.

This dynamic diverges from the expectation that opposition groups will support mass mobilization to enhance their negotiating leverage against an incumbent regime. The systemic opposition's initial refusal to support the January 25 protests and the unresolved tension between it and the antisystemic opposition during the mobilization, moreover, challenges the assumption that opposition leaders are predisposed to pressure authoritarian leaders to expand the boundaries of political contestation.

In this case, popular mobilization exposes elite-driven theories as unable to fully explain a change of leader. Yet the correction should not be to swing in the other direction, because the agency of popular mobilization also proved to be constrained. While the crowds possessed the ability to capture the initiative from state elites and systemic opposition, the leaderless protest movements lacked the ability to shape the outcome beyond incumbent ejection. This limitation may also be, in part, because the speed with which the military relieved Mubarak from the presidency did not give the horizontal organizing approach time to develop. In any case, while popular mobilization mattered, translating the street momentum into a shift in the balance of power dramatic enough to cause full-fledged revolution requires agency beyond the mobilization. Nevertheless, the role of protest movements and popular mobilization—including their limitations—remains a weakness for understanding political transitions. By examining incumbent ejection in Egypt, we can better explain such cases and build more comprehensive theories about how political transitions proceed.

Opposite Directions before the Uprising

The initial impetus for the January uprising came from protest movements that had developed under Mubarak during the last decade. As diverse and divided as these movements were initially, they shared a set of common features, most notably loose organization around nonhierarchical structures and a commitment to an adventurous form of political activism through daring protests, disruptive strikes, and unruly sit-ins.[24] They preferred horizontal organizing over the systemic politics of formal institutions, which they did not trust could (or would) change autocratic practices.[25] The International Crisis Group back in October 2005 characterized the antisystemic opposition as "rejectionist" in their approach, which meant the groups agreed on what they opposed but not on what they wanted.[26]

The first wave of protest movements began in 2000 when NGO and leftist groups formed the Popular Campaign in Solidarity with the Second Palestinian Intifada. Groups organized in solidarity with Palestinians and, later, against US wars in Afghanistan and Iraq. These movements were only implicitly antiregime in their orientation, with their criticism centering on the Egyptian government's foreign policies and not on questions of domestic political reform. A second and more politicized wave of protest movements emerged in late 2004. Building on mass discontent with the Egyptian government's support of US policies in the region, Kifaya, or the Egyptian Movement for Change, held weekly demonstrations beginning in December 2004 and throughout 2005 to demand an end to the rule of Husni Mubarak.[27] They were also staunchly opposed to the prospect of Gamal Mubarak inheriting the presidency after his father retired. No peaceful, organized opposition group had ever called for an end to Mubarak's presidency until Kifaya appeared. Membership in such groups came from a generation of political activists and younger people who were frustrated with the legal opposition parties and the outlawed but tolerated systemic opposition, including the Muslim Brotherhood.

These systemic opposition groups, especially the legal opposition parties, tended to be controlled by aging leaders and were allied with the

Mubarak regime and the security apparatus. While the Mubarak regime actively sought to keep them from developing, there is little these groups could do in terms of fundamentally challenging the Mubarak regime.[28] As the International Crisis Group noted, "A striking feature is that the parties have very little inner life and consequently very little appeal even to those with an impulse for political activism."[29] The Muslim Brotherhood should be viewed as systemic opposition.[30] As Asef Bayat noticed in the 1990s, the Muslim Brotherhood adopted a passive revolution model that was built on slow and incremental reformism. Bayat may have noticed this in the 1990s, but the Brotherhood's strategy of passive revolution has been clear since the 1970s. As the Brothers emerged out of prison after Sadat became president, the group ejected revolutionary members. These forces later became armed groups that carried out violent actions from the late 1970s through the 1990s. The Brotherhood's brand of incrementalism eventually manifested itself in civil society organizations, parliamentary laws, and social relations over time.[31] It was decidedly not revolutionary because the Brotherhood did not seek abrupt change. In Bayat's words, "Egypt, thus, experienced the persistence of an Islamic movement without an Islamic revolution."[32] The Brotherhood never really counted on being antagonistic toward the Mubarak regime or removing it despite the repression they faced regularly. The group hardly ever protested without alerting the authorities. In statements from the mid-2000s, even the Brotherhood's younger members, such as Ibrahim al-Hudaybi, would say things like "Revolutions don't really lead to democracies, just look at Iran. The Brotherhood really wants a democracy in Egypt and it's willing to wait to make that happen."[33] Thus the disdain that most antisystemic opposition had for the legal opposition parties also extended to the Brotherhood.

The emergence of Kifaya encouraged the formation of similar movements, particularly among a new generation of activists. The antisystemic opposition groups shared a disillusionment not only with the ruling party's "reformist" rhetoric but also with the indecisiveness of the largely co-opted established opposition.[34] The distrust, tension, and division between this new sector of antisystemic politics and the systemic opposition was on display during the 2005 mobilizations against Mubarak and hereditary succession.

On July 20, 2005, the Brotherhood participated in a protest at the Lawyers Syndicate in downtown Cairo with several leftist groups, including the Revolutionary Socialists, Kifaya, and the Popular Campaign for Change.[35] It was the first and only time that year that the Brotherhood joined these groups in their weekly protests. While younger members of the Brotherhood and the Left occasionally cooperated, the larger group and its leaders kept the Left at arm's length.[36] It had taken weeks for the groups to reach an agreement about what the protest would look like. The name of the protest was called the National Front. The final agreement was that the Brotherhood would not use Islamist chants, and in exchange, the antisystemic protest groups would not chant against Mubarak. At the appointed time that evening masses of Brotherhood members emerged from all directions, swelling the usual numbers of the protest. For about twenty minutes, the protest, which was watched closely by teams of Central Security Forces, unfolded in an orderly fashion. There was very little mixing between Kifaya and other groups on one hand and the Brotherhood on the other. The Kifaya-aligned groups got frustrated by how subdued the Brotherhood were, and a small group starting chanting against Mubarak (mostly "Down with Mubarak!"). The Brotherhood, almost on cue, would drown out those slogans with chants invoking Islam. The organizers from each side met to discuss a deescalation. Finally, not even an hour into the joint action, the Brotherhood, seemingly on orders, left. Within minutes, the protest's number dwindled to about a hundred. A minority of Kifaya protesters went down the street to the Journalists Syndicate to continue their anti-Mubarak chants. Then with two stationary demonstrations occurring, the remaining protesters at the Lawyers Syndicate went down to the Journalists Syndicate to continue their demonstration for about another hour.

Parallel to these developments in the decade prior to the uprising, there was a rise of protest movements that focused on the socioeconomic grievances of both blue- and white-collar workers, particularly within the state sector. As Joel Beinin and Hossam el-Hamalawy observed in 2007, since 2004, Egypt was experiencing the "longest and strongest wave of worker protest since the end of World War II."[37] While International Financial Institutions lauded Egypt's annual growth rates, which even landed the country a spot on the World Bank's "top-ten" reformers in 2010,[38] most Egyptian citizens not connected to the ruling party despised the neoliberal economic orientation of the Ahmad Nazif cabinet and its policies. The US ambassador at the time claimed that the country's economic reform was a success story before lamenting that "Egypt still suffers from widespread and so far irremediable poverty affecting upwards of 35–40% of the population."[39] Faced with the growing wealth gap that was exacerbated by the upsurge in economic liberalization during the early 2000s, labor groups focused on lobbying the government for more humane wages and improved working conditions. But despite worker hardships, the labor sector did not have a decisive political agenda.

Marsha Pripstein Posusney has shown that there is a long history of Egyptian workers prioritizing their socioeconomic conditions and keeping them separate from wider movements for greater political change.[40] Beinin made similar arguments about the last decade of Mubarak's presidency. As he argued, "Mobilizations of workers and the unemployed infrequently demanded democracy or regime change as such."[41] Even though the labor protests were closer in style to Kifaya than the systemic groups, the overlap between them was not clear. In fact, in the demonstrations of April 6, 2008, there was a split between the nonlabor protesters, who issued political demands, and the labor protesters, who focused on their specific work-related demands.[42] Nevertheless, this is an important moment. Even if labor movements are not choosing to make their demands about politics, it is true that to protest about, for example, corruption or social justice goes straight to the core of the way the system works. During the April 2008 action, younger members in the antisystemic movements started linking fragmented socioeconomic grievances in Egyptian society, particularly as they related to labor, to their calls for transformative political change.[43] It is unclear that they succeeded at that time. Yet, it did enhance the profile of youth in the protest movements as they tried to increase their capacity to mobilize mass discontent into organized demonstrations with a clear anti-Mubarak bent. Yet, a lack of unity remained between the antisystemic protest groups and labor. In many ways, the emergence and development of an antisystemic opposition continued to maintain a cleavage between them and labor while the divide deepened with the formal systemic opposition groups and parties.

When the 2011 uprising began, the protesters expressed anger at the prospect of a hereditary succession and called for ending corruption and police brutality. These demands became articulated around "bread, freedom, and social justice." Egyptian and international media outlets alike discredited them by insisting that the protesters lacked a leader structure as well as clear demands. As the security services' violence and repression ceased to stop the protesters, however, one concrete demand did emerge: Mubarak's resignation. The elites around Mubarak's executive office attempted to stop the uprising, but each time that they tried to get out in front of the protesters, they failed. As Mona El-Ghobashy wrote at the time, "The genius of the Egyptian revolution is its methodical restoration of the public weal. The uprising restored the meaning of politics, if by that term is understood the making of collective claims on government."[44] Yet underneath this change lay a division between the systemic and antisystemic opposition that had developed over the course of, at least, a decade.

The Futility of Systemic Responses

During the initial days of the uprising, an expanding number of protesters from different groups overran the security forces around the country. Then on January 28 the protesters took control of Tahrir Square, the capital's symbolic heart and the epicenter of the national uprising. The security forces were pulled off the streets, and simultaneous "breakouts" emptied some of the capital's jails in an attempt to frighten the population. Neighborhood committees formed to protect the city's various districts as the darkened downtown offices of the ruling National Democratic Party were set ablaze. Rumors spread about the economy's imminent collapse. Meanwhile, the military deployed tanks, armored personnel carriers, and soldiers into the streets to show that it would play a role in resolving the unrest. The army fraternized and built rapport with the protesters.[45] The state's leading generals congealed into SCAF and interacted with Mubarak as they waited to see if the president's dwindling circle could convince people to vacate the squares in exchange for participating in some formal political process. By encircling the protesters in the squares, the army came to surround and contain the masses of gatherings.[46] In only four short days of fighting between the Interior Ministry and the protesters, protests had brought Mubarak's nearly thirty-year presidency to its knees. It became increasingly clear as the uprising progressed that the military would likely factor in its short-term resolution. The army waited out the stalemate between the Mubarak regime and society.

The political dynamic quickly became defined as the protesters versus Mubarak's regime. But the protests did not rally as a unified opposition. The state, systemic opposition, and antisystemic opposition participated during the uprising as separate groups. The division among the latter two allowed parts of the Mubarak state to survive. While such a dynamic had percolated below the surface for years, rarely had the opposition's divisions been on display as dramatically as during the uprising. The differences between the systemic and antisystemic opposition groups crystallized before the protests began. The systemic political groups opposed efforts to stage the January 25 protests, as infamously captured in the Muslim Brotherhood's announcement when they stated they would not participate.[47] Furthermore, systemic opposition parties, such as the Wafd and Tagammu', were not even formally consulted in the lead-up to January 25, and some of their leaders also openly rejected calls for protests.[48]

The tension between the groups was largely the same as it had been since the return of a street protest movement in the 2000s.[49] Yet in a twist on the usual routine, the protesters were able to overwhelm the coercive apparatus as more groups joined the demonstrations.[50] Although the context of the January 25 protests may have been similar to the past, the *scale* of those protests was entirely different. The state initially tried to stop the protests from meeting in central spaces. The police repression angered so many people that by Friday, January 28, the Brotherhood and others joined the uprising, feeling the regime was on their heels. Yet, as the Brotherhood's actions later reveal, the Brothers joined to increase their bargaining power with the state after it was clear the state was in trouble. At no time did it appear the Brotherhood was interested in overthrowing the state. As Hazem Kandil argued, "The political slot was open for negotiations, and the Brotherhood wanted to present itself as the best candidate by appeasing the two custodians of violence [military and security forces]."[51] Yet, their additional numbers sealed Mubarak's fate. Beginning on January 28, the protests propelled into revolutionary territory. When repression failed to secure the position of the elites, and their first calls to meet with the antisystemic opposition were ignored, Mubarak was compelled to renegotiate membership in the ruling coalition. In this moment, observers can glimpse the power of popular protests and the weakness of elite agency to contain such resistance.

The first serious attempt to placate the protesters occurred on January 28, when the army moved troops and tanks into the streets but appeared to remain neutral in the clashes between police and protesters. The armed forces' entrée into the streets blackmailed Mubarak and his supporters into rebalancing internal equilibria of the regime away from the Ministry of the Interior's forces and back toward the army.[52]

This initial step produced a follow-up attempt to dilute the protesters early on the morning of January 29. With the military arriving on the streets the day before, Mubarak appeared on state TV. Saying (or perhaps threatening) that Egypt must choose between chaos and stability, he announced the formation of a new government and the appointment of long-time intelligence aide 'Umar Sulayman as vice president.[53] Sulayman's appointment spoke volumes. Mubarak had ruled his entire presidency without a vice president despite consistent objections from the opposition. Many speculated that his unwillingness to appoint a vice president was linked to plans to pass on power to his son Gamal. Mubarak's appointment of Sulayman was a way of communicating that Gamal's political future in Egypt was over. Relatedly, the appointment accommodated public support, expressed through 2010 in a poster campaign, for Sulayman's presidential bid.[54] Although Sulayman himself repeatedly denied presidential ambitions, his denials failed to exclude his name when the Egyptian public or American officials discussed possible successors to Mubarak.[55] Thus, Sulayman's appointment during the uprising was an attempt to extricate the regime from the polarizing situation between Mubarak and the protesters. Some speculated that Mubarak's fate was tied to the population's acceptance of Sulayman in his new role.[56]

The formation of a new government was also part of Mubarak's attempt to dampen the mobilization. The diminishing regime's strategy was to stem the wounds of mass protests by rotating its elites. By dismissing the Nazif-led cabinet, which had been in power since 2004, Mubarak removed some of the leading agents responsible for the most extensive (and controversial) neoliberal economic reforms in Egypt's history, signaling that the neoliberal era was over. Seemingly taking no chances, the state elites around Mubarak went further still. Neoliberal ministers and some monopoly capitalists, such as Ahmad al-'Izz, that had not fled into exile were arrested. Mubarak also fired and arrested the despised minister of interior, Habib al-'Adli. Perhaps as telling as Sulayman's appointment as vice president, Defense Minister Muhammad Tantawi came to represent the armed forces in the cabinet and even promoted Ahmad Shafiq to deputy prime minister. Furthermore, there was the issue of the president's ruling party. Protesters had torched the building of the NDP during the Friday protests. Thus, by the early morning of January 29, Mubarak and his remaining state elites had changed the composition of the ruling coalition to try to contain the antisystemic demands. The NDP, hereditary succession, and the neoliberal economic reform team were part of the past. The men who operated the coercive apparatus known for egregious cases of torture and police brutality were shoved to the margins of the ruling coalition. Left alone at the coalition's center were the military generals, who were catapulted onto the throne of state power.

Mubarak's new cabinet centered on more traditional and respected figures as well as the armed forces, whose reputation was stellar compared to the repressive Interior Ministry. These elite alterations would have been politically powerful in a noncrisis situation. In fact, had Mubarak carried out such maneuvers a year earlier, it might have preempted the uprising altogether. However, rather than recover initiative and power, such maneuvers during instances of expanding mobilization uncover the impotence of elite power. This impotence resulted partly because the rotation of elites moved the Mubarak regime in the opposite direction that they had traveled since 2004, when "old guard" figures had been incrementally disposed of in favor of the Gamal Mubarak neoliberal team. Yet, during moments of popular mobilization, the monopoly over authority that Mubarak's regime had long enjoyed seemed to evaporate into thin air. Capturing this reversal of power between state elites and protesters, reporter Ashraf Khalil tweeted, "Was in Tahrir 10 minutes after Mubarak gave his speech. Protestors thought it comical. They weren't even mad, just laughed it off."[57] Even though Mubarak's actions failed to alter the dynamic, Egyptian politics nevertheless changed. By adding the military overtly to the ruling coalition (even if to defuse the protests), state elites transformed the political dynamic into a three-sided structure that pitted the protesters against Mubarak and the armed forces.

As Husni Mubarak entered this unfamiliar political world, the state elites recalibrated their attempts to peel the demonstrators away from the streets. As the dust settled from the January 29 cabinet reshuffle, the atmosphere of uncertainty that the regime had hoped to spark by removing the police and turning off the country's internet proved insufficient. Confronted with the inability to stop the protests, Mubarak was nudged onto state TV again and on February 1, made what were previously unthinkable concessions. After again playing on the chaos-versus-stability trope, he announced, "I tell you in absolute veracity that I do not intend to run for the coming presidential election." Prior to that moment, Mubarak and the NDP had always evaded the question about a potential sixth presidential term. While ambiguous about the type of election that would take place, Mubarak indicated that Egypt's transition had begun. As he addressed the nation, silence fell across the squares and homes of Egypt. Mubarak appeared to be more of a frail eighty-two-year-old grandfatherly figure than the source of all neopatrimonial power. The youthful energy of the street mobilization had outflanked him. Yet because of Mubarak's vulnerability, the speech had an effect. If the regime elites' hope was to use Mubarak's weakened state to dilute the various protest movements, it seemed to be working. As Ahmed Kadry reported:

> [Mubarak's] speech was very clever and it went much further than his earlier speech. . . . He stated that he would step down in September but he took away any sign of victory for the protestors by adding that he never planned to run for a sixth term in the first place. He also added that it was only he that could provide stability and peace whilst

> a political transition took place. Protestors continued to call for his resignation once his speech came to a close but their numbers began to dwindle away from the now famous Tahrir Square.[58]

Mubarak's performance revived the notion that he could wrestle the initiative from the protesters. With all that Mubarak's regime had done to the country, Egyptians seemed willing to record the uprising's victory and move on with the transition as the president retired slowly from office.

The following day, however, regime-sponsored violence canceled out any goodwill the previous night's performance achieved. For over sixteen hours in Tahrir Square, thousands of hired thugs (*balṭagiyya*) and protesters battled as the military stood idly by watching the clashes. Some pro-Mubarak agents threw cement blocks off of tall buildings, while other NDP-backed agents rode camels and horses into the crowd, attacking the protesters with sticks and whips. Through bravery, organization, and sheer will, the square held off the continuous assaults. The events on February 2, which popularly became known as "The Battle of the Camel," had deleterious effects on the state elites' ability to end the crisis. It swung the momentum that Mubarak had captured back in the protesters' favor. Reinvigorated, the popular mobilization widened as many of the regular citizens' sympathy for Mubarak transformed into disgust. The demand for Mubarak's resignation hardened and grew louder.

By this point, it is unlikely that Mubarak was running the country. The military was visibly involved when it put tanks on the streets on January 28. After that moment, Mubarak was pushed into the background as Sulayman took the state's reigns, with foreign states communicating through him as opposed to Mubarak or the Foreign Ministry.[59] Sulayman also became the public face of how to whittle down the popular mobilization. He called for a "national dialogue" with the opposition. Such dialogues periodically happened throughout Mubarak's presidency, but had never taken place during a prolonged mobilization. As with the regime's previous attempts, the Sulayman-led spectacle failed to quell the demand that Mubarak leave. It did, however, unmask how the systemic opposition was willing to marginalize the antisystemic sector in favor of protecting and inserting themselves into some semblance of the existing political and social hierarchy.

In an attempt to use the domesticated opposition to reconstitute the exclusive elite arena, Sulayman turned to representatives of Egypt's legal opposition parties, such as Tagammu' and Wafd, representatives of the so-called council of elders,[60] and members of the formally banned Muslim Brotherhood to participate in the dialogue on February 6.[61] The composition of the assembled group was a consequence not of Sulayman's choosing. He invited some antisystemic opposition groups such as April 6 to send a representative, but they declined to participate in the dialogue. As Samer Shehata observed at that time, "The 'national dialogue' is little more than a regime tactic to co-opt the more moderate opposition parties, while leaving the youth protesters out in the cold."[62] Others argued, "Playing catch-up has seen the brotherhood engaging in dialogue with a government that has long kept it outlawed . . . while at the same time trying to avoid accusations of a sell-out from the hundreds of thousands who continue to pack Tahrir Square and who want to see President Hosni Mubarak gone before any negotiations towards a democratic transition can begin."[63] But the state elites again were unable to direct the protests toward an end. The superficial failure of the national dialogue showed the powerlessness of the elites and systemic opposition to alter the situation despite repeated attempts when confronted by mobilization. The systemic opposition was in no position to negotiate with Sulayman's regime on behalf of the uprising because the protesters rejected its credentials as opposition.

The national dialogue, however, did produce a platform for the Brotherhood to negotiate with the outgoing administration. Later, according to defectors from the Brothers' ranks, the initial day of dialogue led to a series of secret meetings between Sulayman and the Islamist group in which the vice president asked the Brothers to send their members home from the square in exchange for an expanded political role.[64] As Sulayman tried to extricate the Mubarak regime out of its predicament, SCAF watched the Brotherhood's actions and realized their goals for the uprising diverged dramatically from those of antisystemic opposition in the streets. They nurtured the Brotherhood as a steadying force. As Muhammad Habib, ex-deputy guide of the organization explained to me in March 2011, "The military realized they could not control domestic stability yet still uphold unpopular foreign policies. They are using the Brothers to serve as this domestic source of stability."[65]

The Limits of Popular Mobilization

The protesters that led the January uprising against Mubarak possessed the ability to shock and immobilize the regime. The success of the January 25 uprising rested on the fact that there was consistent mobilization around the country. While the protests could corner elite actions, they did not, however, have the ability to shape the outcome beyond a change of leader. Because they were leaderless, organized in nonhierarchical structures, and undecided about the type of transition they wanted, protesters could not produce figures that could ably negotiate on their behalf. While some looked to Nobel laureate Muhammad ElBaradei and the National Coalition for Change, which he headed, he did not appeal to important constituencies among the demonstrators or have a national reach. This is not to say a horizontal and inclusive organizing strategy could not have worked, but it seems that such organizing requires time to coalesce. That the military got Mubarak to resign after only eighteen days of protests likely precluded its effectiveness.

Crucially, the remaining elites around Sulayman could move quickly toward incumbent ejection because there existed a systemic opposition that was ready to negotiate as well as willing to lock out the antisystemic opposition groups. As long as the systemic opposition remained loyal to the state, the remnant elites in the reconfigured ruling coalition could effectively neutralize the demands of the revolutionaries. All the incumbents needed to do was find a visible policy to help get the people to declare victory and empty the squares and streets. Given the central core demand was Mubarak's resignation, this became the best, last resort: the military's leadership could force Mubarak to quit and then declare they had conceded to the protesters' central request. Then debate and discussion could begin about the political transition forward.

With the military reintroduced into the ruling coalition, the systemic opposition being included in the country's politics, and the protesters pledged to remain in the public squares until Mubarak quit the presidency, the situation seemed one of gridlock. The armed forces seemed content to wait it out, but then the protesters became recipients of countless reinforcements.

On February 7, the antisystemic labor movement began to influentially contribute to the uprising, tipping the balance in favor of the revolutionaries. Nearly sixty separate strikes—undertaken by fifty to sixty thousand workers in total—started around the country, some with explicitly political demands.[66] They stopped the transportation sector as well as enterprises such as subsidiaries of the Suez Canal Authority, Ghazl al-Mahalla, and Telecom Egypt.[67] In many respects, the strikes were consistent with the growth of labor collective action since 2004. But their timing—beginning at a moment when the political arm of the state could not effect change—increased the prospect that the mobilization would overrun the state and its institutions. Had the situation remained solely about the mobilization in sealed off public squares, the military's strategy to sit tight may have worked. Instead, a perfect storm of labor activity and national mobilization combined with minimal police capacity, and the military, fearing greater contagion effect, was compelled to intercede against Mubarak. While it is impossible to know their intentions, the military's aging leadership (all of whom Mubarak appointed) convened and decided that they had to offer Mubarak up in an effort to mollify the mobilization.

On February 10, Mubarak delivered another state address. If Mubarak's second address tried to tug on the sentimentality of Egyptians, the third one was defiant. He stated that he would pass "some" powers to the vice president and would instigate commissions to amend the constitution. The crowds that had gathered publicly in anticipation of his resignation grew angry, and many feared that anger would lead to clashes between society and any state institution, including the army. The following day, February 11, protesters mobilized in Tahrir Square; by Maspero, the headquarters for Egyptian state radio and TV; and in front of the presidential palace in Heliopolis. As protesters approached the palace, the army turned its tanks' turrets away from them to signal that it stood with the people. Yet this was not an act of defection, because they were not consulting with anyone from the antisystemic opposition. The only contact that had taken place was between the dying regime's civilian leaders and figures from the systemic opposition establishment.

Later that afternoon, the vice president appeared on TV with a general dressed in a suit standing over his left shoulder. Sulayman read a statement announcing that Mubarak had resigned as president and that SCAF was in power. Elation spread among the activists throughout the country; superficially, it looked like an unequivocal victory for mass protests. But the importance of SCAF's intercession into politics should not be underemphasized. SCAF intervened to eject the incumbent in an attempt to save the state. Specifically, it changed the leader in hopes of positioning itself so as to safeguard its long-standing economic privileges and expand its newly acquired political authority. In many ways, it was a return to the corridors of power from which Sadat had excluded the military in the 1970s.

Egypt's uprising produced uncountable changes to politics and society, but it did not create the major opposition divisions. To use Bunce's phrase, the systemic opposition served as "a bridge" for the remnants of the old discredited regime.[68] Even with Egypt's longtime dictator and his National Democratic Party out of the picture, the deposed president's military leaders continued to rely on legal engineering to influence the electoral process, conservative judicial bodies to rule favorably, and the state bureaucracy to return more continuity than change.[69] While conceding to popular demands on symbolic issues, such as putting Mubarak and his associates on trial, the army remained insistent on limiting the scope of the state's institutional change or reform.

Most notably, the country's new rulers left the Interior Ministry and Mubarak's coercive apparatus intact and unchallenged.[70] Repressive practices of the previous regime persisted and were even tightened in some areas. For example, SCAF criminalized labor strikes and demonstrations.[71] Security forces continued to act with impunity as they employed deadly violence against protesters—ironically while the ex-president and his associates were on trial and facing life sentences for failing to prevent violence against peaceful protesters. Despite the 2012 election of Muhammad Mursi as president, the transition process ultimately secured the military's future economic role and political influence. This is unsurprising because SCAF changed the ruling coalition, and as its new minders, used their influence to protect their interests. There is an interesting parallel here to how a national uprising shows the divisions among the state apparatus that apes divisions within the opposition. An uncontrolled uprising also enables jockeying among actors within the state, which permits the ruling coalition to be altered—in this instance the coalition shifted influence from the Ministry of Interior to SCAF. Yet, the larger point remains: had the state fallen because of the popular mobilization alone, SCAF would have never been in a position to secure its interests with such ease inside the vacuum of a transition.

This returns us to the tension within the transitology literature on regime change. Theories on regime change focus on the maneuvers of elites and how they succeed or fail in navigating crises of mass mobilization. If a regime survives, the elites are assumed to be durable, adaptable, or powerful. If a change occurs, a host of elite-centric theories, such as regime fragmentation or individual miscalculation, are often invoked to account for the state's collapse or an imposed transition. Consequently, popular mobilization is explained similarly in the literature: When there is a pacted transition, the popular mobilization is assumed to be the cause because a unified opposition coalition altered the balance of power vis-à-vis the regime toward democracy. When not, reasons are supplied, such as a lack of opposition leadership or unclear demands, to explain an autocratic outcome. Yet, Egypt shows us a different path entirely. An incumbent ejection starts Egypt's political transition. Incumbent ejection initiates a particular kind of political transition in which the leadership is sacrificed while the regime's rump is salvaged through an alliance with the systemic opposition that refuses to push for expanding political space for all. Scholars could better tease out how configurations and linkages between systemic and antisystemic opposition shape an incumbent ejection and how this affects a political transition.

The Other "Revolution"

The 2013 mass mobilization against President Muhammad Mursi also dislocated the lead incumbent. Yet the events of that time do not resemble Mubarak's overthrow. Whereas Mubarak's ejection was a case of popular mobilization stifling and neutralizing executive power and the authority of the state's ruling coalition, the protests that began on June 29, 2013, and culminated in Mursi's arrest on July 3, can be traced to manipulation by the army, Interior Ministry, and General Intelligence Services.[72] Therefore, if the aftermath of the 2011 uprising was about SCAF and systemic opposition trying to get people to demobilize in order to control the transition after incumbent ejection, the 2013 military coup was about manufacturing controlled mass protest to authorize the extralegal removal of an elected president. In 2011, SCAF was powerless to induce change, but in 2013 it held nearly all the levers of power. The irony is that SCAF directed its attention toward the opposition group most responsible for saving it throughout 2011 and 2012.

SCAF and the systemic opposition had tried to bring the antisystemic revolutionaries into the formal processes of the transition, such as through the numerous electoral spectacles, in order to domesticate them and dilute their demands. The events in 2013 were altogether different. SCAF took the counterrevolution into the streets to overwhelm the revolutionaries at their own game. While 2011 produced an incumbent ejection, the mobilization in 2013 helped SCAF end the transition as an experiment as they started the process of constructing a new regime. Rather than Mubarak's team of elites being forced to change their leader by the crowds in 2011, SCAF controlled the change of leadership in 2013. This is not the outcome of a well-designed crowd control plan or the action of a deliberative evil genius.

SCAF likely would have preferred that Mursi remain in the presidency. Observers will never know for certain. But the non-Brotherhood parts of society, which included Egyptians connected to the old regime or sympathetic to the younger revolutionaries, simply would not submit to the out-of-touch, exclusivist practices the elected president pursued. When Mursi became a liability for SCAF, they dropped him quickly. The

2013 intelligence-orchestrated protests against Mursi were engineered on the back of the president's controversial handling of the late 2012 work by the constitutional assembly and in Mursi's constitutional declaration that awarded him sweeping—if temporary—powers. In the face of such governance, people kept mobilizing and placing more pressure on the enfeebled and brittle state apparatus. While Mubarak oversaw a robust autocratic regime, Mursi was merely one player operating in a political arena that had seen power redistributed among the state's agents. Competition, rather than hierarchy, defined Egypt's ever-fragmenting state. SCAF moved against Mursi preemptively because it feared another uncontrolled mass mobilization. The generals had also decided that for their way of life to continue, they would have to get involved in the business of regime-making.

The 2013 military coup brought 'Abdel Fattah al-Sisi and the senior generals in front of the curtain of state authority. Rather than merely run the disrupted Mubarakist state, SCAF would have to build a new regime and fortify the state apparatus. This work remains incomplete at present. While the argument that SCAF's military coup was a return to the authoritarianism of the Mubarak years could be made, there are distinct differences between Mubarak's regime and the post-2013 regime in formation.

The 2013 military coup ushered in an entirely new era of Egyptian politics that is marked with capricious state violence, trivial elections, and a weakened political economy awash with aid rent as the precarity of Egypt's economic situation left it even more dependent on regional states such as Saudi Arabia, Kuwait, and the United Arab Emirates, as well as back in the IMF's grip. The coup also destroyed any relationships between the systemic and antisystemic opposition groups.

The first time that a military coup was mentioned in a newspaper as an option against Mursi was in early August 2012.[73] *Al-Destor* ran a story warning of the Islamization of the state and called for the military to intervene.[74] Mursi had been in power less than five weeks. After that, the military and other security services routinely refused to submit to a chain of command under Mursi's leadership. State-owned Egyptian media outlets, such as *al-Ahram*, reported how SCAF would meet without its "nominal head, President Muhammad Mursi."[75] The military itself issued ambiguous posts and messages on social media sites to combat rumors about their lack of support for Mursi. For instance, after it was rumored that the president was considering changes to the military command structure, a military spokesperson posting on SCAF's official Facebook page denied that SCAF viewed the removal of top generals as "suicide" for Mursi.[76] According to NBC journalist Ayman Mohyeldin, a February 2013 post on another Facebook page close to the armed forces denied that the military would undertake a coup.[77] Yet in January 2013—as lawlessness gripped parts of Egypt after a court ruling concerning the 2012 soccer massacre in Port Said sentenced twenty-one people to death—General al-Sisi issued a statement. The general, whose appointment as defense minister SCAF had secured (whether by persuasion or force), stated, "The continuation of the conflict between the different political forces and their differences over how the country should be run could lead to the collapse of the state and threaten future generations."[78] Such an ominous statement may have been intended to frighten the population into accepting the new president. But, instead, it also fueled a rebellion against him.

If SCAF and the military were unprepared for the uncontrolled mobilization in 2011, they did not make the same mistake before launching the coup to remove Mursi. When attempts to incorporate those with revolutionary demands into the unreformed and counterrevolutionary state institutions or electoral spectacles produced only more mobilization, making Mursi's hold on the presidency even more tenuous, the generals changed tack. Feeding off the popular discontent at Mursi and the worsening economic situation, the military organized a protest movement to go after Mursi and the Brotherhood. If the revolutionaries would not come to the counterrevolution, the generals helped organize for the counterrevolution to take to the streets.

According to initial reports, a new grassroots protest campaign called Tamarrud (Revolt) was established in late April 2013.[79] Tamarrud was originally touted as a descendent of Kifaya. Mahmud Badr, its twenty-eight-year-old leader, would have been just nineteen when Kifaya was founded in December 2004. It is conceivable that Badr had developed some organizing credentials in the interim, but it is also troubling that long time activists did not seem to know him. The other red flag was Tamarrud claimed to have collected more than twenty-two million signatures on a petition demanding Mursi resign as president to make way for new presidential elections.[80] While unquestionably true that most Egyptians were unsatisfied with Mursi at the time—a telephone poll published by Baseera showed that 73 percent of Egyptians aged 20–23 believed the president had not made "a single good decision during his first year in office"—the idea that twenty-two million people signed Tamarrud's petition seems unlikely.[81] I have found no sources that can confirm that twenty-two million signatures were gathered. Similarly, in his rich book on protests in Egypt, Neil Ketchley also noted that it was impossible to independently verify how many Egyptians ultimately signed the petition.[82]

If Defense Minister al-Sisi and SCAF acted ambiguously in their opposition to Mursi, Tamarrud did not. By the time the military's coup machinery began to work, Tamarrud publicly announced on social media and on state TV, "There was no way to accept any half measures. There is no alternative other than the peaceful end of power of the Muslim Brotherhood and its representative, Mohamed Mursi." Furthermore, it issued a warning to the state by imploring "institutions including the army, the police, and the judiciary, to clearly side with the popular will as represented by the crowds."[83] In the aftermath of the coup, Badr claimed that Tamarrud "owns the streets."[84] Yet Tamarrud leaders later revealed, confirming what many had speculated at the time, that different intelligence services had organized Tamarrud members. Tamarrud activist Walid al-Masri admitted to being in constant contact with a group of military officers. He explained, "We didn't ask them for help. They just offered it. And we welcomed that."[85] Another Tamarrud organizer, Muhibb Duss, who was later prosecuted by the government, also corroborated the story. In January 2016, Duss said that Tamarrud founding members Mahmud Badr, Muhammad 'Abd al-'Aziz, and Hassan Shahin met with state and army officials, including al-Sisi, during Mursi's presidency.[86]

The final mobilizations against Muhammad Mursi began on June 30, 2013, the one-year anniversary of his presidency. A mixture of a worsening economy, unfulfilled demands of the revolutionaries, Mursi's paternalistic manner, and the imposition of Egypt's new constitution fueled his undoing over the course of his year in office. By the time of the final protests against him, Mursi sat on top of a state that he never really controlled.[87] No matter how pliant Mursi tried to be to the military or security services, his appeals to the wider political establishment and society went unheard.[88] On July 1, al-Sisi gave the president an ultimatum to step down and accept early elections or be forcibly removed from office—the last time the military would offer the Brotherhood a menu of choices with only bad options.

The 2013 coup was the ultimate tragedy for Egypt's transition. As Mursi was being arrested, military personnel took up positions on the bridges that connected the capital's arterial roads. Soldiers commandeered the state radio and television building. As army helicopters dropped Egyptian flags onto the assembled masses in Tahrir, state TV was prepared for the spectacle, with camera angles perfectly capturing Egyptian pilots in American-made jets skywriting hearts and the colors of Egypt's flag. Meanwhile, US president Barack Obama called for everyone to "show restraint," which signaled that the United States government had accepted Mursi's fate.[89]

Crowds added a popular stamp of approval for the military. State-supported agents and those wanting the state to co-opt them made arguments that the mobilization was the largest demonstration in the history of the world. Reuters cited a source that fourteen million people took to the streets across the country.[90] Others placed the turnout as high as thirty million, which would have been nearly 40 percent of the population. The figures were immediately disproven as impossible.[91] Nevertheless, in a first, state-owned TV broadcast protests, showing crowds assembled in at least twelve different locations around the country. As international media such as CNN called the military's maneuvers and the crowds supporting them a coup, protesters occupying Tahrir Square projected "It is not a coup" in green lasers on the Mugama'a administrative building as the military chased the CNN correspondent from the scene.[92] The systematic coordination promoting the narrative of another revolution was extensive.

Although the coup crushed the revolutionaries' hopes for inclusive political change, the belief that the military took action at the insistence of the crowds also suggested to some that revolution would become more likely as time passed.[93] Others made the argument that the military's intervention would lead to another phase of mobilization in an ongoing transition.[94] This claim echoed earlier arguments that the barrier of fear characterizing the preuprising security state had been relegated to the dustbin of history and assumed, as did most revolutionaries, that society could remobilize instantaneously if those running the state behaved badly. These views were supplemented by other interpretations that watered down what was transpiring. Two analysts at the Brookings Institution, for example, downplayed what Egypt had experienced as a "soft coup."[95] These portrayals served to provide cover for a political contest that SCAF had already rigged to its advantage. What all these views missed was the role of the linkages between systemic and antisystemic opposition groups throughout. The entire process that culminated in the coup had been founded on an uprising in which linkages between systemic and antisystemic opposition groups were divided when they rose up against an authoritarian regime.

Conclusions

Concepts like regime change stress the primacy of elite pacts and defections, the chaos produced by the loss of a patrimonial leader, or opportunistic military interventions. But the Egyptian elites facing uncontrolled popular mobilization in 2011 could only respond with futility to rapid shifts introduced by people power. It was not the maneuvers by elites, but rather the divided opposition configurations, that allowed the state to limp forward, disrupted but with an altered ruling coalition. The revolutionary uprising produced incumbent ejection and collapsed the regime but also structured the transition in a way that favored Egypt's new leaders—the SCAF generals—in the vacuum of a political transition. Such analyses complicate and enrich the dominant approach to transitions and provide an entry point for rethinking regime change, autocratic durability, and popular mobilization.

Notably, whereas the literature tends to treat state elites and formal opposition as separate entities whose interests do not overlap, Mubarak's regime and the systemic opposition were as loyal to one another in crisis as they had been during the last decade of Mubarak's rule. The protests may have forced the generals to repeatedly remake the ruling coalition, but the antisystemic opposition failed to crack the relationship between the regime elite and systemic opposition. In fact, the cooperation between the state elites and systemic opposition reveals just how disciplined they were when confronting an existential threat from the antisystemic opposition. When they could not get the crowds to return to their homes, the military intervened against Mubarak, but there is no evidence that the military ever defected from the regime. SCAF's maneuvers were also not a preemptive coup or a play for power. Sacrificing Mubarak enabled other parts of the state to be salvaged. While military leaders often claim that they intervened to protect the revolution of 2011, the aftermath of the uprising illustrates that they were primarily protecting the revolution—or military coup—of 1952, which brought into place the long-standing political order that successive autocrats then sought to maintain.

The central reason why the military's leadership escaped from the corner that Egypt's revolutionary uprising put it in was that the frequently repressed but systemic opposition groups like the Muslim Brotherhood were so eager to break with the antisystemic opposition in order to serve as a bridge between Mubarak's rule and SCAF's transition.[96] That incumbent ejection is most likely to occur in settings where the links between drivers of popular antisystemic mobilization and systemic opposition are divided effectively creates a drama among a triangle of participants. This design helps explain the continuities that surfaced during a transition after the theatrical fall of a dictator. The battle over Egypt's democratic or autocratic future was just beginning. Yet, this beginning was a production of the divided oppositional linkages on display before, during, and after a national uprising. These divisions allowed the state's remnants to continue to contest politics during an uncertain transitional period filled with elections.

2

Electoral Recalibration?

Transitional Elections and Disempowerment

> The referendum on constitutional amendments equals democracy.
>
> —Text message distributed to every mobile subscriber in Egypt by SCAF, March 18, 2011

> Voting is a release but so is violence. Muhammad Mahmoud was a large scream and voting was a smaller scream. People cast their votes and it showed that they did not want to fight and did not want to boycott. The problem was that voting became the glue for Parliament to keep a repressive regime.
>
> —Activist Wael Eskandar, interview by author, November 2012

The divided relations among systemic and antisystemic opposition groups did not just open an exit for SCAF to eject the lead incumbent as the revolutionary atmosphere spread in January and February 2011. These strained opposition relations seeped into and would define the transition. SCAF was unprepared to govern and as shocked as everyone else by the national uprising. Yet, they had the clout to redesign the ruling coalition as they positioned themselves at the center of the state. They also maintained popular authority to dismiss Mubarak. Yet, despite executing these moves, SCAF had little foresight about their future as the state's masters. They certainly were not thinking about scrapping the transition and committing the task of regime-making. SCAF also needed assistance beyond their supporters. Incumbent ejection did not stop Egyptians from making claims. It did not reintroduce the predictable interactions of Mubarak's collapsed regime or magically repair the fragmenting state. Ceding to a transition process, which SCAF could not have rejected anyway, indicates the military was neither prepared from a planning standpoint to govern nor had sufficient reservoirs of legitimacy to simply take over. Yet, agreeing to a transition does not imply SCAF was a disinterested player. In fact, not only were they interested, they also had international support, weapons, and cash on hand to help blunt the continuing mobilized pressure from below. But even these attributes were not enough. SCAF needed to finesse the transition process and employ certain tools to guide the way. Specifically, the military needed citizens to join in the transition to give time to the fragmented state to calm as well as invest in the political process beyond street protests.

The generals may have not preferred to insert one of their own as president, but they definitely were not there to boost Egyptian democracy. Unsurprisingly the divisions among the opposition relationships, which the Mubarak regime nurtured and had proven so resilient during the initial uprising, played a crucial role into Egypt's turbulent transition. SCAF continued to encourage the split as they encouraged Egypt's Muslim Brotherhood to participate, while teaming up with them to marginalize revolutionary voices. This performance was most on display in the elections held between March 2011 and June 2012. As the quotes above suggest, elections played an outsized role in defining Egypt's transition.

The transition that followed Egypt's uprising was electorally grounded and opened the doors of representative office to previously excluded groups. Yet, despite formal transition processes and the appearance of political change, elections produced new political orders that propped up problematic disempowering continuities from the past. This chapter examines the political work that elections performed during Egypt's political transition because SCAF "electionized" the population and the process.[1]

While Egyptians were electionized during the 2011–13 transition, these contests did not result in greater empowerment for most. For those candidates that did fundraise, develop policy platforms, and campaign as well as for voters that were moved by individual campaigns, the elections were significant and individually empowering. A candidate or a voter might believe the elections were a sea-changing moment. Yet, when we broaden the gaze, the elections allowed SCAF generals to reconfigure parts of the state and redistribute power around themselves while marginalizing revolutionary voices that wanted to democratically restructure the state. Similar to protests and incumbency, SCAF used elections to bring in the systemic Muslim Brotherhood to reinforce the unsettled state, arguing that elections were enough for the revolution to be completed. How, then, do we assess the changes that happened around elections in Egypt?

If Egypt's transitional elections, after years of elections with few choices, can be characterized as enjoying "broad participation from voters" and as "a progressive step towards democratic transition,"[2] they nevertheless anchored into society the notion that the only choice was between the existing state remnants and their Islamist challengers. Transitional elections in Egypt were disempowering to a wider electorate because they structured a narrow choice, which allowed autocracy to be replicated even as they became a mechanism for incorporating segments of the systemic opposition into procedurally free and fair events.

As a secondary argument, elections during a time of regime-making have returned to unexciting moments because the outcomes are never in doubt. The elections since the military deposed Muhammad Mursi do not represent a return to Mubarak-style elections. Rather, they have become a way of redisciplining a restive population and extending the state's dominance into the lives of people seeking political change. Elections in Egypt today transmit a message that citizens will vote as they are told to and nothing else. In such a scenario, wider political participation is not welcome as SCAF tries to build a regime around 'Abdel Fattah al-Sisi while feigning adherence to international norms about convening regular elections.

Although Egypt's transition ushered in elections in which Islamists gained access to the state by winning almost half the seats in Parliament and the presidency, a side effect of the elections was that protests against the unresponsive state became less effective. Elections became an approved alternative to protesting and assembling in the country's squares. SCAF used electoral contests to weaken the power of people protesting and unevenly partner with the systemic Brotherhood.

Elections funneled some participation into these contests, which diluted the unrelenting popular protests and demands on the state. The turnout figures also made the population more legible to SCAF and the state by allowing the elites to see how different parts of the country vote. SCAF was able to do so because the repeated elections were characterized by real choice, higher turnout, and a lack of state interference—a stark contrast to the electorate's previous experience during the Mubarak years.[3] In this way, individuals might feel empowered while overall elections also led to collective disempowerment because they (and developments around them such as constitutional declarations) anchored SCAF and the military's privileges into the state while attacking the resiliency of the protest opposition. Elections, therefore, remained spectacles that limited the population's ability to contest state power or reject certain types of governing practices. While the actors might have changed during the transition, autocratic hegemonic practices and interests continue to electorally marginalize democracy advocates that protest in the streets. As British journalist Jack Shenker argued, "The attempt to . . . democratize our societies beyond their electoral systems is the principal battle of our generation, and revolutionary Egyptians are on the frontline."[4]

The case of Egypt and the changes from the Mubarak period to the SCAF-led transition to al-Sisi's presidency provide an opportunity to examine and compare elections in the same country during a relatively short time period under three sets of conditions: "stable" autocracy, a transition, and during the construction of a new authoritarian regime. This comparison forces us to develop a nuanced understanding about elections after an uprising. As the Egyptian case shows, successive elections between March 2011 and June 2012 recalibrated an exclusivist political arena.[5] The elections were a real-life theatrical performance that citizens took seriously, whereby new actors blended into the remnant and unreformed state apparatus while the electorate obstructed revolutionary thinking, horizons, and possibilities.[6] While the transitional elections did not resemble those of the late Mubarak period because there was real choice, little state interference or forgery, and an active and open campaign period, the contests nevertheless continued to serve the state's expansive bureaucratic interests and revive its older discourses. The group of revolutionaries, who refused to accept the offer to exchange street politics for voting booths, pointed out the disempowering effects of elections, continued to protest, and faced increased violence from the state.[7]

After reviewing the literature on elections as a new mode of transition and examining transitional elections in other cases, this chapter discusses the five times that Egyptians voted between March 2011 and June 2012. I detail the case of Egypt as well as use discourse analysis, participant observation, and interviews to build a more comprehensive middle-range theory on elections in transitional contexts.[8] Then I examine how elections changed again when the military encouraged the population to authorize a coup, thereby producing subsequent presidential and parliamentary elections organized by military intelligence. The most recent elections in Egypt appear far more circumscribed than those during Mubarak's presidency. In fact, they are likely the most closed elections in the modern history of Egypt. As a consequence, elections under al-Sisi's presidency are even more controlled and less effective for extending state power into society than even the autocratic contests under Mubarak.

Transitional Elections

Within the literature on authoritarian durability, elections play a central role in sustaining such rule.[9] The literature's findings are correct in that these often-rigged contests had few constructive or empowering effects for the electorate. But some do exist.[10] States and regimes in places like Egypt have used parliamentary and presidential elections to fortify executive autonomy, settle intraparty conflict while advantaging ruling-party incumbency, distribute patronage, reproduce clientelist networks, and display state power in ways that made citizens feel powerless.[11] The literature is robust, but the electoral productions are not a linchpin for preventing mass citizen revolts, incumbent ejections, or regime changes.

While most researchers showed the deleterious political effects of elections in the Arab world before the uprisings, they also thought that should regime dynamics change, then elections could be significantly more important in potentially democratizing a polity. In the words of Ellen Lust, "The question of democratization is rarely, if ever, on the table. . . . In the absence of political or economic shocks, elections inherently help to maintain the status quo."[12] The question of the region's elections is important because when some postuprising Middle Eastern and North African countries, such as Egypt, began transitions, the generals used elections as a tool to guide and claim an advantage over the process.

When these real-world developments occurred, a large literature on elections as a mode of transition already existed. In the mid-2000s, Staffan Lindberg had directed a large research project that brought together top scholars working on different regions to assess the role of elections during political transitions. The key argument in the introduction to the book he subsequently edited was that elections were likely the central causal mechanism of transition.

Unlike the early transitology literature, in which elections were either absent or served as an indicator of consolidation, the newer scholarship argued that democratization by elections is the crucial mode of a transition. As Lindberg explains in the preface of the book, "Elections are not only indicators but also a mode of transition themselves, whereby electoral processes and incentives under certain conditions play causal roles in furthering democratization. However paradoxical it may seem, we argue that elections are not only an undeniable constitutive part of democracy, but their practice can also in itself foster democratization."[13] While the argument that Lindberg derives from the group's work states that elections can result in democratization, autocratization, or regime reproduction, there is an explicit sense that successive elections over time eventually lead to more pluralistic and inclusive political societies. As he argues, "The more elections, the more democratic the regime and society in general."[14] Yet, competing research argues that the structure and context of electoral systems is more crucial to explaining whether elections promote democracy or representation as opposed to what the contests themselves reveal.[15]

Yet, as Lindberg explains, "Elections as a mode of transition can be a factor in both democratization and in autocratization but do not play much of a role at either end of the spectrum."[16] While there is evidence produced that elections can move countries in either direction, Lindberg claims that for more countries in the transitional middle than not "elections have become a causal factor in democratization."[17]

Viewing elections as causal factors of an eventual outcome places a disproportionate amount of analytical weight on this type of contestation as opposed to other types of political contention. Furthermore, relying on elections as the new mode of transition implicitly includes some political actors and excludes others. Namely, it excludes people and groups that choose to not participate in the contests. Because the theory gives elections a central role, it implicitly accepts a logic in which official state processes are more important than others. Focusing only on the role of elections occludes the impact of other, less measurable processes on democratization or autocratization, which elections cannot capture with all their data.

Elections, like other elite-state or hierarchical initiatives, seek to organize and discipline a society's politics. After the initial shock of Egypt's uprising, elections became the tool that served to redirect energy always from the street and into more containable institutions, which those in power will always favor. People in the street are harder to control or manipulate, so the strategy for SCAF's generals was to promote elections as the next phase of the transition, when, really, they are more of an effort to end the period of unpredictable protests as quickly as possible. To accent the point, SCAF even deployed the language that anyone remaining in the street was an enemy of the revolution, since revolution was now advancing toward its electoral phase.

In this sense, SCAF's generals used elections to bless those forms of politics that were permitted and condemn others that were forbidden. This productive disciplining is particularly evident when accounting for who writes the rules that govern elections and what those rules say. It means that elections can be procedurally free and fair and still limit a society's politics in binding ways. Elections reflect and advantage those with access to power rather than society at large. There is more at stake in elections than the process of democratization or autocratization.

Transitional Elections in the Wild

Regime change through elections is a theoretical model that explains how a country transitions from autocracy to something more pluralistic. A researcher must accept the assumption that it is elections that are primarily doing the work (and, even then, the process of transition is not uniform). In the literature on democratization by elections, the cases of Serbia (formerly part of Yugoslavia) and Mexico stand out as representative.

In Serbia, Slobodan Milosevic's electoral defeat in 2000 indicated a rapid transition from autocracy toward democracy. After Milosevic signed the Dayton Agreement in 1995, his regime, lacking more enemies to fight outside of Serbia's borders, grew more repressive at home. The opposition that emerged was divided, with leaders of the various opposition groups frequently quarreling with one another. Most notable were the public spats between the country's two most famous opposition leaders, Vojislav Kostunica and Zoran Djindjic.[18] Evidence suggests that the electorate would have not voted Milosevic out of office in favor of the weak opposition. Beginning in 1998, however, two opposition groups emerged that organized across the various opposition groups and brought unity to their ranks. When Milosevic called for early elections after amending the electoral law in 2000, the opposition carried out a disciplined campaign that produced an electoral victory for Kostunica, who won 51 percent of the vote. Then, the opposition also mobilized the wider population to ensure that the incumbent respected the result.

The two organizations that forced the opposition groups to overcome personal and political differences could not have been more different. The strategy of the student movement Otpor (Resistance), which emerged in 1998, was to recruit, plan, and build networks around the country. It organized itself horizontally on a nationwide basis with lots of foreign support.[19] At the height of its influence, seventy thousand people claimed to belong to the leaderless movement. In the lead-up to the 2000 presidential elections, Otpor organizers locked the systemic opposition leaders in a room and forced them to agree to unify in order to oust Milosevic.[20] Indeed, even political rivals Kostunica and Djindjic agreed to work together, with the latter backing the former as presidential candidate.[21] The second organization, the Center of Elections and Democracy, was an NGO that sought to advance methodologies in public-opinion polling. It also improved electoral infrastructure such as voter support and cleaning up electoral rolls. As figures from what would have been seen as the systemic opposition met with different parts of the regime, the message was not one of acquiescence or docility. They were there to establish the limits of what the opposition would cede and what it would not accept from the incumbent regime.[22]

After Kostunica won the election, Milosevic sought to buy time and counter the opposition's victory, but the opposition mobilized the population from across the country to march on Belgrade. Additionally, the opposition got one of the largest energy companies to strike in protest of Milosevic's tampering. Confronted with the election results and growing protests, parts of the regime around the president defected. Milosevic was left no good options but to concede. Kostunica became president and appointed his former rival Djindjic prime minister.

The electoral regime change has yet to create a flourishing democracy. While many Serbs remain unsatisfied with the lack of economic growth and their new politicians, Serbia now has regular elections and transfers of power, and is far less autocratic than it was when Milosevic was leader of his party (1989–2000). The literature betrays its own argument about the centrality of elections by valorizing the "mobilizing" work of the opposition.

If Serbia represents a case of a rapid electoral regime change that was safeguarded by a strong mobilized opposition, Mexico's electoral transition represents a more incremental strand. The Institutional Revolutionary Party (PRI) dominated the politics of Mexico between 1929 and 2000. No other party recorded a parliamentary majority, much less sent a candidate to the presidential palace during this time. Yet in 2000, the candidate of the National Action Party (PAN), Vicente Fox, won 43 percent of the vote to become president. The case of Mexico, which is similar to that of Taiwan and South Korea, represents another instructive model of electoral regime change. As Dorothy J. Solinger has argued, these cases show "the outcome of a lengthy process of unraveling of single-party domination."[23]

Several developments have to occur for single-party rule to be eclipsed. Solinger elucidates six prerequisites: regime commitment to elections, opposition parties, a history of electoral reforms, gross corruption within the ruling party, defections from the ruling party, and a charismatic opposition leader.[24] Mexico met all of these conditions. It held elections regularly beginning in 1917, had an opposition tradition that dates back to the independence (1821), and experienced five electoral reforms between 1987 and 1996. The PRI elites also corruptly blended the ruling party into the state, which beginning in 1986 produced offshoots from the party due to differences over economic austerity plans. Furthermore, Mexico had trained alternative candidates in the charismatic Vicente Fox as well as Cuauhtémoc Cárdenas of the Party of the Democratic Revolution (PDR). Even with all these conditions in place, a transition requires time.

Each time the PRI initiated electoral reforms—in 1987, 1990, 1993, 1994, and 1996—it was a response to popular mobilization. Once the playing field was leveled legally and defections began to take a toll on the PRI, the opposition began to gnaw away at some of the PRI's traditional bases of support. When Fox emerged victorious, he did so with only 43 percent of the vote. The PRI's Francisco Labastida claimed 37 percent, and Cárdenas earned another 17 percent. Procedurally, groups such as The Carter Center reported the election to have been one of the cleanest ever observed.

The variable of oppositional configurations is murky in such incremental and anticlimactic electoral regime changes. The PAN and PDR did not partner in a coalition against the PRI during the 2000 election. The parties tried, but negotiations fell apart and each selected its own candidate. In this instance the separate candidates most certainly took away from the PRI's potential voters, which enabled a path for an opposition victory. At first glance, such transitions speak more to the internal collapse of the dominant party than to the constellation of opposition configurations. As Schedler argued succinctly, "The Mexican transition looked like a distinctly postmodern phenomenon characterized by multiple absences: no collapse, no foundational elections, no big pacts, no constitutional assembly, and no alteration in power."[25]

Yet in cases where there is a slow decline of a ruling party as the electoral rules are leveled and splits from the party occur, the newly acquired spaces of contestation make possible a political learning that in turn gives rise to a type of oppositional strength. As Solinger rightly notes, "More of the voters cast their ballots *against* the winner than *for* him. *Had the ruling party still contained the faction that split off from it, it would have had a majority.*"[26] Thus, the weakening of the dominant party contributed to the strengthening of the opposition. Given that there was no pact between the systemic opposition and soft-liner state elites, the Mexican case does not fit neatly into the third-wave model of democratization, nor does it exemplify the more popularly driven fourth-wave model.[27]

In Egypt after Mubarak's departure, elections had higher voter turnout, increased choice, and cleaner processes, which suggests, at least on the surface, that empowerment—if not democratization—is one possible seedling. Given that new actors were thrust into the ruling coalition and previously illegal groups performed so well electorally and occupied a near majority of Parliament as well as the presidential office, the case of Egypt is not about regime reproduction. Thus, we are left to view Egypt's transitional elections as having neither autocratizing nor replicating attributes. But what if they also did not democratize?

A deeper interrogation of Egypt's transitional elections suggests another aim was at work: namely, the establishment, by elites and their formal competitors, of an exclusivist political arena that marginalizes the voices of revolutionary political change and contains unruly and ongoing protest actions. Elections became the mechanism for emptying the streets and rechanneling political energies into more controllable institutions. Perhaps if the uprising had been given time to result in a revolution, we would have seen elections contribute to a more democratized polity. But Egypt's transitional elections deviate from the theoretical expectation that posits elections as potentially democratizing. Elections also reflect underlying balances of power. Thus, the case of Egypt teaches us about what elections do in transitional settings as a larger historical process of political, social, and economic change unfolds.

Egypt's Transitional Elections

Egypt held more elections than any of the other Arab countries that saw uprisings in the 2011–12 period. If you were one of the country's fifty-one million eligible voters after Mubarak resigned, SCAF invited you to cast a ballot on five separate occasions: the constitutional referendum in March 2011, the People's Assembly (Maglis al-Sha'b) legislative elections in November 2011–January 2012, the Shura Council (Maglis al-Shura) legislative elections in January–February 2012, and two rounds of presidential elections in May and June 2012. With the exception of the Shura Council election,[28] each yielded high turnouts,[29] provided voters with a competitive choice,[30] and were free of routinized interference by the notorious security sector.[31] The difference between these transitional elections and elections under Mubarak, such as the final parliamentary elections under Mubarak's presidency in December 2010 that Mona El-Ghobashy described,[32] could not have been starker.

Rather than reveal people power, however, the elections of Egypt's transition anchored and reconstituted older discourses while bringing new agents into the state's representative bodies. This reduced political competition to two parties—the military supported state and the Islamists—while excluding revolutionary voices of change. Ultimately, the elections had an exclusionary as opposed to an empowering effect. In this respect, Egypt's elections deviate from the theoretical expectation that they will produce more inclusive change—much less democratize a political order—after a dictator falls and a political arena is forced open.

The initial vote Egyptians participated in following Mubarak's forced departure was a national referendum on nine emergency amendments to the constitution, held on March 19, 2011. This electoral spectacle structured voter choice between the revolutionaries on one hand and the army and Islamists on the other. The crowds wanted a dramatic political transformation. The generals and Islamists pined for stability in a reconfigured political arena, but not in ways that enabled revolutionary thinking or politics. The parliamentary elections for the People's Assembly (Maglis al-Sha'b), which occurred in November and December 2011, replicated this choice between those who had endorsed the "legitimate" official representative arena (both Islamists and non-Islamists) and those who did not (revolutionaries). The presidential contest, which happened in May and June 2012, reduced the competition to a choice between Islamist rule or the unreformed and fragmenting state. Yet, even the Islamists had consented to leaving the state alone. Thus, over the short duration of fifteen months, the electorate was forced to choose between accepting the remnants of the Mubarakist state or watching power be shared between these remnants and the Brotherhood. This incremental but regressive electoral design sidelined the prospect of more inclusive and revolutionary change because it narrowly circumscribed electoral choice. Egypt's 2012 presidential election concluded the process of elite-led electoral calibration to marginalize revolutionary participation in the state's affairs. The elections of the transition produced a civilian president and state continuity, and they gave unprecedented influence to the military, who were unaccountable to anyone but themselves.

During the transition, elections ultimately configured a political arena that not only tried to wear down popular mobilization and minimize the power it projected but also encouraged the newly elected figures to accept the state's surviving actors. The elections produced incentives for compromise between whoever emerged victorious and the state's unelected bureaucrats that favorably structured continuity. In a real sense, the idea is that the actual players in the elections are not relevant (i.e., Islamist or not). It is that the elections are a signal that deeper social transformation is off the table. This is not unique to Egypt in 2011–12. As in Indonesia after Suharto's 1998 overthrow, the opposition that got absorbed into the transition's electoral networks "were the organizations which had been most deeply affected by the politics of compromise, survivalism, and deal making" under the old order.[33]

For the previously systemic opposition and groups conditioned to capitulate to the Mubarak regime, elections gave a sense of empowerment for individuals and groups. The experience of a candidate running, winning, and entering the state's institutions generated a willingness to meet the remnant state elites halfway in Parliament and the presidency. This investment in the system lowered the likelihood that any unpredictable or dramatic change could occur from outside the electoral frame. Such an alignment ensured that people pushing for greater change would continue to be marginalized. Elections, therefore, countered the powerlessness unleashed by an uprising that surviving elites felt in a fragmenting state.

Ultimately, SCAF's strategy of overseeing an electoral transition failed even if the disempowering effects bought them some time against the protests. SCAF wanted elections to dilute and eventually stop the street protests and continuous mobilizations around revolutionary grievances.

While the multiple elections did divide the efforts of people in the streets, the generals did not entirely control the process because a hearty core of citizens with claims to make continued to articulate mobilized demands on the state. Mursi's presidency and the unstated pact between the Brotherhood and the military came under intense pressure because of relentless protests. Seeking to preempt further uncontrolled revolutionary mobilization, the generals, together with military intelligence, orchestrated a coup to abort Egypt's turbulent transition. The coup also ended Egypt's first experience with procedurally free and fair elections. The military intervention also indicated that SCAF had changed course and was committed to building a new regime.

The Beginning: The Constitutional Referendum

After granting Mubarak a few chances to get the protesters out of the country's major squares, his failure to do so forced the hands of the generals to eject Mubarak from the presidency. The army's first move to stem the crush of protests was forcing Mubarak to resign and retire to Sharm al-Shaykh. While protesters debated about whether to continue to press for control of the transition, Mubarak's resignation on February 11 peeled too many protesters off the streets. With the numbers in the streets ebbing and SCAF in complete executive and legislative control, the process of deliberate electioneering began. This strategy of electionization was identical in its aim of ejecting Mubarak in that both tactics tried to convince protesters to leave the streets and squares.

The first national vote of the transition, a constitutional referendum, would take place just five weeks later. In the referendum, Egyptians would vote yes or no on a package of constitutional amendments on the presidency's eligibility requirements, term limits on the office, and the executive's expansive powers. The amendments, nine in total, were formulated by a constitutional committee that SCAF, which promised a quick six-month transition to civilian rule, had convened. The committee's eight members included prominent scholars, a former judge (Tariq al-Bishri), and a former Brotherhood parliamentarian (Subhi Salih). Upon receipt of the committee's recommendations, the generals announced that there would be a national referendum on the amendments, to be held March 19. Following the announcement, Egyptians debated the best course forward.

Previously banned Islamist organizations, such as the Muslim Brotherhood as well as Salafi groups, supported constitutional changes. Brotherhood leader 'Isam al-'Aryan argued, for example, that voting "yes" prepared the ground for drafting a better constitution. He also argued that the speed in holding the referendum prevented counterrevolutionary forces and pro-Mubarak factions from mobilizing. Approving the amendments quickly would prevent, he explained, the emergence of another authoritarian pharaoh and would transfer sovereignty away from the people.[34] Furthermore the Muslim Brotherhood members around the country hung signs equating a "yes" vote with Islam and political stability. Echoing the old Mubarak theme of stability versus chaos, the Brotherhood message was that a "no" vote meant the country would face an uncertain fate. The Salafis, for their part, encouraged a "yes" vote because the amendments continued to safeguard shari'a law as the principle source of legislation. Thus, the Salafi pitch also became one that equated acceptance of the amendments with religiosity. Although technically neutral, SCAF sent text messages to all Egyptian mobile subscribers instructing them to participate in the referendum because a "yes" equaled democracy.[35] Amr Hamzawy, along with other rising liberal politicians, felt participating in the vote and approving the amendments would help to establish a more vibrant democracy. He also said that "accepting the referendum's results was a must for all political actors."[36] Other public intellectuals expressed that a "yes" vote was necessary because it kept SCAF on a strict timetable that would ease them out of politics more quickly.[37]

Despite the voter mobilization efforts, others noted the deleterious structuring effect that the referendum had. Namely, it prioritized top-down change over addressing bottom-up demands. Islamist columnist Fahmi Huwaidi argued that the referendum created a problem for the transition. He viewed the referendum in terms of whether to accept an elite-led process, which would marginalize the very people that started the uprising. Thus, "the referendum turned the national consensus into a political dichotomy" that decreased the ability to bridge the divide between the elites and those horizontally organizing in society.[38] Huwaidi's analysis pointed to how transitional elections serve as the anchoring frame for politics. His warning, however, was not heeded. Other commentators refuted his criticism by emphasizing that for the first time Egyptians would have their vote counted and praised the new levels of political competition between liberal, secular, and religious positions.[39]

Many of the revolutionaries lobbied for a "no" vote because of how the referendum itself would hamper their potential reach. Although writers framed their opposition in terms of a lack of transparency, they recognized the referendum was taking on an increasing "Islamist against revolutionary" hue in public discourse. In addition to calling for a temporary constitution before elections began, many activists, such as Wa'il Qandil, thought the referendum would initiate an environment in which revolutionary groups would be poorly suited to performing well when parliamentary and presidential elections followed.[40]

On March 19, 2011, Egyptians turned out in unprecedented numbers at polling stations around the capital and country, stretching Egypt's voting infrastructure to capacity. State officials announced that 41.9 percent of the electorate voted.[41] In the end, 77.2 percent of those who cast ballots favored adopting the constitutional changes against 22.8 percent that opposed. Just as the level of voter turnout was new, so were other differences from past election days on display. The Interior Ministry's security forces were not present, nor did the state bus in voters or bribe people on streets. Although some cried foul, the vote proceeded with minimal irregularities. From my research observations, many people, particularly in poorer neighborhoods, saw their "yes" vote as an expression of support for SCAF's leadership role in the transition.[42] Many who claimed they voted "yes" expressed a genuine belief in the military's benevolent, stabilizing role.[43] This point is important. The referendum in March 2011, as well as the subsequent elections for Parliament and the presidency, met the standard of democratic. SCAF's repeated attempts to use the ballot box to substitute for street politics cemented the split between the country's systemic and antisystemic opposition; SCAF achieved this development with elections that were more or less open.

By holding a referendum instead of just decreeing the amendments into existence, SCAF created a sphere in which Egyptians had to, in a sense, side either with the military or with forces pushing for ongoing street mobilizations. That the amendments passed with a supermajority provided SCAF with a snapshot of who supported them. The data showed them and the population how the country voted at the district level and also revealed the strength of SCAF's support to the wider population. The referendum made voters legible to SCAF in ways no other vote in Egypt ever had, given the state's manipulations in those previous exercises. The fact that there was unforced turnout, a competitive choice on offer, and a lack of state interference provided a stamp of electoral legitimacy unknown to any previous leader. The referendum felt empowering but anchored a SCAF-led transition. This was a sleight of hand by SCAF. People experienced a positive spectacle that generated autocratic political effects. The vote pushed those seeking to join the formal political arena into one camp while those that rejected the exercise got placed on a secondary path of political exclusion. In this way, the referendum authorized some to be heard while silencing others.

Although the referendum did not stop the revolutionaries' mobilization or dictate the terms of the impending transition, it initiated a process. SCAF wasted little time after the referendum results were announced. SCAF used the implementation of the amendments to further consolidate its authority. Just four days after the referendum, on March 23, it used an executive order to unilaterally decree the nine amendments to be in effect. Furthermore, it tacked an additional fifty-four articles that legalized SCAF's role in the transition. SCAF's unilateral constitutional declaration also affirmed many restrictive laws from the Mubarak era. The declaration emptied the referendum of meaning but still gave SCAF the ability to claim, in the words of one activist, "You had your say. You can participate during an election. But no more protests."[44] Moreover, the same day as the constitutional declaration, Prime Minister 'Isam Sharaf approved a law that criminalized protests deemed harmful to Egypt's economy.[45] Introducing a discourse that the unreformed state media services disseminated, SCAF targeted protesters and the restive labor movement by deriding their demands as "special interests" (*fi'awī*).[46]

If SCAF wanted to win acquiescence from the revolutionaries, it did not. Protests continued and often resulted in increased levels of state violence that reached new segments of society. Arrests, torture, and hostility toward the revolutionaries began to wear down their opposition. Furthermore, nearly twelve thousand military trials were used to try civilians between March and November 2011,[47] female protesters were subjected to virginity tests, houses of worship for the Coptic Christian minority were attacked, and the families of revolutionary martyrs were beaten.[48]

If the constitutional referendum set the stage for this repression, the People's Assembly elections that occurred in three stages later that year configured the political arena again in an even more disempowering way.

The Prize: Parliamentary Elections

Between the referendum and the 2011 parliamentary elections, the army, police, and state thugs attacked protesters on numerous occasions.[49] Protesters continuously sought justice for victims of violence committed by both the former regime and those currently in power. On July 8, for example, a number of protesters chanted for the fall of Field Marshal Tantawi.[50] A routine began to emerge: SCAF would act repressively and then retreat by offering a concession. After protesters occupied Tahrir Square in July 2011, the military finally acquiesced and put the former president on trial.

As the protests continued and targeted SCAF rule (*hokm 'askr*) throughout the summer, revolutionaries worried about the electoral law that would be written to govern the elections. Details were not forthcoming. Less than two months before the elections were scheduled to begin in late November, SCAF announced there would be a mixed system whereby two-thirds of the seats would be determined by proportional representation while the remaining third would be based on individual candidacy.[51] Most independents, as well as nascent politicians who had gained fame through participating in the uprising, felt this arrangement weakened their ability to win because a predominately list system would give an advantage to more established groups, such as the disbanded NDP and the Muslim Brotherhood. Activists also emphasized that the districts were designed under the old regime and favored candidates and groups with large war chests of capital and the ability to deliver constituent services. The revolutionaries had neither. These concerns were disregarded as the three stages of elections, scheduled to occur over six weeks, began on November 28. Those seeking entry to Parliament worked on establishing coalitions and campaigning. The design of the electoral system became a source of resentment for revolutionaries, who felt the transition put political participation and input beyond their reach.

In the weeks leading up to the elections, SCAF also floated the idea of passing a constitutional declaration, known as the al-Silmi document after the deputy prime minister, that would have limited the authority of elected institutions vis-à-vis the military. The army's budget would be discussed in secret parliamentary committees, and a special council, whose composition would be half military and half civilian, would be created to liaise between the state's elected officials and the unelected armed forces. A number of political parties and groups approved the constitutional principles.[52] Others were outraged. Disputes about what to do about the al-Silmi document forced many into the streets the week before the parliamentary elections.[53]

Supporters of the Muslim Brotherhood, Salafis, and revolutionaries gathered in a large protest in Tahrir Square to express their discontent with SCAF's handling of the transition. The Brotherhood was particularly upset that after its organizational prowess paid electoral dividends, the al-Silmi document would impede its ability to govern. This is further evidence that the elections themselves were not being manipulated, but the process and distribution of power afterward would rob the contests of some of their meaning. Revolutionaries focused on the fact that elections were being organized in a way that likely limited their ability to win. The memory of the recent October 2011 Maspero massacre remained fresh, as were the reminders that there had been no real progress in reforming the state security sector or Interior Ministry. The revolutionaries felt groups such as the Brotherhood were in an alliance or pact with SCAF to secure a negotiated Parliament without them. When the joint protest over the al-Silmi document ended and the Brotherhood and Salafis left the square, security forces, with military support, provoked a street fight by violently trying to disperse a sit-in by the families of revolutionary martyrs.[54] What followed was violence that raged for days on Muhammad Mahmoud Street, one of the streets that branches off of Tahrir Square.

The battles were symptomatic of the military's failure to competently run the transition. As people battled the security forces, others milled around in Tahrir, discussing whether boycotting or voting in the parliamentary elections was the best course of action.

Analyzing the Muhammad Mahmoud battles is central because the elections that followed formalized the split of the transition between generals as incumbents, challengers that wanted to contest politics in state institutions, and other participants that viewed entering into elections and state institutions as effectively handing the state back to the military or giving it to the Brotherhood. As Hesham Sallam has argued, the parliamentary elections formally created the "universe of the transition" and the "universe of the revolution."[55] The fact that many questioned the strategy of voting or boycotting is telling. As Wael Eskandar explains, "Voting is a release but so is violence. Muhammad Mahmoud was a large scream and voting was a smaller scream. People cast their votes and it showed that they did not want to fight and did not want to boycott. The problem was that voting became the glue for Parliament to keep a repressive regime."[56] While this focus on street protests continued among the activists, other parts of society seemed overwhelmingly in favor of minimizing the mobilization and supporting a formal political field governed by elections and representative institutions.[57] This is not unsurprising, yet the ramification was that roughly the third of society pushing against the Brotherhood and the remnants of the old state became effectively locked out of the transition—an exclusion that would be solidified months later during the presidential election.[58]

TV and newspaper commentators overwhelmingly supported the parliamentary elections and convening of the Parliament. Some analysts close to SCAF made arguments that the elections could save the country. The revolutionary forces were portrayed as too divided, which had led to violence at the Muhammad Mahmoud battles and threatened to undermine the whole transition. As 'Abd al-Magid argued, "Elections turn out to be the last opportunity to get out of the bottleneck. It is also the last option among other worse alternatives for the transitional period."[59] Other commentators who had criticized how the referendum was handled surrendered to the idea of carrying on with a flawed transition. Islamist-leaning Huwaidi, for instance, felt that the elections would bring clarity about the strengths and weaknesses of Egypt's political nascent parties and groups as well as help limit the power of SCAF's feckless leadership.[60] Those who remained defiant argued that the electoral infrastructure of the Mubarak years had never been fixed and that the elections would be marked by vote buying, corruption, and other forms of fraud.[61] As the elections began, the state media and generals flooded the country with a message and images that suggested that the revolutionaries caused instability and violence.

Like the referendum before it, Egypt's parliamentary elections were procedurally free and fair. People voted in record numbers, with over twenty-seven million out of nearly fifty million eligible voters participating (54 percent). The state's overt attempts at interference did not cloud the outcome. There was also substantial choice: in addition to individuals, voters could choose from nearly fifty registered parties. Furthermore, rather than one party controlling the rest, the parliamentary results produced a mosaic that favored the Islamist-leaning parties but had slices, even if disproportionate ones, for many contenders. The Muslim Brotherhood's Freedom and Justice Party (FJP) earned 49 percent of the vote, while the conservative Nur Party gained 24 percent. Non-Islamist groups such as the Egypt Bloc, New Wafd, and Wasat won another 10, 7, and 3 percent of the vote, respectively. The Revolution Continues bloc, which was where most of the candidates favored by revolutionary protesters were, won a mere nine seats, or less than 1 percent of the vote. Diversity and the appearance of democracy aside, the parliamentary elections served an anchoring tool by determining who would legitimately engage with SCAF over the future constitution and how would elected legislative authority matter. The inability to win entry or the outright rejection of the process meant exclusion from the next serious consultations. In this way, we can see how Islamists found the process empowering while, overall, the contests gutted the prospect for wider revolutionary change.

No previous election in post-1952 Egypt had ever produced a result that carried such credibility for political elites. However, as Sallam argued, "SCAF [saw] the recent elections as a way to channel unruly dissent into an organized sector that it [could] easily manipulate and control through legal engineering and limited pacts."[62] Yet, this only applied to those in society that entered such electoral races. Indeed, having just spent time, energy, and capital to be elected, few of the newly minted parliamentarians seemed willing to challenge SCAF or push it into a place whereby it might cancel the election results. In this respect, given the choice between siding with the military or revolutionary change, the newly elected chose the former. More divisively, however, the 2011 parliamentary elections magnified this split within Egypt's opposition and pulled powerful actors and groups into the camp of the SCAF-led transition and away from those demanding more radical political and economic change or social justice.[63] Therefore, the elections were empowering for those that participated while disempowering for the wider aim of democratizing the state.

With representatives produced through a clean electoral process, even if the rules advantaged systemic trends, some Egyptians expressed they wanted life to return to normal and the constant protest actions to cease. While many disagreed with the ideologies of some of the groups elected, they had voted for the transition to move forward. Through elections, SCAF had constituted a path to marginalize people who demanded change while structuring compromise from those that won inclusion and became invested into the political order.

After the lower house was selected, SCAF asked the electorate to return to the ballot box again to choose deputies for the upper Shura Council. Of all voting opportunities after the uprising, the Shura Council produced the least enthusiastic turnout—a mere 15 percent.[64] The council's powers remained legislatively limited after the uprising, and it does not have the same resource distribution capacity as the People's Assembly, which leaves many confused as to what purpose the council serves.[65] In the words of one analyst, "Voters do not believe that the Shura Council is politically important."[66] Not anticipating much gain, Egyptians stayed away from these elections. This is not to say that these elections were unimportant. The results in the Shura Council elections echoed those of the People's Assembly and further entrenched the Brotherhood's FJP and other groups within the formal elite arena.

The elected Parliament was embattled even before it convened. In many respects, the gridlock between SCAF, its appointed cabinet, and the parliamentarians was the result of each group testing where its authority stretched as well as how to cooperate. A constituent assembly was created to discuss drafting a new constitution, but it ended acrimoniously after being dissolved by a court order in April 2012. Not only did this leave people unpleased with the Parliament, but it left Egypt without a constitution as the country drifted toward presidential elections. Moreover, it left SCAF in a dominant position.

Despite the high turnout, voter choice, and lack of state interference, the outcome of the parliamentary elections cemented divisions among those seeking to challenge or govern post-Mubarak Egypt. The ambiguity allowed SCAF to make decisions but also use the veneer of temporarily ruling the transition. Those civilians, who ran and entered Parliament, came to share the systemic worldview of the new state incumbents. They came to accept SCAF as a foundational political actor while adopting the logic of the unreformed state's elaborate bureaucracy. Groups like the Brotherhood may not have liked it, but they became proponents of incremental reform rather than advocates for a radical break from the emerging transitional political order. While the state structure included new actors and was more diverse, the antisystemic opposition was excluded from participating in policy creation. Thus, an exclusivist political arena was constituted to guide the transition as it lurched forward. The electorate was effectively split in thirds, much like the state-systemic–antisystemic opposition triangle that allowed SCAF to eject Mubarak and lean on the Muslim Brotherhood to dilute protest demands while the group also helped balance the disrupted state by not trying to reform it.

The Consolidation: The Presidential Election

The presidential election upped the stakes of the formal transition. It also was the maturation of a process that SCAF oversaw. The elections themselves were not manipulated. Again, high turnout, little state interference, and real choice characterized the vote. But SCAF and the courts intervened in ways before the presidential election runoff concluded that suggested that manipulation happened in the offices of the state rather than the country's voting booths. After a registration period that witnessed the Muslim Brotherhood reverse its promise not to run a candidate, the group fielded two contenders: Khayrat al-Shatir and Muhammad Mursi.

The so-called remnants (*fulūl*) segment also produced three candidates: ʻUmar Sulayman, Ahmad Shafiq, and Husam Khayrallah. Popular choices among the revolutionaries were neo-Nasserist politician Hamdin Sabahi, former Muslim Brother ʻAbd al-Munʻim Abu al-Futuh, and socialist lawyer Khalid ʻAli. Sulayman and al-Shatir eventually were disqualified on technicalities, but that still left a field of twelve candidates vying for the presidency.

The excitement and apprehension over the presidential elections were palpable. One writer noted that voting for the president would formally end the first republic and give rise to a more democratic second republic.[67] The famous novelist ʻAlaʼ al-Aswaʼni argued the opposite. He denounced the elections as unfair, citing the lack of transparency, the way the rules preserved SCAF's interests, and the fact that not all candidates had the same opportunity.[68] Beyond this interpretation, others framed the vote differently. Public intellectual Usama al-Ghazali Harb argued shortly before the election that the Egyptian president has always been important in shaping the state before warning that many of the candidates lacked the experience necessary to run the country's affairs. He noted that the field could be divided into "primary," "secondary," and "revolutionary" candidates.[69] By creating such a schema, this prominent commentator in Egypt's largest newspaper implied the revolutionaries were not to be taken seriously compared to other contenders. While this dismissal was not determinant, it captures the dilemma that most Egyptians unaffiliated with the state or the Brotherhood faced.

The Muslim Brotherhood mobilized its networks for its candidate. It was unclear whether the remnant faction could do the same, given their poor showing in the parliamentary elections months earlier. The revolutionaries debated and argued about their course of action. Many remained uncomfortable voting for an ex-Islamist (Abu al-Futuh), but also felt a socialist (ʻAli or Sabahi) would never have broad appeal. In the end, they split their vote between Sabahi and Abu al-Futuh. This allowed Brotherhood apparatchik Muhammad Mursi and former air force general Ahmad Shafiq to slip into the second round with nearly 25 and 24 percent (respectively) of the initial vote in May 2012. It arranged a showdown between the state apparatus and the formerly excluded Islamists. Academics, such as

Ellis Goldberg, rightly pointed out that the revolutionaries were a sizable voting bloc, but the lack of agreement among them split their vote.[70] Many revolutionaries emphasized that their top two candidates combined for nearly 38 percent of the vote and so actually outgained Mursi and Shafiq by at least a margin of 13 percent. Nevertheless, per the electoral rules, when no candidate won 50.1 percent of the first-round vote, only the top two entered into the runoff.

The public mood of hope turned bitter. The election runoff was the dynamic many Egyptians had been hypothetically warned about for three decades. Mubarak frequently told society that the alternative to the state's rule was the Islamist forces assuming control of the state. While it is impossible to know if this prophecy influenced how people voted during his long tenure, the prospect had become real for voters during the transition. Would the electorate choose the candidate of the state or the Islamists?

Calls to boycott the election immediately surfaced.[71] People pining for personal freedom or social justice would not be satisfied with either candidate winning the presidency. This produced two kinds of boycotters. Some actively boycotted because they felt the electoral design was a sham. These people continued to protest and intentionally spoiled their ballots. Others passively boycotted by not voting because of the lack of a likeable candidate. Islamist thinker Fahmi Huwaidi called the runoff's design "the biggest mistake."[72] He noted that formulating the runoff in such a fashion forced a choice between a civil state or a religious state that would leave the electorate unsatisfied. While some, such as al-Aswa'ni, refused to make the choice, others expressed frustration with having to make this choice.[73] Others not wishing to boycott but repulsed by both options were left to "hold their nose" and vote Mursi.[74] Despite the presidential election consolidating a disempowering experience for Egyptians, those that did commit to the election experienced a different empowering reality where voter turnout mattered and every vote counted.

Both candidates intensified their campaigning in the period before the presidential runoff on June 16–17. Shafiq's rallies resembled less enthusiastic NDP rallies but were large. Jihan Sadat, Muna 'Abd al-Nasser, Isma'il 'Usman of the Arab Contractors, and former NDP apparatchik Mustafa al-Faqi, as well as other so-called remnant luminaries, came out to remind the base to vote for a "secular" state, which was a deliberate swipe at the Islamist competition.[75] Comparatively, the Brotherhood's rallies were big and held across the country. Each side hurled unproven allegations that the other side was using money, jobs, food distribution, the promise of services to secure votes, and threats.

The lead-up to the vote provided extraelectoral drama that structured an outcome regardless of who won, because the military's powers expanded and the presidency's powers were curtailed by SCAF and the courts. This is seen in three key events that took place before the presidential runoff. It began on June 13, three days before the vote, with a SCAF law that enforced an earlier Justice Ministry decree allowing the military to arrest civilians.[76] As Hugh Roberts notes, "This is a remarkable thing to do in the middle of a democratic presidential election but it was just the first, teasing move in a three-part maneuver."[77] The following day a second ruling by the courts came in that changed the dynamics entirely. The Supreme Constitutional Court had ruled against the law passed by Parliament in April to bar Mubarak-era figures from high politics.[78] In the Delta province of Gharbiyya, Shafiq's campaign head could barely contain his excitement. As he exalted in his man's judicial reprieve, his phone rang again: the court had ruled that the law governing the previous parliamentary elections was unconstitutional.[79] This ruling allowed SCAF to dissolve Parliament. The Muslim Brotherhood, which commanded 49 percent of the assembly elected over the previous winter, was out. The court transferred legislative powers to SCAF.

In Cairo, particularly among the revolutionary forces, these developments affirmed the widespread judgment that the runoff was fixed. Some decided to vote for Mursi to deny victory to Shafiq. Others planned to boycott by not participating in the vote. Still others boycotted by scrawling "Down with military rule!" across their ballots, thereby invalidating them to make the boycott legible as an intentional and active rejection. For Shafiq's campaign head, however, the verdicts were extra advantages. He was not even worried that he did not have the province's voter rolls. Shafiq's campaign was based on *'aṣabiyya* (group solidarity), he said. "We have reintegrated the big families of Gharbiyya," he explained, rattling off the names of eleven families that were urging a vote for Shafiq.[80] At that moment, a member of the Zahran family called to share his happiness over the court rulings

Nowhere were the Shafiq backers more coolly confident than in Minufiyya, the province to Gharbiyya's immediate south and home of Shafiq's patron and fellow air force general Mubarak, as well as several of the ex president's top cronies. In Minufiyya's first round, Shafiq had routed the other candidates, amassing 586,345 votes to second-place Mursi's 203,503.[81] But even here, the Muslim Brotherhood hotly contested each locale. As one Mursi campaigner said, "We are here to close the gap, not to win."[82]

The Sadat School in the Minufiyya town of Talla offers a tiny but illustrative example of how empowering the vote was for the participating campaigns.[83] As the polls closed on June 17, a judge sequestered all the cell phones in the room as her five poll workers began to sort and count the ballots. Soldiers were stationed outside, and a brigadier general ordered, "If there are any troublemakers, shoot them." The only noise outside the school came from a crowd that had gathered to chant, "The people and the army are one hand!" Two campaign representatives, one loyal to Shafiq and one to Mursi, watched like hawks as the workers placed counted ballots in stacks of fifty. It was not close. Of the 2,341 votes, Shafiq had taken 1,725 (73.1 percent), while Mursi won 583. But as the judge finalized her paperwork, Mursi's representative protested. There was a problem with the numbers. One ballot was missing. The previous day, a woman had entered with a precompleted ballot—whether she voted for Shafiq or Mursi was unclear—and when she tried to take another empty ballot, she was arrested. But there was an irregularity in the final count.

Two recounts later, Mursi's representative remained unwilling to certify the results. The brigadier general on duty ordered sternly, "I don't want any noise from you. Shut up! Sign the papers!" He ordered a police officer to confiscate the Brotherhood representative's phone, which, at that moment, began to ring. The general shook his head contemptuously. The Mursi representative said, "You should not have done that. Now, the group [the Brotherhood] will be outside wondering what happened to me." The general erupted, "So help me God, if that group comes here and causes a problem, I will arrest everyone." The outnumbered representative did not flinch. "Sir, I don't understand why you have to speak to me in such a disgusting way." Exasperated, the army officer ordered the judge to submit the results without the Brotherhood representative's signature. Instead, the missing vote was invalidated, and the general left the room mumbling, "All this trouble over one vote."

All the district-level votes were tallied before places like Talla sent results to the governorate office in Shibin al-Kum. The heavily guarded aggregation center was quiet. Inside, several Mursi campaigners live-streamed the updates from Cairo. They showed Mursi ahead nationwide, but his lead was not insurmountable. Bent on keeping the state's vote counters honest, Mursi's team in Minufiyya had done their own aggregation. One of them waved a copy of what the results should look like—78,702 votes for Shafiq to 33,731 for Mursi. When the official count was announced over a shoddy public-address system, Shafiq had 78,701 votes, while Mursi had scored 33,731. Mursi's team rejoiced at their accurate numbers. They did not seem to mind that Shafiq was missing a vote.[84] This example underscores how empowering these contests were for committed participants while they ultimately insulated SCAF as the real source of political authority.

Despite the hiccups, the only international election observation group, The Carter Center, viewed the vote as procedurally clean despite reservations about the Supreme Constitutional Court effectively disbanding Parliament on June 14 as well as another SCAF constitutional declaration on June 17.[85] SCAF's constitutional declaration on the second day of the runoff election effectively gutted the presidency of its traditional powers. It was the final nail in the coffin of any hope that the presidential election would extricate Egypt from politics dominated by the military. Effectively restoring the post-1952 Free Officer regime, the declaration changed the Egyptian presidency, with its autonomy vis-à-vis other state institutional actors and opposition, that Sadat had constructed in the 1970s and Mubarak had expanded for nearly three decades. Egyptian and foreign researchers began to call Mursi "President Asterisk," a reference to the way his power was qualified by the lack of a Parliament and the powers the military had taken with their new constitutional declaration.[86]

Nevertheless, the popular excitement surrounding the election and the impending announcement of its winner carried the day. Though SCAF may have rendered any potential president impotent in its last-minute power grab, the spectacle of the election was overwhelming.

The national vote count was so methodical and meticulous that the result took over a week to announce. The army was placed on alert around the country because of fears of violence after the announcement. On June 24, Egypt's Supreme Presidential Election Commission declared the winner and confirmed that Mursi took 51.7 percent of all the valid votes, while Shafiq won 48.3 percent. Nearly 52 percent of Egypt's fifty-one million eligible voters had participated.[87] Thus, it appeared that most of the revolutionaries, who had effectively split their vote among three candidates during the first round, broke toward Mursi. While he was nowhere near a revolutionary, they voted for him because they feared that if Shafiq were brought to power, he may make good on his threat of revenge against those that had been calling for change across the previous sixteen months.[88] David Kirkpatrick's description of Shafiq's address at Egypt's American Chamber of Commerce days before the election gives a glimpse into why the revolutionaries were worried: "The well-heeled audience cheered as Mr. Shafik suggested that he would use executions and brute force to restore order within a month [of his election]."[89]

After the results were announced, Mursi supporters and some revolutionaries filled Cairo's iconic Tahrir Square to celebrate a victory over Mubarak's old allies. But Egypt's presidential election was not merely a story of a long battle that produced the country's first elected civilian president. Rather, it was the culmination of a process that SCAF's generals promised: a handover of power through popular elections that were not fraught by violence, state interference, and the tomfoolery of the ancien régime. As Hazem Kandil captured the dynamic, "Army members do not see their leaders as devious or complacent: the revolt demanded democracy, and SCAF has indeed organized free elections—'What else do the revolutionaries want?' they keep asking."[90] Furthermore, given the high turnout, candidate choice, and lack of interference on election day as well as the fact the former opposition figure had won, SCAF felt vindicated by hosting a fair election, despite its violence and mishandling of the transition. SCAF also had little to worry about: the military isolated a potential President Mursi or Shafiq before either was announced as the victor of the election. Egypt's leading generals had a long-game strategy to capture Mubarak's executive authority, and they emerged as the election's actual winner because they positioned themselves to be in charge of the country.

Indeed, even if SCAF had minimally fulfilled its promise to return the country to civilian rule, they had also effectively used elections to configure the electoral arena such that certain politics became legitimized and others marginalized. This configuration forced actors to decide whether they were going to demobilize and join institutional processes. Then, as an added guarantee, SCAF cornered the victor of the presidential election with the June 17 constitutional declaration. The winner was left in a position of continuous compromise and capitulation to SCAF's wishes. Therefore, the military council used elections to create a political field designed to exclude the voices of huge swaths of the population clamoring for change, while those that participated and won had to bend the knee to the unreformed state that had the military at its apex.

Rather than the 2011 uprising leading to flawed elections that may or may not have empowered greater numbers of Egyptians in the future, the military used transitional elections to redistribute power in a way that ensured their influence in the political system became unassailable. Elections were just the tool of choice that decorated SCAF's power play. Despite convening procedurally free and fair elections, and also including systemic opposition groups like the Muslim Brotherhood to help the state regroup after the uprising, the goal of isolating street protests only worked partially. Elections determined which kinds of politics were acceptable and which were not. While these electoral processes shrunk the size of those protesting in the streets, the ongoing mobilization still continued. This suggests that, even though SCAF hoped elections would be the antidote to uncontrolled mobilization, the military's continued interference before and after elections kept bringing people into the streets.

SCAF worked overtime with parts of the state apparatus to undermine the process of having consequences that would limit its ability to act politically. Elections were also a mechanism to bring in and attach the revolutionary waves of street activism to the state's formal institutions, which divided and diluted the numbers making demands on the state. In its aim of regaining power, SCAF succeeded spectacularly. In its aim of neutralizing revolutionary mobilization, it failed. This forced the military generals and intelligence services to make another grand spectacle a year later in order to complete the restoration of the post-1952 Free Officers state. Feeling that elections had reached the limit of their utility to structure outcomes, the military planned and executed a more regressive form of politics—a coup d'état—when faith in the elected presidency appeared to be fraying. They conducted a coup premised on mobilization. When the military leadership realized that there was no bringing a core of revolutionaries into the voting booth, they decided to take counterrevolution into the streets.

Disempowering Elections during Transitions

The transition's elections gradually fortified military officers at the center of the state. Since Sadat's presidency, the military's role in politics had declined,[91] with Mubarak and his team of managers fortifying the structures that he inherited after Sadat's assassination until he established an enormous amount of centralized autonomy. The 2011 uprising disrupted this arrangement, and the collapse of Mubarak's regime left a vacuum that SCAF filled. Yet the generals needed to assume the powers they sought incrementally. They used the symbolism of the presidential office, which had been gutted of its autonomy, the hope of a real Parliament, and Egypt's largest and best organized opposition group—the Muslim Brotherhood. The mechanism that tied all these together was elections.

While citizens had voted in procedurally fair contests, which was a novelty, SCAF accumulated power and designed a hierarchy to persuade the citizens to adhere to their authority and fall back in line with the routines a recovering state apparatus offers. Elections in Egypt's transitional setting never included the option of popularly dictated, empowering democratization. They were about responding and exploiting the disruption of the 2011 mobilization to soothe the unsettled political order. That the elections served to strengthen the authority of the state-supported elites has arguably left society frustrated with the practice of elections and democracy, which came to be seen as an empty shell wrapped up as a grand spectacle of hope and change. Others have come to view the entire process cynically. As Wael Eskandar argued, "Elections were used to pacify and undermine the revolutionary movement."[92]

Elections—in of themselves—do not really matter as much as the context and environment in which they take place. In Egypt's case, military generals used the supposed empowering tool of elections, which are propped up by decades of international normative propaganda, to incrementally sap the power of popular mobilization while incrementally installing themselves as politically unchallengeable. Yet as the state's continued fragmentation shows, the process does not necessarily end with the military winning the political control in a decisive or final way. The elections were stopgaps that moved the transition process along, but even those ultimately failed because of popular dissatisfaction, because their demands were not being considered—much less addressed. This continuing mobilization necessitated SCAF's intervention against Mursi in June 2013. The elections might have bought the generals some time, but ultimately the protests continued in response to SCAF's manipulation of the environment around the contests.

The referendum on the constitutional amendments boiled down to a question of whether the military or the revolutionaries should lead the transition. Then, the parliamentary elections provided opportunities for groups favoring different versions of the SCAF-rule to prevail over those demanding more extensive change. It also unleashed intra-Islamist competition between the Muslim Brotherhood and the Salafist groups. Finally, the presidential election restructured the political arena into a question of whether the old state or the Islamists should rule Egypt.

Elections during Egypt's transition prompted a process whereby the military would insert progressively more safeguards to protect themselves and their interests against more expansive electoral change.[93] The military generals used genuine elections to reinforce the opposition divide and slow the protests while designing measures that insulated their institutions from electoral results. Thus, elections configured the political field in a way that secured antidemocratic and antireformist enclaves of autocratic interests while a "democratic" spectacle transpired. As a result, the elections were emptied of their potential to be transformative and empowering on a societal level.

Using elections to perform the political work of creating and remaking a political arena to legitimate some actors and marginalize others diminishes the prospects of popular democratization. While elites cannot control electoral outcomes entirely, they can design systems that push politics in more preferable directions for them. Thus, in Egypt, remnant military generals in a fragmenting state manufactured a false choice of either "the state" or "the Islamists" as a way to eliminate other, potential revolutionary options. Electoral processes, then, are not suggestive of a simple process of democratization or autocratization.

Elections help design a political field during formal transitions. This trend does not just apply to transitions in Egypt or other states. Transitional elections have done important work for constituting new social practices in other regional contexts. As William Liddle reminds us in the case of Indonesia after Suharto, the surviving autocrats convinced the opposition to "stop trying to overthrow Habibie through civil disturbance . . . and start planning for elections."[94] In previously autocratic states that saw successive elections in which the opposition came to power, protests were marginalized, and average citizens became frustrated and disappointed with the lack of democracy, development, and change.[95] This was the road that SCAF forced Egyptians to take. It was not happenstance. It was manufactured, given how the rules of the election were structured, how courts ruled in favor of status quo groups, and through a constitutional declaration.

Egypt's transition was scheduled to end when Mursi took his oath of office on June 30, 2012. The transition produced some dizzyingly impressive theater—from the sight of Mubarak on trial in a courtroom to scenes of Mursi touring the presidential palace—but democracy was never on the menu of options. Headed by SCAF, the military has become more powerful politically and economically than at any time since the days of Nasser, to the extent that comparisons with the ruling Pakistan Army are not misplaced.[96] And for all SCAF's appearance of bumbling and shows of bowing to the people's will, its greatest accomplishment was that it accrued much of this authority at the ballot box while Egyptian citizens voted on other things.

Between Mubarak's ouster in February 2011 and the July 2013 military coup, SCAF called the Egyptian people to the polls five times. Mursi asked them to come out once. Three occasions proved particularly momentous: the March 2011 constitutional referendum, the 2011 wintertime parliamentary contests, and the presidential runoff in June 2012. In each of these three instances, the generals pulled a bait and switch, gutting the voting of meaning after it was over. Days after the first referendum, SCAF unilaterally decreed an additional fifty-four amendments that the public had never seen. Then the parliamentary elections helped to construct an elite arena that marginalized and excluded the revolutionary forces from negotiations of a transitional pact between the Brotherhood and the army.[97] The elections thus produced two parallel universes: one of the transition and one of revolution.[98] Key political forces, including the Brotherhood, helped balance the country while SCAF reestablished the state's control and encouraged those in the street to go to the ballot box and accept the formal political institutions. Finally, minutes after the presidential polls closed, SCAF mooted the last exercise with its second constitutional declaration.

The experience of Egypt's turbulent transition suggests that choice and spectacle are not mutually exclusive. The outcomes were not preordained; in the presidential race, the rulers' preferred candidate lost. Yet the actions, announcements, and rulings surrounding the elections assisted in installing the military as a supraconstitutional force in the political system while it promoted an image of Egypt as polarized between two, and only two, views: that of the remnants (*fulūl*) and that of the Muslim Brotherhood (al-Ikhwan). SCAF played these poles off one another in monarchical fashion while simultaneously tamping down the politics of the street. This polarizing process—rather than democratic empowerment—was the legacy of Egypt's transitional elections.

Elections after the fall of a dictator do seem to have other negative effects for those interested in continuing street protests to open the debate about moving forward more widely. They transform and harden the lines of an opposition that continues to struggle against unreformed state apparatuses and elitist political projects. At the same time, they help justify the elites' use of greater state violence against a segment of the population that publicly refuses to participate in the grand legitimizing spectacle. The violence during the Muhammad Mahmoud protests in November 2011 is one example. The December 2012 referendum on the new Egyptian constitution, which was dubiously rammed through during an all-night session, is another case in point. After the formal handover of power from SCAF's generals to Muhammad Mursi, the civilian president maintained an interest in continuing to electionize the governing processes in order to secure mandates and make cases for getting what his interest group wanted. Rather than bring in a wider range of voices, Mursi and the Muslim Brotherhood used an electoral referendum to integrate their document into the state apparatus. The eruptions of high levels of mobilization and state violence underscore how elections—even if characterized by a lack of state interference, increased choice, freedom to campaign, and higher turnouts—fail to say much about the quality or direction of a political transition. In fact, viewing transitional elections as a status report could provide an altogether misleading narrative.

No one was foolish enough to argue that elections in places like Egypt were free or fair before the 2011 uprising. Turnout was always low and usually imagined by state bureaucrats. The state also used all manner of shenanigans to ensure it won. Within five weeks of the toppling of Mubarak, however, SCAF employed elections to encourage broad voter turnout and invited much public debate. The constitutional referendum as well as parliamentary and presidential elections transformed overnight the possibilities of institutionalizing elections as emancipatory, if flawed. While some decried the unfairness of the overall process, the elections were generally free and fair procedurally. This gap between the structural and the procedural aspects betrays that the elections were about something other than empowerment. Rather, they produced a tightly constrained choice that directed society toward reaccepting the politics of the state as well as its new master—the leading generals of the armed forces.

Elections in the Time of Regime-Making

Elections after the 2013 coup have become meaningless affairs. While the transition elections were actually procedurally legitimate, the practice fell apart after the coup against Mursi in July 2013. While SCAF tried to use fair elections to reduce street protests and get opposition into more controllable state institutions, the generals' constant manipulation of the context around the contests soured some Egyptians' views on elections. Despite SCAF shifting manipulation away from the voting booths and toward context (a reverse process from the Mubarak era), Egyptians continued to protest state manipulation. SCAF's use of elections allowed the generals to carve up the already divided antisystemic and systemic opposition. Yet, when the strategy failed because mobilization continued deep into Mursi's one-year presidency, the protests encouraged the military to end the transitional experiment and attempt to build a new regime to stand on its own.

There were even fewer voters showing up to cast ballots or run as opposition in postcoup elections than during the late Mubarak period. 'Abdel Fattah al-Sisi secured 96.1 percent of the vote in the elections of May 26–28, 2014. His opponent, the leftist Hamdin Sabahi, barely managed to secure 3 percent. In April 2018, al-Sisi outdid his performance four years earlier by securing reelection with 97 percent of the vote. More Egyptians cast write-in votes for international Egyptian soccer star Muhammed Salah than for the formal candidate on the ballot.

The Egyptian government formally designated the Muslim Brotherhood a terrorist organization in December 2013 and has subjected the group to extreme state repression. What remains of the Brotherhood boycotts all elections now. Yet, the ghost of Mursi's 2012 election continues to haunt the general-turned-president. One ramification of the transitional elections was that because Mursi won an election where 52 percent of the electorate turned out and provided him with 13.3 million votes, those aligned with the state and wishing to install al-Sisi had to prove their candidate's popular support surpassed Mursi's.

Given that in the two years following Mursi's election Egypt's electorate expanded to 53 million eligible voters, the government was under pressure to produce a similar turnout. Before al-Sisi's presidential election in 2014, a justice ministry decree was issued that allowed those failing to cast a ballot to be fined. The decree, however, did not seem to be enough of a threat to compel many to participate. Al-Sisi himself claimed in the days before his first election that he expected turnout to be 80 percent. It was not even close. News reports and video footage mostly showed empty polling stations. Then, on the second day of voting, which was supposed to be the final day, the state declared a public holiday to allow a third day of voting. This, too, failed to drive people to the polls. When announcing the results, officials claimed that 47.5 percent of Egypt's eligible voters participated in al-Sisi's election. It is hard to believe anyone finds this number credible. Far surpassing the bar of Mursi's 13.3 million votes, al-Sisi was said to have accumulated 23,780,104 votes in 2014, which is almost a laughable claim. While powerful states like the United States congratulated "the winner of Egypt's presidential election" and looked "forward to working with" President al-Sisi, groups that monitored the contest between Shafiq and Mursi issued statements of dire concern. As The Carter Center said in a statement days before al-Sisi's 2014 election, "Egypt's political transition has stalled and stands on the precipice of total reversal."[99] In fact, by this point, the process had already gone over the cliff.

Other elections in Egypt have also proven to be an organizational challenge for the state. While before the uprising it was common for the NDP and security establishment to coordinate on parliamentary elections, in the absence of having a ruling party, the responsibility has fallen to the security establishment alone. Given the competition between the various security services, military intelligence, which was al-Sisi's institutional home before the uprising, was given the task of organizing the vote. In his masterfully researched "Anatomy of an Election," an unparalleled piece of analysis on a state's organization of an election in the Arab world, Hossam Bahgat describes how military intelligence rigged the first postcoup parliamentary elections in January 2015. Bahgat shows how military intelligence set up an infrastructure of news coverage, liaison officers with bags of cash, and national, governorate, and district coordination to curate a pliant Parliament. As he stated, "More than a year after the election of the president, parliamentary elections were inescapable. The first such elections in four years, they would need to produce an assembly that poses no challenge to the presidency's tight grip on the political sphere, although the political landscape had shifted radically in the post-revolution period."[100] The elections, which took place between October and December 2015, returned a nearly opposition-free Parliament.

Upon being seated, the 2015 Parliament immediately passed all but two of the declarations al-Sisi had issued when there was no assembly. Almost from the moment the assembly was seated, parliamentarians routinely argued that the constitutional term limits on the president needed to be changed. In August 2017, Parliament sought to amend article 140 of the constitution to change the presidential term limit from four to six years.[101] The parliamentarians argued that the 2014 constitution was shortsighted and written in a time of political "instability." Explaining that "the constitution is man-made it is not to the word of God," Helwan MP Isma'il Nasir al-Din, for example, argued that circumstances have changed and people should correct mistakes like short term limits.[102] The burden of conducting nationwide elections, which the transition set as a precedent, is weighing on the minds of those that work to orchestrate such contests. Furthermore, calls to change presidential term limits are arguably less controversial than other legislation that the Parliament has passed, such as prohibitions on NGOs, social media, and journalism as well as aggressive antiterrorism laws, or the extension of the state of emergency. As veteran civil society researcher Bahi al-Din Hassan, who directs the Cairo Institute for Human Rights, argued, "Many of the laws passed since January 2016 share the common attribute of assisting the authorities in rolling back the freedoms won in the January 25 uprising."[103] While this legislative crackdown in the assembly may draw comparisons to the preuprising parliaments of Mubarak's presidency, the present Maglis al-Sha'b is operating under a military government within a state working with less cohesion and capacity than what Mubarak oversaw.

Likewise, the preuprising and postcoup elections were vastly different. The elections in postcoup Egypt are fanciful compared to those held in the late Mubarak period because al-Sisi's regime-in-formation has yet to build even shell institutions that Mubarak readily had at his disposal. The state as ruled by al-Sisi looks so precarious that the rickety state Mubarak guided appears to be a juggernaut in comparison. The result is that elections in al-Sisi's Egypt are manufactured and without choice.

This does not mean we are likely to see another uprising anytime soon. The state repression—also a sign of a brittle, fragmenting, and incoherent state—depresses people's ability and willingness to participate. If meaningful elections allow a state to see its citizens and make their preferences legible to the outside world, it is nearly impossible to know what Egyptians are thinking politically now. We could assume, based on the rigged turnout and results, they love al-Sisi, but this is unlikely. As has been the case for far too long, Egyptians do not get a say in how they get ruled unless they revolt. Since the generals do not speak for their citizens, elections will continue to tell us little more than how insecure the regime-making project is or how far away from being reconsolidated the state may be. After all, now we can compare the elections under al-Sisi to those under Mubarak in terms of how they are conducted and organized.

More interestingly, we can see in the events not just a story of Egypt's journey from a regime's factitious elections to real elections and back to imaginary ones, but the politically anchoring work elections do during a transitional period. The case of Egypt also reveals the normative constraints elections place on elites who have access to military power, are further backed by regional and international powers, and are willing to use violence in weakening, fragmented states. The question of democratization is certainly more complicated than whether the tool of elections is empowering for a society. Elections might tell us many things about a society, but whether it is a democracy or autocracy is just the most superficial assessment. In Egypt, treating transitional elections as isolated events or as a series of empowering events disguises more than it illuminates about the political dynamics at work.

Along with the transition's elections dividing the systemic and antisystemic opposition further, elections as a formal process also normalized the use of state violence on the bodies of those publicly refusing to participate. While the transition's elections might have tried to stem the potential expansion of street protests and the demands protesters generate, they also facilitated the generals' ability to deploy more state violence. While the violence escalated as the transition proceeded, the generals unleashed even more state violence as they began regime-making after the coup in 2013.

Ironically, the generals focused their postcoup violence on the systemic opposition group that helped them steady the state during the transition. This observation reveals SCAF's concern over any group capable of winning a procedurally clean election. Yet, the escalation of state violence against the Muslim Brotherhood has also been used against the marginalized revolutionaries after the regime-making began in 2013. Before the transition began, SCAF had few options but to oversee the process, try to protect their interests, and deflect democracy while controlled elected civilians provided a veneer of cover. When that possibility began to extinguish, SCAF stepped into the fray and decided to build a new regime at the center of the state apparatus. To erect this construction, they targeted all critics with lethal state violence as well as mass incarceration and travel bans. If al-Sisi and SCAF succeed in building a new regime, it will be on the corpses of their citizens.

3

State Violence as Life

Regime-Making and Counterrevolution

Egypt is currently experiencing the most violent period in its modern history. Each time this statement gets uttered, it seems impossible. And, yet, corporal state violence on Egyptian bodies escalates without interruption. Relatedly, new laws, mass incarceration, death sentences, and movement restrictions also increased after the uprising that ejected Mubarak began and then again after the coup. Like Egypt's uprising and transition, the deployment of state violence by leaders was a process. The state's leading generals, housed in SCAF, emerged as the de facto leaders of a political transition, which they electorally grounded. As the country conducted more and more elections, which cemented the divisions among the opposition groups, the contests also opened up pathways where SCAF could use state violence more frequently.

While the generals often said they had no intention of using force against Egyptians during the uprising or transition, unleashing state violence increasingly became their default move as well as their current president's decision. Two quotes animate the change from not using force to deploying it regularly. In December 2011 SCAF Major General Adel Emara told the press, "The armed forces does not use violence systematically. We exercise a level of self-restraint that others envy. We do not do that out of weakness but out of concern for national interests."[1] Six months later, embattled SCAF Field Marshal Muhammad Husayn Tantawi issued a public threat at a military training center. As he proclaimed, "God Willing, we'll cut the tongues of those who make false allegations against our troops and men."[2]

The images of organized state violence are burned into the psyche of participants and observers of Egypt's uprising.[3] There were the photos of singer Rami Esam's bruised back after the military tortured him in the Egyptian National Museum, reports by victims of military doctors conducting virginity tests on women, videos of soldiers using their armored personnel carriers to run over predominately Christian protesters at Maspero, images of soldiers stomping on the woman in the blue bra by Parliament, videos of security forces dragging dead bodies along the ground like garbage, and other videos of snipers shooting at the heads of Brotherhood protesters at the Republican Guards Headquarters.

Scholars watched this violence and nearly always mention it in their accounts but then do not treat state violence as something that needs to be theorized. Others have noticed a similar dynamic in other contexts.[4] With respect to the Middle East, as Laleh Khalili points out, while some feel that focusing on violence in the Arab world advances clichés, prejudices, and stereotypes about the region, it is a mistake to avoid the subject, because violence and "other forms of coercion" help replicate "institutions of state."[5] One could add that state violence also assists in regime-making. If researchers want to understand how violence helps a disrupted state build, change, or replicate regime hierarchies, then state violence and repression need to be studied on their own terms.[6] While it is still early, publications are starting to emerge that tackle state violence directly.[7] This chapter explores patterns of state violence and political transitions and then examines what lessons, if any, the case of Egypt reveals to us about this topic during uprisings, transitions, and regime-making.

Theorists have, however, considered the phenomenon of state violence generally.[8] Few works focus on state violence as causal.[9] Rather, state violence shows up as an effect—mostly as a result of design limitation in a "weak" state. As Nazih Ayubi once argued, "The contemporary Arab state is obsessed with power and strength and it may indeed be strong in terms of its 'body'. But the violence of this state is in reality an indication of its weakness and fragility: the (coercive) apparatus may be powerful but the state as a whole is weak because it lacks rationality and because it lacks the necessary moral, ideological, and educational supports."[10] It seems ironic that researchers studying one of the world's "least free" regions have not published more scholarship about how elites there use state violence to create or maintain regime practices of domination in a society.[11]

State violence is understood as a sign of weakness, not strength. Hannah Arendt argued decades ago, "It is insufficient to say that power and violence are the same. Power and violence are opposites; where one rules absolutely, the other is absent."[12] This is a great quote, but does the observation hold? James Ron notices a dynamic in his research about state violence in frontiers and ghettos. As he argues, "States are more likely to use police-style methods in institutionally dense settings, but more destructive tactics in institutionally thin arenas."[13] When elites are housed in states that maintain their inherently unstable position of dominance over oppositional social forces, state violence is reactive and limited. While physical coercion is the most visible strategy for maintaining authoritarian rule, it is also the option least frequently deployed by a regime.[14] Most governments use their organized means of coercion (arms, military troops, police, and jails) "to maintain what their rulers define as public order."[15] According to the logic of Tilly's argument, the reason government elites choose policing rather than unleashing physical state violence is because force has limitations in that it does not resolve political problems. Yet, not all state violence is a sign of brittle weakness.

Elites in autocratic states can use repression, but it is not the default or automatic response. Tools such as elections, patronage distributed through ruling parties, and official pageantry are available to officials to manipulate politics to the state's advantage and transmit the message that resistance is hopeless.[16] If those tactics fail, then robust security forces lie in wait. As long as the security forces are paid, have transnational political support, and remain willing to repress, citizen attempts to change a regime are unlikely to succeed.[17] When state violence is used in such scenarios, deaths do occur but not in high numbers. They are usually sporadic or individual. In these instances, state violence is an effect because something causes it—an inability to incorporate demands from society, poor political calculations by elites, or a mistake or excess by security forces. These regrettable instances are mostly defensive attempts to contain dissent in order to preserve existing relationships within society.

What happens in states when society disrupts an autocratic status quo in rapid or dramatic fashion? How does it affect how elites deploy state violence? As the protests in Egypt built momentum and forced SCAF to dump long-time incumbent Husni Mubarak, security forces and state-sponsored plain-clothed "thugs" (*balṭagiyya*) killed many people. During the initial eighteen days of protests, at least 846 people died.[18] This was not premeditated state violence. The violence was an effect of the rapid collapse in daily routines and a shift in the balance of power between the state elites and social forces. The generals, who had been thrust into leading the transition in Egypt's withering state, were not trying to create a new political playing field. They were trying to not be swept away with Mubarak, the NDP, and various neoliberal businessmen under the pull of people power.

After SCAF assumed authority over the transition, though, a new pattern of violence emerged. The state continued to fragment as protests continued. Episodic escalations of state violence produced increasingly high death tolls, frequently a cluster of deaths during a single incident. Although the state used violence more widely and more frequently during this period than during the previous regime, the violence was preservationist and appeared aimed at protecting a fragmenting state facing sustained popular mobilization. We see an inverse relationship in which state violence rises as state capacity diminishes. The pattern continued through the period of SCAF's leadership as well as the one-year presidency of Muhammad Mursi. This inverse relationship also explains the increase in state violence as a state undergoes the changes from the status quo to being disrupted but not overthrown.

The pattern morphed again in July 2013, when the elected president was deposed in a coup. After the military arrested Mursi and installed a civilian interim government, state violence intensified as SCAF began to create a new regime. At first, the military's high command ordered an escalation of state violence through appointed civilian lackeys. Then, once 'Abdel Fattah al-Sisi formally became president, the military began governing in the open. One need only look at the death toll after the coup to see that the security forces have been killing citizens at an increasing rate. On the surface, academic research suggests this was inevitable; there is ample evidence that military coups produce increases in violence.[19] Yet the expectation of an increase in violence does not capture the changing power relationships or the political work the state violence attempts to accomplish. State violence, like the transition paradigm, focuses on outcomes but not the process of more repression being incrementally normalized in society. The violence in the postcoup period is not defensive and is dissimilar to the state violence of the late Mubarak period and the transition under SCAF and Mursi. This violence is also not intended to revive the old regime's relationships with society.

Rather, state violence after the coup has been used to create a new political regime. Although Egypt's generals after the coup were not building a state from scratch, the state violence after the July 3 coup has helped engineer a new political reality as the generals write new rules of engagement between the state and its citizens. The state's violence has been premeditated and planned.[20] There is precedent for this kind of violence, as Vincent Boudreau has shown in his work on state building and repression in Southeast Asia. As Boudreau argues, "State crackdowns allowed new dictators to shake themselves free of the old system."[21] Constitutive state violence, in this sense, can be seen as causal because it is deployed to reconfigure and isolate the social forces that could potentially resist an attempt to establish a new regime order. Part of creating a new political order means, as Tilly reminds us, leaders "eliminating or neutralizing their rivals inside" the country.[22] Therefore, the state violence everyone witnessed after the postuprising turmoil is not about containing a failing order but creating a new one.

As al-Sisi tries to build a new regime on the ruins of the uprising, state elites in Egypt are deploying deadly force more frequently than at any time in post-1952 Egypt. This chapter looks at how elites in Egypt are using counterrevolutionary state violence as a constitutive process to build an exclusivist political order and a new regime. By detailing the events from the late Mubarak period to the transition under SCAF and Mursi to the period after the July 2013 military coup, I develop a theory on state violence to show the constitutive aspects and transformative character of state violence after a political transition.

State Violence under Mubarak

As Mubarak was being ousted, Western media outlets constructed a narrative in which an oppressive dictatorship was being dislodged by a nonviolent protest movement wielding social media and inspired by the octogenarian Gene Sharp.[23] It was a feel-good story, but it bore no resemblance to the process unfolding in Egypt.

Violence was a hallmark of the Mubarak regime. Residents and visitors to the Arab world before 2011 witnessed "slow violence" as part of everyday life in the region.[24] This violence included plainclothes officers or riot police selectively attacking protesters, security personnel and informers watching from street corners, activists receiving invitations for "chats" from interior ministries, and videos of people being tortured in police stations mysteriously (or intentionally) being released on the internet.[25] The arbitrary and rotating imprisonment of activists was the political norm.[26] These repressive tactics serve as a deterrent to society and give those who wish to be politically active a reason to pause or not act. But people living in these societies challenged such slow state violence anyway.

Domestic groups and independent journalists bravely struggled and published researched reports about the quotidian abuses committed by the incumbent regimes. Nevertheless, this type of slow violence became normalized, even if despised, by many. In fact, some have shown that the repressive character of the region's authoritarian regimes encouraged parallel social structures to help people cope with such slow violence.[27] These informal avenues help people intentionally stay out of their state's way. Sometimes the state recognized the informal gains made by people.[28] Other times not.

As in most autocratic states, elites in Mubarak's Egypt did not draw from a wide enough social base to be able to win over their critics or institutionally incorporate their opposition. When the power of persuasion and the blocking of avenues into institutions could not contain society's oppositional forces, security forces were dispatched. State violence under Mubarak was functional and aimed at solving problems that politics could not in order to maintain the status quo.

An exemplary instance of this phenomenon is the 2005 parliamentary elections in which the illegal Muslim Brotherhood won 20 percent of the seats. The night before the voting started, a prominent figure from the ruling party argued that "the best way to deal with Islamists is through politics, not through security means or using a security mentality."[29] But after the first two rounds produced seventy-six seats for the Brotherhood, security intervened to limit any more opposition gains in the third round of voting. Nine people died in the last round and only twelve more Brotherhood candidates were elected.[30]

During the late Mubarak period, it was a challenge to distinguish where the presidency, the ruling NDP, and the security services started and ended. They blended together as a cohesive unit: the president announced or approved policy, the party would do its best to implement the directive, and the security services would enforce order when the party failed. A background of low-level, reactive violence was the norm.[31]

The state's response to the Kifaya movement in its first year is instructive. Kifaya was founded and held its first protest in December 2004. From early 2005 until the presidential election that September, it held nearly weekly protests challenging Mubarak's presidency and the idea of hereditary succession. The protests took place across Cairo, including outside the gates of Cairo University, at the Journalists and Lawyers Syndicates, and in Sa'd Zaghlul, Sayyida Zaynab, Lazoughli, Zaytun, Matariyya, Imbaba, 'Abdin, and Tal'at Harb.[32] The protesters, who would usually number between one hundred and seven hundred, were usually encircled by the Central Security Forces and not allowed to move. But, on occasion, they did march, such as at a protest in Cairo's Shubra district on June 22, 2005.

Every time Kifaya met in any part of Cairo, the Central Security Forces were there and set up a cordon around the group. Most of the time, protesters interacted with the Central Security Forces, talking to them, giving them water, perhaps handing them a flower. Protesters would sometimes attempt to provoke a confrontation, but the security forces would let it pass without a response. Only on three occasions did security forces attack the protesters that year. During a constitutional referendum on May 25, 2005, state-supported agents sexually assaulted women protesting on the steps of the Journalists Syndicate in order to shame them back into their houses. And when Kifaya held a protest in Bab al-Luq on June 30 after Mubarak accepted the formal nomination as the NDP's presidential candidate, plainclothes thugs rushed the crowd, putting an end to the protest. The third instance was on the day of the presidential election, when the regime mobilized to stop protesters from gathering in places like downtown or Bab al-Sharaya, the home parliamentary district of Mubarak's primary competitor, Ayman Nur.

This is not to suggest that protesting during this time of Mubarak's presidency was safe or without risk: security was omnipresent, and rarely were protests allowed to freely assemble or move. Furthermore, during this time, the regime frequently targeted activists, harassing them, torturing them, and trapping them in a legal swamp of politicized charges.[33] Rather, this background suggests that there were limits to state violence under Mubarak. Security forces could not just open fire on protesters, and the military had not deployed into the streets en masse since the Central Security Forces revolt in 1986.[34]

In the decade leading up to the uprising, the military was one of several equals on the ruling coalition. It was not first among them and had not been since the late Sadat period.[35] While members of the military undoubtedly contributed to behind-the-scenes policy decisions and served as governors of the country's numerous provinces, Egypt during this period, as some analysts have correctly argued, was an archetypal "state-security" state rather than a military state, as it would have been labeled in the 1950s and 1960s.[36] After al-Gama'a al-Islamiyya's insurrection in the 1990s and the onslaught of protest activity from labor and groups such as Kifaya in the 2000s, the Interior Ministry's web of spies, police, and informants came to compete with the military for resources from the state.[37] It was the Interior Ministry that became responsible for local order on the various street corners and neighborhoods around the country.

The last decade of Mubarak's rule also saw increasing street activism, from protests against hereditary presidential succession to labor unrest.[38] Yet even in this politically resistant climate, large-scale lethal violence against the public was not an option Mubarak's regime exercised. The dictatorship kept its boot firmly on civil society's neck, but it did not choose to snap it in two. It is unclear that the regime ever permitted the security forces to kill activists during the 2000s.[39] More apparent were allegations of torture by the police and the State Security Investigations Service. Although security forces could not be held to account, killing dissenters was a line not many in the Mubarak regime wanted to cross willingly. When deaths occurred, they were likely unintentional.

The now well-known case of an Alexandrian man named Khalid Sa'id reveals the exception to the rule because the authorities did kill him in 2010.[40] The outpouring of popular outrage following the murder of Sa'id illustrates how under the Mubarak regime, lethal state violence was so beyond the norm that when it did occur it provoked a national scandal. On June 6, 2010, two police officers got into an altercation with Sa'id in Alexandria's Sidi Gabir district and subsequently beat Sa'id to death in the stairwell of a building. The pictures taken at the morgue, which show his disfigured face, galvanized Egyptians, who circulated the pictures alongside photos of Sa'id when he was alive. People amplified the case of Sa'id because he was a regular person. They used the tragedy to say that if he could be brutally murdered, anyone could be a victim. Marches commemorating his death took place in major Egyptian cities, and activists established the "We are all Khalid Sa'id" Facebook page.[41] Sa'id's death was a particularly egregious instance of state repression. People were shocked at the savagery of the state's agents, and while they did not revolt, they organized to clearly send a message that this type of brutality was unacceptable.[42] Even though this resistance did not produce accountability, it is instructive to compare the outraged response to the death of a single person, who was probably killed accidently, to the responses to the increasing number of deaths after Mubarak was overthrown. Less than a year later, as lethal state violence became normalized, individual deaths were no longer followed by the same widespread level of outrage or commemoration even if they generated immense social pain.

Although one should not diminish the ferocity of state violence under the Mubarak regime, remnant elites that battled to save the state from imploding after January 25, 2011, unleashed increasing amounts of state violence against Egyptians. Differentiating between the types of state violence can help explain the variation and escalation. Under the late

Mubarak regime, state violence remained an option of last resort, or, at least, a selective tactic to stop opposition gains when nonviolent politics failed. The politically disobedient were handed over to the court system or beaten in the street by thugs not in official uniform. Security officials liked to say beating someone or humiliating them back into their homes was a way of "teaching someone a lesson." In this sense, state violence was an infrequently used tactic that sought to help preserve the status quo. Since Mubarak's overthrow, however, the default of Egypt's elites is to quickly deploy greater levels of violence. State violence now reaches new and more diverse segments of society, including those that previously had been relatively secure.

Incumbent Ejection, Collapsed Regime, and a Vacuum

From the start of the protests in January 2011, there were violent confrontations between demonstrators and the security forces. The security forces were meticulous in their preparation for the protests. For the first four days, activists braved water cannons, tear gas, and assaults on squares by the forces of the Interior Ministry. The canal city of Suez resembled a war zone.[43] The protesters chased security forces out of the streets by physically confronting and defeating them. At the end of the initial eighteen days of the uprising, at least 846 people had died.

After the military stepped in on January 28 and was forced to "retire" the long-serving president on February 11, many wanted to believe that the Egyptian uprising had unleashed a linear progression toward democracy. But while initially Egypt's uprising could be characterized as a "revolution-in-process" whose outcome was undetermined,[44] and while there can be no doubt that revolutionary activities gripped Egypt after the January 2011 uprising began, counterrevolutionary forces responded to maintain some semblance of a fragmenting state with a regime that had collapsed. What Egyptians ultimately experienced was an incumbent ejection.[45] Leaving the disrupted state apparatus intact deleteriously affected the prospects of wider inclusive change, because although coalition members, such as leading NDP figures, got dropped, the state was not overrun. Thus, some could argue that no revolution ever actually took place.[46] SCAF's

Machiavellian political maneuvers, together with the Muslim Brotherhood's opportunism and governing incompetence and the fact that the state apparatus remained largely Mubarakist, allowed enough elements to survive to prevent state collapse. In fact, while the protests were happening in February 2011, scholars such as Ellis Goldberg accurately noted that the course the military would likely pursue would be one of "Mubarakism without Mubarak."[47] Nine years after the uprising began, plenty of Mubarakism remains.

But despite the Mubarak holdovers, the members of the ruling coalition after the July 2013 coup maintain different power relationships with each other and with society from those that existed in the late Mubarak period. The events since the coup indicate strongly that the unreformed police and the army will be the central players in determining Egypt's near-term political trajectory.[48] Other pro-state figures will reemerge as servants and implementers of the security establishment's agenda. Yet al-Sisi does not govern a cohesive regime. At best, he is overseeing and managing competition between different parts of the state that sometimes compete and sometimes cooperate.

While new parties formed in the wake of General 'Abdel Fattah al-Sisi's coup and subsequent election, and many have former NDP members, any large single ruling party will need to be constructed from scratch. The situation is unlike when Sadat transformed the Arab Socialist Union into the National Democratic Party by decree in the 1970s. Any party that is created as al-Sisi leads the efforts to build a new regime will be utterly subservient to its military overlords and their wishes. People that participated in the governing of Egypt under Mubarak's long tenure may return to official positions, but it remains to be seen if those personalities and offices will have the authority they had under Mubarak's dictatorship. For instance, crony capitalists that profit from and support the military's substantial business ventures, some of which are buttressed by wealthy multinational corporations, will likely form any eventual regime's civilian business face.[49] But other research suggests that this end point will be a much more tumultuous journey than assumed.[50]

What has fundamentally shifted in Egypt in the age of regime-making is the stark and profound power of the military, manifested in the figure of al-Sisi. Since his election in May 2014, the system has morphed into one in which executive power flows exclusively into and out of the offices of military intelligence, while al-Sisi and other officers influence politics in ways that lack the slightest modicum of transparency. In this way, the new regime-in-formation will be entirely different from the one Mubarak oversaw because it will be narrowly centered around the army's generals.[51]

The popular mobilization that shocked and muted the old Mubarak elites allowed for these alterations in Egypt's ruling coalition. The military under former Defense Minister Muhammad Husayn Tantawi, who governed SCAF and the country for the first seventeen months after Mubarak's ouster, used the uprising to secure the generals' place at the top of the hierarchy as they tried to salvage what remained. But SCAF was unprepared when it took over in February 2011 and incapable of politically engineering such an outcome alone. The generals needed help from the systemic opposition, and they found such support in the seemingly politically patient wings of the country's oldest civilian organization, the Muslim Brotherhood.[52] Beyond this, the military resorted to systems of discipline that they trusted. For example, under SCAF's leadership, nearly twelve thousand civilians, including protesters and workers, were referred to military tribunals between February and December 2011.[53] This figure exceeds the total number of civilians tried in military courts during the thirty years of Mubarak's rule by nearly a factor of six.[54]

When SCAF directly ruled, the Brotherhood served as willing agents to bring about the change that established and insulated the generals at the apex of state authority. As the Brotherhood waited for parliamentary and presidential elections, it dismissed criticisms of SCAF when it employed violence against protesters and used military trials against civilians, and it obliged SCAF's wishes not to reform the state apparatus when it did win parliamentary seats and the presidency. The Brotherhood gave the institutions that had exerted repression against them for decades a pass and, consequently, undermined the projective capacity of the protesters' mobilization. When given a chance to run for Parliament or the presidency, the Brotherhood jumped at the opportunity to show off its national organizational capabilities while together with SCAF electionizing Egypt's transition.

Even when the newly elected president Muhammad Mursi overreached, such as with the November 2012 constitutional declaration granting him sweeping temporary powers, he sought to insulate and protect the security services and permanently expand the army's reach into political life. This was best seen in articles 197 and 198 of the constitution, which passed in a referendum in December 2012. The articles prohibited parliamentary discussion or oversight of the military's budget, established the fifteen-person National Defense Council, and legalized military trials against civilians in more expansive ways.

The Brotherhood, however, could never overcome the suspicions of its detractors in society or the generals. Other Islamist groups felt that Mursi and the Brotherhood sought only power, not a march toward "true" religious rule. The non-Islamist constituencies worried about Mursi's seeming disregard for their concerns, token appointments, and lack of serious effort to include their voices. In many respects, the Brotherhood's actions in power confirmed what many thought, which had been conditioned by thirty years of Egyptian and international speculative discourses about the ruling intentions of Islamists.[55] Lastly, but most decisively, the generals that commanded SCAF and the armed forces never really accepted that over the long term, Mursi and the Brotherhood would be subservient. Brotherhood spokesmen had publicly acknowledged that they had designs on establishing civilian control over the military in the future. This was the ultimate deal breaker in what turned out to be a tenuous political pact.[56]

As we have seen, there are, at least, three kinds of state violence: defensive/reactive, preservationist, and constitutive. There is no debate about the increasing amount of state violence in Egypt. Yet signs of this state violence were present long before in different forms. The increased violence that we see, therefore, is the violence of the process of regime formation at work—that is, the regime collapsed during the initial eighteen days, but SCAF generals have been trying to build a new one since July 2013. This regime-making project was underpinned by cascading state violence as SCAF broke with the transition and tried to construct new practices with their own hands. The number of deaths resulting from deliberate military and police violence against different segments of Egyptian society reveals a pattern in which state violence changes over time. When an autocratic regime develops a status quo, state violence is limited and reactive in order to preserve existing inequalities in the distribution of power between the state and society. When the state is disrupted and becomes more fragmented, elites increasingly deploy state violence, but it is again defensive and intended to reestablish the disrupted hierarchy and end the popular mobilization. When elites decide the social forces from the older political order no longer can participate, they use constitutive state violence to create a new political field, as they forge a new regime by destroying the social forces of the older order. In this instance, state violence becomes causal and constructive in engineering the structure of politics.

From Preservationist to Constitutive State Violence

Over the seventeen months of SCAF rule, thousands were injured and over one hundred were killed. Between March and June 2011, security forces used electric prods against protesters in the squares as activists were beaten and females subjected to army-sanctioned virginity tests in the Egyptian National Museum.[57] In June, security forces clashed with families of the initial uprising's martyrs outside the Balloon Theater in Cairo. Nearly six hundred protesters were injured.[58] On October 9, 2011, the violence qualitatively escalated when the military killed twenty-eight protesters at Maspero in Cairo.[59] The following month security forces killed another forty-one (and injured over one thousand) in the battles on Muhammad Mahmoud Street the week before the first parliamentary elections after Mubarak's ejection.[60] Nineteen protesters died (and over seven hundred were injured) at the hands of the military at the Cabinet Offices sit-in in January 2012,[61] and another fifteen were killed in protests near the Interior Ministry in February 2012.[62] The security forces killed twelve more protesters at the Defense Ministry sit-in between April and May 2012.[63]

Others died while the security forces were either absent or deliberately unresponsive. After instigators started the clashes at a football match in Port Said in February 2012, clashes between citizens left seventy-nine dead and over one thousand injured.[64] After twenty-one people, who were mostly Port Said residents, were sentenced to death for involvement in that incident, more clashes between citizens and the police happened and left another forty-eight people dead in Port Said in January 2013.[65] And in December 2012, shortly after Mursi's constitutional declaration, Brotherhood supporters attacked protesters at the Presidential Palace, leaving another nine protesters dead.[66] There were also the lynching murders of four Shi'i in a Giza village in June 2013.[67]

This state violence under SCAF was wider reaching than it had been under Mubarak and began affecting new segments of Egyptian society. At the same time, it remained reactive and preservationist—an attempt to stave off uncontrolled change to the machinery of governance. In the aftermath of al-Sisi's coup in July 2013, state violence ceased to be about reestablishing a semblance of the regime's practices as they had been under Mubarak. The elites in the postcoup state use organized violence to help create a new regime while simultaneously transforming Egyptian political society. Instead of being an effect, state violence is used causally to change existing relationships as well as engineer new ones.

After Mursi was removed from office, whatever tacit or unspoken pact the military and the Brotherhood had made collapsed. The existence of the Brotherhood became a threat to SCAF's governance and control. Furthermore, procedurally fair elections, on their own, were not going to successfully extract the new governing elite from the tumultuous situation of the state fragmenting around them. SCAF had used elections to guide the transition. They could not coup Mursi from power and then reuse the tool of credible elections. The failed pact and the relentless popular mobilization threatened to undermine the state and produce revolutionary changes beyond the military's control. The preuprising state and its transitional aftermath had run its course. The state needed to be reinforced and a new autocratic regime created. At this point the military began to use state violence to restructure Egypt's political arena. As Andrea Teti has argued, "The repressive wave aimed at the Brotherhood was *useful* to the 'deep state.'"[68] While the concept of the "deep state" can be ambiguous, what Teti points out is important in that state violence shifted from its defensive or preservationist forms to constitutive as SCAF tried to redefine politics and make a new regime.

After Mursi was relieved from the presidency, his detention prompted protests from the Muslim Brotherhood and his electoral supporters. At first, protesters gathered at the Officers Club at the Republican Guard headquarters, where the president was rumored to be held. Two days after the coup, security forces shot and killed five protesters near the headquarters. As is often the case, the state's use of lethal force produced more popular mobilization. A few days later, there were reportedly two thousand people sitting in across from the Republican Guard headquarters. In the early hours of July 8, 2013, security services supported by the military used sharpshooters and others to open fire as protesters performed their dawn prayers. The security forces killed 51 to 61 people, according to different reports, and wounded 435 more in under four hours.[69] In comparison, two police officers and one solider were also killed during this second assault. The interim government legitimized these assaults by alleging the demonstrators tried to "raid" the Republican Guard headquarters. The military urged protesters to remain peaceful and respect the military and other sovereign institutions. This incident led the military and government to launch a propaganda campaign they touted as a war on terror.

The government's campaign transformed people's perceptions of the Brotherhood. It enabled well-deserved social skepticism of the Brotherhood to become vociferous opposition by creating what Stuart Hall and others have called a "moral panic."[70] The narrative that the state could collapse if the Brotherhood continued minding the presidency, as well as the idea of the "Brotherhoodization of the state" regularly invoked in the press, set up other popular discourses and constructed an atmosphere of fear-mongering for people to accept and promote the Brotherhood's dehumanization. Politics were pushed into a state of ideological displacement, which Hall describes as "when such discrepancies appear between threat and reaction, between what is perceived and what that is a perception of," allowing the institutions of state to induce a moral panic that advantages their ability to recapture or exert social control.[71] The moral panic around the Brotherhood, which saw ordinary citizens cheer on the military's next move, was the death knell for civilian politics in postuprising Egypt.

The dehumanization process began with a popular notion that the Muslim Brotherhood and its supporters were a bunch of "sheep" (*khirfān*).

As Sarah Carr noted, the framing "suggest[s] that Morsi supporters are all members of the Muslim Brotherhood, and are all unthinking androids programmed by the Supreme Guide."[72] The Brotherhood's supporters responded by labeling its opponents infidels or *fulūl* (Mubarak regime holdovers). The polarizing rhetoric led to much dehumanization in the aftermath of the coup. The army seized on this dynamic and further encouraged it. With all sides degrading one another, military leaders were in a position to whip up—with the full weight of the state behind them—popular support as they planned the violent regime-making alteration of society. What happened next changed the post-1952 landscape of Egyptian politics.

The anti-Brotherhood campaign was not without precedent, however. The generals and the state also relied on thirty years of international and domestic discourse about Islamists' autocratic "intentions" as they exaggerated the actual exclusivist tendencies of Mursi's presidency.[73] After all, SCAF had committed many of the same excesses Mursi had without widespread social pushback. The abstract target of the "counterterrorism" offensive became the faceless Brotherhood's anticoup coalition. The Brotherhood became a homogenized enemy of a state that was backed by the military and enjoyed broad social support. Those who were anti-SCAF, opposed to a coup on principle, or may have even voted for Mursi in the presidential election but identified with more revolutionary change, were left with no perch to inject nuance into the polarizing dynamic of the Egyptian state versus the Brotherhood. The weight of SCAF's targeting the Brotherhood engulfed the nuanced political positions of the middle despite their not having affection for either actor. The generated atmosphere left most revolutionaries, unaffiliated people, and people connected to the state's actions on one side against the Brotherhood on the other.[74]

The physical target of the war on terror became Cairo's al-Raba'a al-'Adawiyya and al-Nahda Squares, where the largest anticoup coalition had been camping out for weeks following Mursi's arrest. Other smaller protests around the country also demanded that Mursi be reinstated as president. The media railed against the secretive and nefarious Brotherhood in society's midst. As posters of al-Sisi appeared everywhere around the country and as the sweet shops in posh parts of Cairo began selling cupcakes with his picture on them, the state elites used the state apparatus and public discourse to cynically construct a political context whereby social forces and ordinary citizens authorized mass state violence against their fellow citizens.

Having laid this groundwork, al-Sisi, with the full backing of the state bureaucratic machine, convened a rally on July 26, 2013, that was impossible to escape in the newspapers, radio, TV, and internet. Clad in sunglasses and military uniform, the general appealed to people to rise up and give the state a mandate to "combat terrorism." In response to being labeled terrorists, the next day more Mursi supporters started a march to Raba'a Square to join those already there. As the procession on the Sixth of October Bridge made its way, security forces fired on the marchers by Ramsis Square. According to Human Rights Watch, plainclothes forces as well as snipers shot and killed at least ninety-five protesters.[75] Most victims had kill-shots to the head, neck, or chest. One police officer was also killed, according to the Interior Ministry. It was the largest death toll in a single protest since the initial unsettled days of January 2011.

In early August, the total number of protesters killed since the June 30 coup was nearly two hundred.[76] As the weeks passed and the political tensions rose, SCAF thwarted an American and European plan to resolve the problem.[77] State violence at that point was not merely an option for the postcoup government: it was a necessary part of a strategy to dismember and break the Brotherhood's nationally organized networks. The goal was to eradicate the Brotherhood by using state violence to *unorganize* them.

The calculation seems to have been that having deposed Mursi, there was no way for the new elites to peacefully resolve the sit-in short of allowing Mursi to return as president. They also could not allow an organized Brotherhood to resume their role as an opposition force. Disposing of Mursi by a coup could push this systemic group into the arms of the antisystemic opposition. The experience of the previous year's competitive presidential election campaign, the promise that elections are a mechanism for the politics of compromise, and the coup that dislodged Mursi meant that more preservationist state violence could not resolve this predicament.

The situation reached its climax on August 14, when the government broke up the sit-in at al-Raba'a al-'Adawiyya Square, then on day forty-five. At 6:30 a.m., the security forces, both police and military, unleashed a coordinated attack on the protesters that lasted for twelve hours. The attack began with tear gas and bird shot fired at the square's entrances. The state quickly escalated the level of force, using snipers from rooftops and helicopters, ground forces, bulldozers, and armored personnel carriers. A report by Human Rights Watch documented that the security forces used live ammunition, leaving "hundreds killed by bullets to the heads, necks, and chests."[78] At least 817 people are reported to have died, but the number could be over 1,000. While the government had issued public statements that they would clear the square with force, they had never set a deadline or let people know through the media when it would occur. Protesters that managed to escape claim they never heard the audio warnings the government claims they repeatedly gave before the operation commenced. As Human Rights Watch documented, security forces attacked all five ways into and out of the square and blocked any safe passage out until the end of the operation.[79] Even those injured or surrendering were not allowed out. In many instances, they were shot at instead. Despite allegations that the pro-Mursi sit-in had many armed elements, people mostly defended themselves with rocks, Molotov cocktails, and fireworks.

Without an escape, most people moved from the edges of the square to its center. After several hours, the security forces made their final push to claim the square. The mosque at the center, and the medical clinic next to it, were surrounded. They forced the doctors out and ordered the corpses to be left. Then, around 5:30 p.m., the police likely set the mosque, other buildings, and tents on fire. Security arrested nearly eight hundred people, and detainees were beaten and tortured and some summarily executed on the spot.[80] Human Rights Watch claims it was the largest state massacre of citizens in a single day in recent world memory. As its report explains, "By way of contrast, credible estimates indicate that Chinese government officials killed between 400–800 protesters largely over a 24-hour span during the Tiananmen Massacre on June 3–4, 1989 and that Uzbek forces killed similar numbers in one day during the 2005 Andijan Massacre."[81] Sharif Abdel Kouddous, a journalist who has covered Israeli bombings of Gaza, civil war in Syria, and the uprising in Bahrain, and who was in Raba'a covering events, called the clearance of the square on August 14 the "single bloodiest day that I have witnessed as a journalist. Somewhere in the range between like 600–800 people were killed in a matter of hours. And in one place."[82]

Images of the corpses appeared on blogs, Facebook, Twitter, and in the international media.[83] Egyptian state TV played a loop of aerial footage that showed the destroyed square while the announcer calmly read the official government statements, which claimed that the government did not attack the protesters and that the Brotherhood was lighting the fires in the torched square.[84] The images and the state's dispassionate description was a declaration that the Brotherhood was no longer permitted to exist in, much less resist, the postcoup order.

Less than two days after the Raba'a massacre, protests again erupted after Friday prayers in Cairo's 'Abbasiyya district. The Brotherhood had called for a "day of anger." Demonstrators began a march near Ramsis Square. Police again fired on them, and in clashes that lasted over six hours, killed another 120 people.[85] In the six weeks following the July 3 coup that ousted the first freely elected president in Egypt's history, more than at least 1,150 protesters died in five different cases of mass state killings of protesters.

The arrests of national, governorate, and district Brotherhood leaders followed, as did the flight into exile of many of their members. All of this ensured that the Brotherhood was unable to exist as an opposition party waiting in the wings to threaten the regime again in the near term. The violence qualitatively changed the character of the Brotherhood. The organization that so many researchers have studied over the years no longer exists.

Today, state violence appears to be more limited than in the weeks that followed the military coup. Still, the state uses violence more frequently than in the initial transitional period. Protests remain prohibited, with the seeming exception being around subsidized bread.[86] In most cases, the government blocks protests from even happening. On rare occasions, people succeed in gathering for a protest. For example, in 2016, there were demonstrations protesting al-Sisi's agreement to give Tiran and

Safir Islands to Saudi Arabia, but the government broke these up quickly.[87] While the threat of lethal corporal state violence remains a possibility, as the instance of security's 2015 murder of Shaimaa al-Sabbagh shows,[88] there are also other violent effects that include imprisonment and other repression like movement restrictions.

If the Brotherhood was the regime-makers' first target after the coup, they were not the only ones targeted. The situation on the whole is one in which activists of all stripes languish in prison, websites are censored, NGOs have been shuttered, rights are routinely trampled on, and parts of Cairo and the country have become no-go areas for people who do not reside there or for those researching political topics. Observers continue to witness this elevated constitutive violence. Egyptians live with it in totalizing ways. For example, Human Rights Watch describes police stations and prisons as having "an assembly line" of torture, and the capital's district of Matariyya has been described as one of the most dangerous places in Egypt because of its connective location.[89] The study of torture and trauma as well as their continuities before, during, and after the revolutionary atmosphere is showing up more in the scholarly literature.[90] There is good reason for this development. In 2015, according to the now closed al-Nadim Center for the Rehabilitation of Victims of Violence, almost 500 people died in custody while 676 more were tortured.[91] The subsequent years have been terrible as well: in 2016, the Egyptian Coordination of Rights and Freedom reports, another 14 Egyptians died from torture while in custody and said their lawyers received 830 torture complaints.[92]

Furthermore, forced disappearances, or being put "behind the sun" as this tactic is known in Egypt, are also skyrocketing.[93] In a 2016 report, Amnesty International puts the number of people who disappeared in the 100s.[94] The al-Nadim Center documented 464 cases of forcible disappearance at the hands of the state.

The construction of new prisons, mass incarceration, and holding political prisoners is also a new normal. When President al-Sisi appeared on *60 Minutes* in the United States during January 2019, he claimed that there were no political prisoners in Egypt.[95] This statement contradicted one he made in June 2015 when he claimed "there are innocents in prisons."[96] All data suggests mass incarceration not only encouraged the construction of nineteen new prisons between 2011 and 2016,[97] but also that these prisons are being populated by political prisoners.[98] As the Arabic Network for Human Rights Information stated in their report, "New prisons in Egypt came, unfortunately, not as a result of the increase in population, but rather due to a policy of random arrests, unfair trials and unjust laws passed after July 3, 2013, such as, the anti-protest law and the decision to increase pre-trial detention periods, as well as the widespread impunity policies."[99] According to *Wikithawra*, they claim to have documented the arrest and imprisonment of nearly forty-one thousand people between July 3, 2013, and May 2014.[100] An additional twenty-six thousand more were arrested between 2015 and 2016.[101] It is estimated that roughly sixty thousand prisoners in Egypt are being held for political views and actions rather than criminal activity. This figure accounts for nearly 56 percent of all people being warehoused in the country's jails.

Prison time is also deceiving as Egyptian authorities continue to innovate on what it means to be imprisoned. For example, recently, there have been two prominent cases of political prisoners being released after completing their unjust sentences. While photographer Mahmud Abou Zeid (known as Shawkan) and activist Alaa Abdel Fattah have been released after completing five-year prison sentences, both are required to report to their local district police station each day, where they complete a twelve-hour stay between 6 p.m. and 6 a.m. the following morning. Both would have to follow this routine for the next five years, but Alaa Abdel Fattah has been rearrested without charge and returned to full-time incarceration.[102] Many others also will live like this under this new wrinkle of being freed and imprisoned each day over years. This state-stipulated situation also acts as an effective travel ban. If you have to report to the police station every day, there is no traveling inside or outside of Egypt.

If not under a de facto travel ban, the state now also relies on the movement restriction of a travel ban on "more than 30 of the country's leading human rights defenders and threatens to jail them at any moment."[103] Of the list of notable rights activists and journalists, Hossam Bahgat occupies a prominent place on the state's travel ban, which he discovered at the Cairo International Airport in February 2016.[104] Longtime rights leader Gamal Eid also is not permitted to travel abroad.[105] 'Aida Seif al-Dawla, a former cofounder of the now government-disbanded antitorture NGO al-Nadim, is also not allowed to leave.[106] The airport is also a site of prolonged disappearances and, if fortunate, where expatriate Egyptians, journalists, and scholars only just find out if they are permitted to enter the country. According to Daftar Ahwal, as of March 2016, there were a total of 554 cases of "politically motivated banned entry" at the airport.[107] This included 534 cases in Cairo's airport, 18 cases in the Borg el-Arab Airport in Alexandria, and 1 case each in the airports in Hurghada and Luxor.

This use of movement restrictions dramatically increased after the coup. Daftar Ahwal documented 35 cases during the SCAF-led transition, 21 during Mursi's presidency, and then 279 and 218 under 'Adli Mansur and al-Sisi's rule between July 2013 and February 2016.[108] The breakdown of the numbers includes 274 Egyptians, 81 "Arabs," and 199 people with other nationalities.[109] The prisons being constructed, the jailing of political prisoners, and the bans on activists too prominent abroad to jail disguise the fact that many Egyptians have been reduced to a life in exile. Regime-making built on state violence and its omnipresent threat has produced another exodus from the country. One recent report noted that "many more migrants have left Egypt than in previous waves of politically motivated migration, and they are much more diverse in both identity and motivation for departure."[110]

The state attacks organizations as they do people. Al-Sisi and company also use a new 2017 law to shutter offices of potentially activist NGOs. Over two thousand NGOs alone have been closed, their assets frozen, and some of their staff arrested because they are linked to the Muslim Brotherhood.[111] Yet, this crackdown on NGOs is wider than just Brotherhood-affiliated NGOs. The state targets all NGO groups that *might* potentially contest it and its budding regime.

The state's violence is no longer reserved for just Egyptian citizens, either. In January 2016 Italian PhD candidate Giulio Regeni, who was studying labor activism, disappeared on his way from Cairo's Dokki neighborhood to downtown. The next month his body was discovered on the side of the Cairo–Alexandria Road. It was badly bruised and showed signs of torture. His neck had been snapped in two. The way he died suggests his murder was at the hands of the state's security forces.[112] Egyptians say that he died "like an Egyptian." The security forces' likely role in the murder of Regeni is a direct consequence of the constitutive state violence the coup and regime-making injected into politics.

These developments are terrifying for people trying to participate politically. As journalist Amira Howeidy observed generally about the dynamic, "You never know which security branch is responsible or in charge any more. It's unpredictable. That's what makes everything dangerous. You cannot see it coming."[113] Beyond the competing security and intelligence agencies, a regime needs institutions such as parties and political organizations. It needs spectacles like elections and people whose actions reflect belief in the ruling vision rather than fear. For now, al-Sisi's regime-making attempt has many sticks and few carrots. While it would be comforting to believe that this situation cannot go on forever, a terrible status quo can go on for a long time, as any student of Mubarak's Egypt can attest.

The current state elites seem intent on not only repressing dissent but also trying to erase the crimes of the recent past.[114] In November 2013, the government transformed al-Raba'a al-'Adawiyya Square by adding a monument to honor the police and military in its center. The roads have been repaved to conceal the blood stains and the mosque was repainted. As the *New York Times* reported, the redesigned square leaves "no hint of the violence except the bullet holes in lampposts and homes."[115] It is not just landscapes that are changed to cover up the repression: many of the participants and witnesses have been silenced. Photographer Mahmud Abu Zeid (Shawkan), for example, was arrested on the day of the Raba'a massacre and was held for nearly six years before being released in March 2019.[116] Amnesty International noted there were nine charges against him, including a life sentence and the death penalty for the pictures he took that day.[117]

The state has also expanded its use of mass death sentences, and there are days where multiple people are executed by the state. For example, the state sentenced 529 Muslim Brotherhood members to death in March 2014. There is consistency in these mass death sentences. The state tried 739 defendants from the Muslim Brotherhood and sentenced 75 of them to death in September 2018. The London-based organization Reprieve claims that 2,159 Egyptians have been sentenced to death between January 2014 and February 2018.[118] Most of the executions started after the assassination of public prosecutor Hisham Barakat, who was blown up by a car bomb outside of his home in July 2015. As the state's chief prosecutor, he was responsible for signing death sentences and filing charges. Dissenters killed Barakat because of his facilitating role. Since his assassination, the state has employed capital punishment with greater frequently.

The use of mass death sentences is having an effect at the gallows, where all capital punishment is done by hanging. For comparison, consider that Mubarak's regime executed 11 people in the final three years of his presidency.[119] The increases in state execution have been dramatic. According to one news report, Egypt ranked sixth in the world behind China, Iran, Saudi Arabia, Vietnam, and Iraq for the number of people a state executed (43) in 2018.[120] Egypt executed 1 person in 2011 and 0 in 2012 and 2013. Then, 15 people were executed in 2014, followed by "at least" 22 in 2015, 44 in 2016, 35 in 2017, and 43 in 2018.[121] As of April 17, 2019, the Egyptian state has already executed 15 people in the first three-and-a-half months of the year including 9 executed on the same morning in February 20, 2019.[122] The state killed 15 at once on December 26, 2017.[123] Execution day happens on Tuesdays. The state does not inform the family that their husband, brother, son, or friend is being put to death. They find out afterward. The use of capital punishment has become a complementary feature of regime-making Egypt as executions continue to rise even as mass death sentences decline. The problem is that the state's use of violence necessitates more repression to counter evidence of its crimes as well as baits violent responses from society.

Not all the state violence is legally bound or processed to a conclusion of state-sanctioned capital punishment. Some of these executions surface in the form of extrajudicial killings, which is happening at a much greater rate than formal state executions. Almost immediately after Hisham Barakat's assassination in July 2015, a violent new trend appeared according to Amnesty International.[124] The al-Sisi-led state is allowing for the extrajudicial executions of targets in busy city streets and desolate desert landscapes. According to an exhaustive report by the British wire service, Reuters, shoot-outs between security forces and unidentified victims occur. These happen a lot. Reuters noted that between July 1, 2015, and December 31, 2018, there have been 108 shoot-outs that resulted in 465 people killed by the state's security branches based on Interior Ministry statements.[125] Another six suspects did not die and only sustained wounds. These figures account for an astounding "kill ratio of 98.7-percent."[126] The Interior Ministry also publishes pictures of corpses of "liquidated terrorists" surrounded by guns on their Facebook page.[127] The photos come off like the trophies serial killers keep from their murdered victims, except the Egyptian state celebrates its killings by sharing them publicly. The state does not try to cover the murders up or enjoy them in private. While the death is reported and visible, the only story that gets relayed is the state's version of events. In fact, in the case of 302 of these murdered people, the ministry neither supplied the deceased's name nor a location of their killing.[128]

In comparison, extrajudicial killings happened during the state's war with the al-Gama'a al-Islamiyya insurgency during the 1990s,[129] but the state left the practice dormant during the 2000s. Yet, even in the 1990s, this practice was not as regular or expansive as it has become as al-Sisi tries to forge a new regime.[130] Jacob Greene and Allison McManus noted the novelty of this development. As they reported, "Cases of extrajudicial killings . . . are a relatively new phenomenon. Though thousands of alleged terrorists have been reported killed in military operations in Egypt's North Sinai province (and to lesser extent, in its Western Desert), killings outside those isolated areas were once rarely seen."[131] The phenomenon is spreading outside of Sinai, however.

While the state's Interior Ministry and its legions of security and police forces resume overseeing the daily repression across the Nile Delta and Valley, the military remains in an ongoing theater of war in Sinai. Political unrest in Sinai has been an enduring problem for the Egyptian state. During 2004 and 2005, there were a number of bombings and attacks on tourist sites in Sinai's beautiful Red Sea coastal cities of Dahab, Taba, and Sharm al-Shaykh.[132] Mubarak's government responded with unrelenting pressure and collective punishment against the towns of al-'Arish and al-Shaykh Zuwayd.[133] At one point, the Mubarak state had arrested 2,500 people for hotel bombings for which they had no suspect. Instead, the state defaulted to collective punishment of the peninsula's northern residents. Torture became endemic.

This dynamic in Sinai really got away from the Egyptian state after the uprising.[134] If the state fragmented in other parts of the country, it seemed to disappear in Sinai. The vacuum enabled violence to thrive. An insurgency appeared first as Ansar Beit al-Maqdis before adopting the name Islamic State. The militants began to roam around North Sinai. They attacked the Egyptian military, and the armed forces responded against the militants. Some researchers, like Ellis Goldberg, have focused on exploring the history of Sinai and its relationships to Egypt's state to escape the immediacy of news analysis.[135]

This cycle of violence fueled both sides and morphed into a brutal war between the Egyptian military and these Sinai militants. The state's only response has been militarization of the conflict.[136] Occasionally, these exchanges result in extremely lethal ends, which set the next stage of this serialized conflict. In 2012, militants killed sixteen soldiers in one attack. This instance initiated tit-for-tat exchanges that continue to the present. It is not uncommon to see stories in the press that exclaim that the army has killed fifty-two militants, as in 2018,[137] or an attack by the militants has killed twenty-six soldiers and wounded another thirty-three, as in 2017.[138] A frequent refrain in the media coverage is that the numbers or events cannot be independently verified. In fact, most honest reporting admits upfront that "while no one knows the exact composition or origins of the different militant groups based in Sinai, many believe past state crackdowns on the area might have fueled their growth."[139]

As Sinai has become Egypt's killing fields, Egyptian soldiers are beginning to claim the war against the guerillas is unwinnable and that "Sinai is our Vietnam."[140] It appears completely beyond the Egyptian state's ability to end the conflict. Residents of Sinai claim the tactic of extrajudicial killings is prominent in the northern Sinai city of al-'Arish.[141] Egypt's president reached out to an external expert on militarization and collective punishment to help shift the balance of power in Sinai. Al-Sisi has admitted on American TV that Egypt was coordinating with Israel in Sinai in unprecedented ways.[142] A *New York Times* correspondent exposed the secret military cooperation with Israel almost a year earlier in

February 2018. As David Kirkpatrick reported, "For more than two years, unmarked Israeli drones, helicopters and jets have carried out a covert air campaign, conducting more than 100 airstrikes inside Egypt, frequently more than once a week—and all with the approval of President Abdel Fattah el-Sisi."[143] Yet, while war simmers in Sinai, a cycle of violence extends beyond attacks between the state and adherents of the Islamic State.

On one level, observers such as Mohannad Sabry argue that if Egypt's state can only show up in Sinai with militarized options, there can be no resolution or peace.[144] On the other hand, there are 450,000 people trapped in northern Sinai that also experience the brunt of the trauma that a years-long militarized conflict brings. As is often predictable in such situations, the shops of al-'Arish have shuttered, civilians frequently are killed at the hands of the military and the militants, cell networks are often disabled by the state, schools are empty, and daily curfews turn into months of having limited access to the outdoors. The war has turned Sinai into an apocalyptic living situation for its residents, the near majority of whom do not belong to the Islamic State or desire to see their state engage the tool of collective punishment, which steals their lives, time, political agency, and economic well-being.[145] The residents of Sinai—especially those in the northern governorate—remain hostages to this militarized reality, with no escape as Egypt's state and its militant resistance remain locked in a fight with no end.

Egypt's new rulers may not need to use long-term state violence to realize their political project. But, currently, state violence has proved instrumental in helping them try to forge new repressive practices and governing regimes in most places except Sinai. This repression will, as sure as day follows night, plant the seeds for future resistance and social struggle. No matter how state violence is used in creating new political realities, there remain internal contradictions for the Egyptian state that may postpone revolution, but not permanently crush its prospect. State violence is used at different times for different reasons. The latest iteration of state violence in Egypt is a deliberate attempt to politically engineer a new regime out of the ashes of the older usable order.

Egypt's uprising and transition showed that divided opposition relations allowed the new military leaders to keep those involved in initial mobilization from cooperating with one another. By nurturing an already de facto split among the opposition during the uprising, SCAF pursued incumbent ejection to contain damage to the disrupted state rather than trying to outsprint a revolution from below without one. The generals maintained these divisions while electionizing the population during the transition. In addition to further damaging the prospects that systemic groups like the Brotherhood and antisystemic groups may ever team up against the state, the strategy failed to deliver a sustained transition. People continued mobilizing and questioning the quality of the process. All of these maneuvers involved inherited structures that SCAF used to make decisions about how to insulate their position and entrench their privileges in the state. These maneuvers also involved an interplay between constrained agency within such structures. With respect to the political economy of Egypt's revolutionary process and SCAF's violent regime-making exercise, the generals might have met a match that they cannot divide or outflank on their own. Egypt's political economy of social revolt remains the largest continuity in this journey from the Mubarak period to al-Sisi's regime-making. Egypt's political economy also presents issues and poses questions that do not have easy solutions and which repression cannot offset.

4

An Uprising against Neoliberalism?

The State, Military Inc., and the Political Economy of Egypt

Perhaps the longest running conversation in post-1952 Egypt is a debate about what role the state should play in the economy. Either side of the January uprising produced a different view of the state of the economy. In December 2010, right after the most rigged parliamentary elections of Mubarak's presidency, Gamal Mubarak lauded the progress of economic reform. As the president's son said, "We need to immediately start a second wave of reforms . . . that are more ambitious and more daring. Much has been achieved but the goals are far greater."[1] A year later Interim Prime Minister Kamal al-Ganzuri teared up in front of journalists while announcing that "the economic situation is worse than anyone imagines."[2] The neoliberal elite in Egypt watched their fortunes change in a dramatically short period of time.

The January 2011 uprising in Egypt cemented continuities such as the division between systemic and antisystemic opposition groups. It also introduced changes with respect to elections and state violence. But what about the economy? Some credit neoliberal economic policies as responsible for the uprisings.[3] The origins of the 2011 uprising are not found in neoliberalism alone. To understand the uprising, its aftermath, the coup, and the current regime-making project requires seeing the longer continuities of the state's fiscal health.

When Egypt's uprising began in 2011, many observers pointed to the state's neoliberal economic practices as the reason people took to the country's streets and squares. As Angela Joya argues, "The revolution is a product of decades of neoliberal economic policies that were carried out with the use of political repression by the state security forces."[4] In this version of events, Mubarak had overseen the implementation of a set of neoliberal policies that made cronies rich and tore apart schools, health care systems, roads, and other infrastructure as well as social services. Since the early 1990s, Egyptian politicians helped restrict labor laws, reverse land reform, lift subsidies on some everyday goods, withdraw certain public services, privatize state assets, allow free market competition, and liberalize foreign currency exchanges. As international capital penetrated Egypt, the standard of living got worse for all except the country's extremely wealthy.[5]

State employees' pay stagnated, workers' rights were rolled back, oligarchs reclaimed the land of farmers, and ordinary consumers' cost of living went up, stretching finite household budgets and making life unbearable for many. Additionally, the state's capacity to referee the disparities through political negotiations was weakened. By the final years of Mubarak's presidency—after decades of such changes—"the hegemony of the neoliberal order . . . had become complete."[6] These changes wreaked havoc on people's lives and led to a rise of protests a decade before the January uprising. The incremental decline in the standard of living eventually pulled the disparate protests together into an uprising that led to Mubarak's ouster.

Yet, since agreeing to an IMF structural adjustment program in 1991, Egypt has always pursued a different kind of neoliberalism than most assume. Contrary to what neoliberalism would recommend, the state never withdrew from society. The structural adjustment process Cairo unleashed simultaneously maintained the state's subsidies while reallocating wealth into the coffers of connected capitalists. Tim Mitchell noticed this preservation of the state's involvement in the economy long ago and argued, "The neoliberal program has not removed the state from the market or eliminated 'profligate' public subsidies. These achievements belong to the imagination. Its major impact has been to concentrate public funds into different, but fewer hands."[7] Over a decade later Walter Armbrust extended the critique and noted, "Egypt did not shrink its public sector, as neoliberal doctrine would have it, as it reallocated public resources for the benefit of a small and already affluent elite . . . the very limited function for the state recommended by neoliberal doctrine in the abstract was turned on its head in reality."[8] The neoliberal prescriptions of the Washington Consensus did not undo the Mubarak regime alone; the cage that imprisons those who administer Egypt's economy has a longer history.

Neoliberalism alone did not lead to Egypt's 2011 uprising; rather, the uprising originated primarily from the gradual, steady, and continuous economic decline of the state's fiscal health over decades.[9] Neoliberalism helped drain the fiscal health of the state, but it did not create its structural weakness. The gradual and steady decline of economic health over decades was visible in the state's own annual budgets,[10] and this structural weakness had long nurtured conditions ripe for a social revolt. The political economy of Egypt remains defined by a state that was erected in 1952, after the Free Officers Revolution from above.[11] The political economy of Egypt's uprising, transition, coup, and regime-making attempt, therefore, is a story of historical continuity rather than abrupt change.

This dilemma of the state's fiscal health is the same that faced every Egyptian president since the 1970s. If leaders of Egypt's state maintain services, subsidies, and social expenditures they cannot pay for, the state's debt will rise and fiscally the economy will grind to a halt slowly, necessitating external financial interventions to prop up Egypt's money pit. But if politicians chase the neoliberal dragon, they court the ire of Egypt's numerous civil servants, factory workers, and neglected poor. Pushed aggressively enough, neoliberal reforms will dismantle the post-1952 state and collapse an already frayed ruling bargain. Furthermore, neoliberal reform and regime-making seem incompatible unless extreme state violence accompanies the project.

In any of these scenarios, the situation is practically impossible to govern without increasing state repression in the short, medium, or long term. Yet even this securitized response to the population's economic grievances causes the state to fiscally exhaust itself. As political economist Amr Adly put it, "The reproduction of the post-independence state is the trap. If you do nothing and let it continue, the fiscal crisis undermines the state. If you liberalize the economy, you undermine the state. Instead, it's a bloated civil service, new and more police, and piecemeal cuts that produce protests."[12] Neither populists nor neoliberals, Egypt's new military leaders remain cornered unless they reshape the state and the less controllable social forces that inevitably clash with it to create politics. As Ayubi argued during the 1990s, "Under the impact of fiscal crisis or at least fiscal constraints, they now feel the need somewhat to reduce the economic role of the state, they find it difficult—owing again to their structural weakness—to 'impose the market.' The end result may well be weaker, if still repressive, states lording it over stagnating economies."[13]

That the state's new military minders chose not to use the 2011 uprising as an opportunity to change course suggests that the political economy constraints on the Egyptian state loom much larger than the durability of any particular regime's practices. If the similar inputs produce the same outcomes, conditions on the ground will gradually worsen as the state's fiscal health continues to deteriorate. This will especially hold true if aid disappears or if another area of rent, such as tourism revenue, drops unexpectedly. As conditions worsen, they will necessitate increasing the already unprecedented levels of state repression to contain dissent and protests. Even then, the script of such an effort's failure has already been written because such support props up a model that has already produced a revolt. Egypt's political economy remains ripe for social revolt, even if people are not routinely mobilized in the squares. Yet this also does not mean that another uprising in the short run is inevitable.[14]

Before Egypt's Uprising

Research by the late Samer Soliman refutes that Egypt's 2011 uprising was caused by neoliberalism alone. Instead, he shows the uprising was linked to the state's declining fiscal health caused by crisis spending. Looking at the state's budgets over a thirty-year period, Soliman reveals a steady decline of the state's fiscal health as state expenditures outpaced revenues. As he argued in the wake of the uprising,

> The Egyptian state today functions on roughly half the revenues (in terms of percentage of GDP) as it did when Mubarak first came to power in 1981. Oil and gas revenues, Suez Canal returns, and foreign aid are no longer sufficient to feed the state coffers and make up for low tax

> revenues. Fiscal crisis is a dilemma for any authoritarian regime, as its stability depends not only on political repression, but also on buying the loyalty of segments of the population. . . . But a regime can delay the political consequences of fiscal crisis for only so long.[15]

Soliman notes that in autocratic regimes, when revenues rise for any reason, such as investments, aid, or other access to rents, there is a corresponding rise in state expenditures in the form of subsidies and social provisions. Accordingly, when revenues drop so does the funding of goods and services to the people who expect to receive them. Successive years of declining revenue thus present autocrats with a dilemma. Governing elites have little inclination to cut the expenditures as drastically as neoliberal doctrine, IMF Structural Adjustment Programs, or even the drop in state revenues would warrant. Therefore, when state revenues decline, so do state expenditures on people—but never as much as the decline revenues dictate. This difference between money coming in and going out contributes to a country's deficit and determines how citizens experience these incremental normalizing cuts in social expenditures.

Egypt witnessed a continual and slow drop of state revenues during Mubarak's presidency. The high point for state revenue as a percentage of GDP was 1984. Following that year, in addition to tax-based state revenue being one of the lowest in the region, the country saw declines with respect to percentage of GDP in foreign aid, other rent revenues, and taxes.[16] After 1991, there was an even more precipitous drop in foreign aid and Suez Canal revenues as a percentage of GDP. The sources of state revenue from petrol, Suez Canal remittances, and foreign aid dipped to their lowest levels after 2005 and then either flatlined or dipped during the last five years of Mubarak's rule. For example, foreign aid accounts for over 14 percent of the GDP in 1992 and about 4 percent by 1995; it and fell to under 1 percent after 2003. The percentage continues to drop until 2010, except for a slight increase in 2008.[17] Compare the static or declining revenue of these rents in figure 1. While there is a spike in aid after the military coup in 2013, the revenue as a percentage of GDP is perpetually declining.[18]

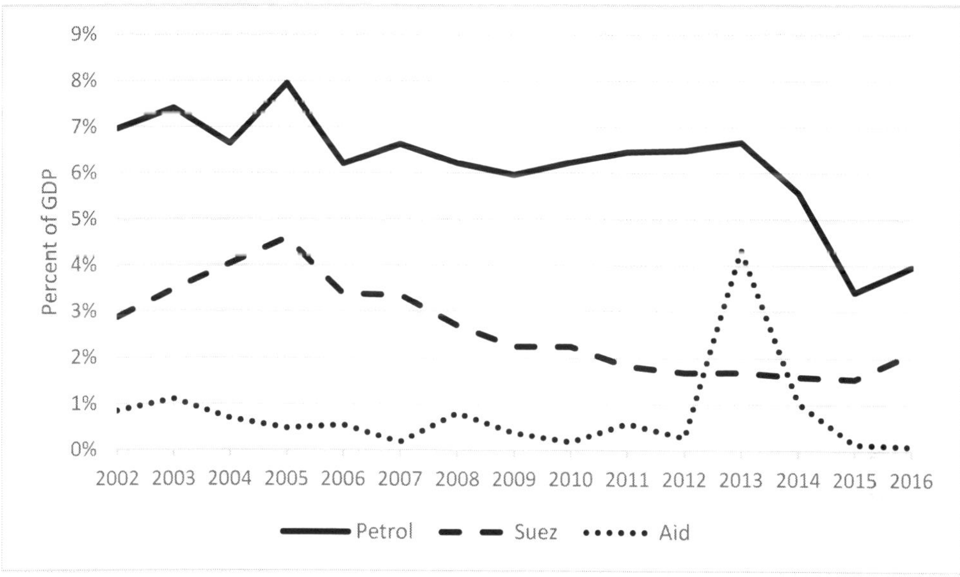

1. Value of revenue sources (petrol, foreign aid, and Suez Canal), 2002–16. Shown as a percentage of GDP.

This trajectory indicates that Egypt's uprising in 2011 comes after nearly thirty years of steady deterioration in the state's fiscal health in which declining revenues forced cuts in state expenditures on society.

To maintain minimal political stability elites had to maintain payouts, and they favored funding that benefited security specialists and civil servants rather than society as a whole. Elites also had to manage how important sectors such as the military were incorporated into the regime's base as the state's fiscal health worsened. The percentage of GDP for a sector like military spending might not have changed as revenues declined, but the actual dollar amount did over time. To keep the military included in the ruling coalition, elites allowed the military to offset this decline by investing in commercial areas that "earned the army considerable financial independence from the national budget."[19] Furthermore, elites also gave military officers preferential access to existing social services, consequently restricting society's access to them. This largely created Military Inc., which is similar to the term "Milbus" borrowed from Ayesha Siddiqa to describe the military's businesses and role in consumer production in Egypt.[20] As military spending declines with a drop in state revenues, citizens feel a tighter pinch because their services are reallocated to the military to offset the officers' potential pain. This trend is consistent with the declines in other areas of the economy, such as education or health care.

While all other economic indicators traveled south with state revenues, the expenditures on the security sector and civil servants remained constant or increased. For the Mubarak regime, security became paramount. In Soliman's words, "The security mentality prevailed over the political approach to government."[21] Accordingly, the expenditures on security and policing as a percentage of GDP increased almost 1.5 percent between 1987 and 1997, when the state was combating al-Gama'a al-Islamiyya insurgency.[22] This number grew again during the 2000s as Habib al-'Adli, the interior minister, routinely pleaded for and secured budget increases to deal with the protests taking place daily in the streets, communities, and factories around the country because services were stretched beyond capacity.[23] 'Aida Seif al-Dawla has shown that by the mid-2000s the Interior Ministry's budget came to total more than combined allotments of the health and education ministries.[24] Even when society signaled through protests that the expenditures were not enough, rather than redirect some of its limited funds to social services and infrastructure, the state preferred to increase spending on security to preempt and contain dissent. Spending on security was a way the regime could ensure its main allies—the security forces, police, judges, military, and civil servants—remained on its side. This continued crisis spending on security, in turn, exacerbated the original problem. In effect, the state elites under Mubarak gave up on the population long before the uprising in 2011.

Compounding its crisis spending, at no time was there a coherent neoliberal plan for the state to withdraw from the economy or society. The neoliberal policies tried by the Ahmad Nazif government, which formed in July 2004, merely exacerbated the existing and growing inequalities. It is highly contested whether neoliberalism can actually work as a prescriptive set of policies. Unraveling polities and heightened repression, rather than salvation, flowed from the International Financial Institution's (IFI) neoliberalism. Yet neoliberalism never meant that the Mubarak regime ever would empower its population or relinquish its security apparatus's grip on society. As Soliman noted:

> This tendency towards tightening security controls is characteristic of authoritarian regimes as they decline, and it reflects their decreasing power with respect to the rising power of social classes. The dwindling resources of the state are catalysts for this shift in the relationship between the regime and society in Egypt, in particular the entrepreneurial, middle, and working classes of society. This process of readjusting the power relationships between these sectors of society and the regime paves the way for political change.[25]

With his meticulous research showing glaring disconnects in the state's budgets over the years, Soliman produces research that shows this incremental and slow-cooking political economy of social revolt. Egypt's budgetary allocations kept its society on the constant brink of a revolutionary situation.

Egypt under Mubarak did not have a strong state.[26] Its lack of revenues and budget discrepancies did not allow for the state to develop. But the logic that flowed from this state of affairs was to fund security policies and civil servants in order to contain contentious civil society, labor, and protest groups. The goal was to keep such groups from connecting with each other and less organized than the state. This approach worked until it failed in 2011. It was impossible to know when it would fail, but the chance always existed, given that Egypt's political economy was ripe for social revolt.

Not only do most of the non-oil states in the Arab world look like Egypt—and therefore perpetually exist in a political economy of possible social revolt—but they also condition state-society interactions in ways that structure how revolutionary scenarios play out. The contradictions of Egypt's political economy are embedded in its state formation. These do not allow a clean break from the past. Neoliberalism may exacerbate the economic crisis of the exhausted Nasserist state. But the protesters' rejection of neoliberalism means that their demands defaulted to a reconstituted statist model of economic policy that has already failed. Such focused claims about neoliberalism also misdiagnose the economic origins of the revolt.

Egypt's Uprising

The story is almost cliché now. In the decade preceding the uprising, the IMF and World Bank lauded the performance of Egypt's macroeconomic growth.[27] The president's son, Gamal Mubarak, and his fawning technocrats set the topics of annual NDP meetings and brought the Davos agenda into the NDP. At the time, the minister of finance, Yusuf Butrus Ghali, barely even tried to explain emerging inequalities, preferring instead to rely on people's endless patience.[28] As the ship drifted into shallower waters, these technocrats and "crony globalizers" became victims of a neoliberal glitch.[29]

The neoliberal faces of the government were the first to go to jail or into exile as the uprising caught fire, while old-guard NDP members retired and disappeared back into society. State bureaucrats and factory workers were given time off. On February 7, everyone was due back at work. But the labor movement continued to withhold their labor, which proved to be the deciding motivation for the military to nudge Mubarak from power. Joel Beinin's research shows that production in central industrial sectors dropped by 60 percent during the week of state-mandated vacation.[30] Mubarak was left with a handful of loyalists, while the army acted as the buffer between a collapsing regime within the fragmenting state and the population. We will never know how long the army would have waited out the crowds because its hand got forced on February 7—about seventy-two hours before Mubarak resigned.

Hesham Sallam lays this point out in his lucid work on Egyptian workers and their participation in the uprising. Sallam shows that in addition to an uptick in worker strikes in the month leading up to the January 25 uprising, workers in some locations, such as Mahalla al-Kubra and Suez, actually formed the majority of the revolutionaries demanding change.[31] The protesters and security forces in these industrial areas engaged in some of the most violent exchanges during the initial eighteen days.

But it was February 7 that turned the screw for the military. Thousands of workers who were expected back at work went on strike, bringing a halt to the country's economic life. As Beinin wrote, "When business resumed, some fifty to sixty thousand workers declared strikes at dozens of work places, including strategic enterprises like the subsidiary companies of Suez Canal Authority, Ghazl al-Mahalla, the Cairo and Alexandria Public Transport Authorities, and Telecom Egypt. Medical doctors also went on strike."[32] Private labor unions as well as workers of public companies stopped working. While some called for the end of Mubarak's regime, the majority focused on the legions of "mini-Mubarak" managers that oversaw their labor. They insisted that their managers stop behaving like autocrats and also demanded better pay and benefits. In addition, thousands of farmers from Asyut blocked highways with flaming palm trees to protest bread shortages, while homeless people set a government office on fire in Port Said.

There was only one industrial labor force that kept working during the initial uprising: military factory workers, who are also often army conscripts, continued to work while the military deployed tanks and soldiers to protect the factories. These industries are often heavily financed or owned by Gulf investment firms. In fact, foreign companies such as the Kuwaiti conglomerate Kharafi National publicly lauded the military's protection of investments during Egypt's unrest.[33] The army also went to great lengths to ensure that the ports and oil and gas facilities operated as usual during the uprising.

Despite these exceptions, the strikes produced a decisive blow to Mubarak: the conclusion one is left to draw is that SCAF's generals worried the strikes would spread even further, threatening state collapse and revolutionary political change. With the prospect seeming increasingly likely the longer Mubarak held on, SCAF generals ejected the president in hopes of salvaging the state. Once they decided to act, the generals tried to suppress the strikes through negotiations to buy time. As Sallam said, "One of the first things that the Supreme Council tried to do after taking power was to bring an end to strikes [which] suggests that work stoppages were a source of deep concern for the generals."[34]

It was the economic grievances that took protests beyond the urban squares, where a largely immobile crowd could be easily contained, but the volume of these gatherings put the final nail in the coffin for Mubarak's presidency. As Hossam El-Hamalawy argued in an interview, "The workers struck and that was it—the game was over. The machines wouldn't run. There would be no money coming in. The cars won't move. The buses won't move. The factories wouldn't open . . . the subject was finished."[35] After the army ejected Mubarak, the Muslim Brotherhood as well as some revolutionary protesters withdrew from the squares. The resulting decrease in the number of active protesters meant the military could begin to draft a strategy to counterbalance the thousands of people withholding their labor or making claims on the state.

While no single sector or group alone caused the fall of Mubarak, each played a crucial role, and the pressure they collectively exerted pushed the military generals to act against Mubarak. The challenges of Egypt's economy remained, however, and the military's stake in the economy seemed to grow rather than lessen as their former competitors from the discredited ruling class faded from view. The Mubarak-era practices of crisis spending would not only continue but also spike dramatically after the ejection of the long-time president.

SCAF's Transition

On February 12, 2011, freed from the constraints of the Mubarak regime for the first time in nearly thirty years, and with the state limping along, citizens undertook the business of reimagining the class lines that Mubarak worked to maintain. Describing the popular cleaning campaign of public spaces, Jessica Winegar observed, "The burst of beautification immediately following the removal of Mubarak was both literal and metaphorical." But, as she noted, "The intense focus on cleaning could reproduce the logics of power that led to the revolution in the first place."[36] Like the citizens, the army used the uprising to give the appearance of change while reproducing the crisis spending that characterized Mubarak's presidency. Indeed, crisis spending accelerated after the overthrow. Most media outlets attributed the economic downtick to the disruption of protests.[37] But it was the aggressive outlay of expenditures that exacerbated the political economy of social revolt. It continues to be strained today.

One of the first orders of business for SCAF, which was reconstituted under the leadership of long-time defense minister Muhammad Tantawi, was to combat those with economic grievances. The people were not attacked by security forces. They were hired by the state. SCAF was in state salvation mode and reinforcing the state's foundation was the priority. The generals sought to rein in the discontent of state employees as they tried to keep government ranks cohesive. The expansion of the public sector in the year following the uprising is telling. In 2010, Egypt had 5.6 million state employees. After the revolution, the state hired an additional 900,000 workers.[38] As analyst Hani Shukrallah told the *New York Times*, "Everyone is looking for money, and there's none to be had."[39]

This increase meant that the overall spending on civil service employment more than doubled between 2009 and 2014. In 2009–10, state workers' salaries amounted to LE 85 billion. By 2013–14, that figure had risen to LE 178 billion, accounting for 25.4 percent of the state's public expenditures.[40] What the numbers cannot tell us is how many of these new employees were temporary contract labor. It is also hard to disaggregate the data to identify in which sectors the new hires were occurring. Housing construction and petroleum industries, which are closely connected to Military Inc., were the heaviest employers in the public sector according to one report.[41] Yet overall expenditures on public sector employment increased from 7 to 8.9 percent between 2009 and 2010 and 2013 and 2014. The amount of money spent on wages increased both in absolute terms and as a percentage of all public spending and GDP.[42] This crisis spending is more aggressive than that of the late Mubarak period except for the expenditures rising between 2007 and 2008. In figure 2 one can see the dramatic jump beginning in 2011. A dramatic jump can also be seen in the deficit as a percentage of GDP. In the years of high growth under Mubarak, the growth continued to produce a deficit that represented −6.7 percent in 2007, −6.9 percent in 2008, and −8.2 percent in 2009–10. In the aftermath of the uprisings, the gap between revenues and expenditures grew even wider, bringing the overall deficit as a percentage of GDP to −10.5 percent in 2011, −14.1 percent in 2012, and −12.8 percent

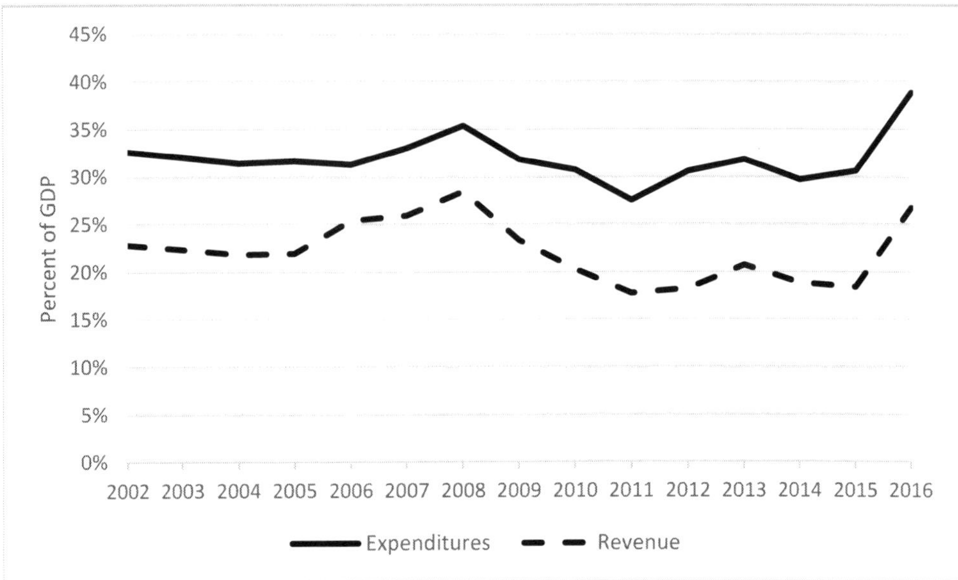

2. Public expenditure and revenue trends using data from Egypt's Ministry of Finance, 2002–16. Shown as a percentage of GDP.

in 2013.[43] The widening gap of crisis spending after the uprising underscores continuity rather than change.

As figure 3 shows, the IMF has different numbers, but the direction of the economic trends suggests the same dynamic: a widening gap caused by expenditures outpacing revenues and the increasing fiscal weakness of the state.[44]

The uprising is not what caused the collapse of the economy. This is not to say that the uprising did not play a role: businesses closed; tourism rents, which accounted for 12 percent of the GDP, dropped by 35 percent; foreign investment stopped in civilian sectors; and the generals used the foreign reserves to help cover losses. Foreign currency reserves dropped from $32 billion to $18.2 billion during 2011.[45] Not only did SCAF use reserves to cover costs but they also tried to keep the Egyptian pound from depreciating. Yet despite the declines in production, investment, and rent, state expenditures on public sector wages, subsidies, and handouts jumped sharply. Regardless of whether they had the revenue after

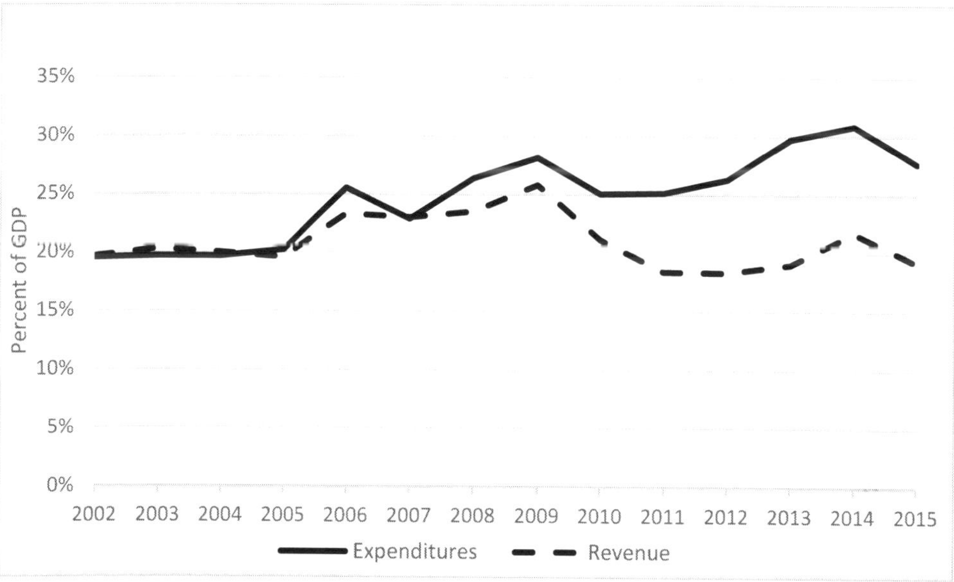

3. Public expenditure and revenue trends using data from the IMF, 2002–15. Shown as a percentage of GDP.

Mubarak was ejected, SCAF committed more resources to shoring up support among state employees and discouraging further protests. The spending spree did not stop with salaries. To insulate the military and its businesses from possible demands, SCAF ordered the Central Bank of Egypt to distribute monthly bonuses of nearly LE 2,400, or US$400, to middle-rank officers.[46] It is this spending—and not declines in tourism, work stoppages, or the other economic disruption caused by social revolt—that explains the sharp decline of Egypt's economic growth indicators when the economy contracted from nearly from 6 percent growth in 2008 to –4 percent growth in 2011.[47] Although the economic indicators would improve in 2012 and 2013, growth at levels near 6 percent did not return until after 2014.[48] In figure 4 we see expenditures on salaries against total outlay of subsidies and social benefits as well as interest.[49]

The generals were also concerned about the continued protests by workers. While Egypt's schoolteachers, one of the largest sectors of government employees, went on strike in September 2011 and demanded better

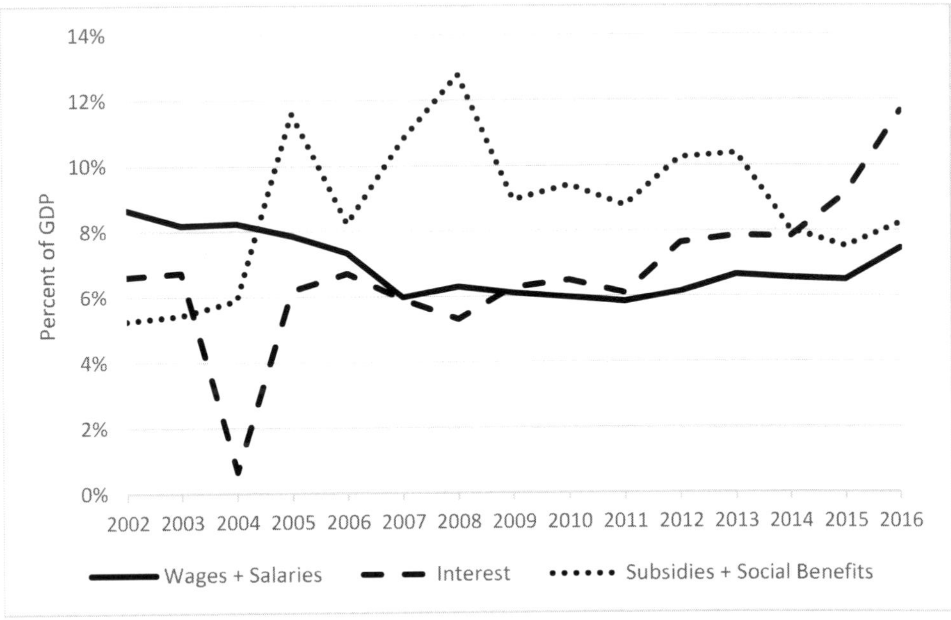

4. Breakdown of Egypt's expenditures by category, 2002–16. Shown as a percentage of GDP.

pay and benefits, factory workers continued to demand an expansion of their rights as well.[50] As Beinin shows in his research, "Strikes continued despite the effort to criminalize them. Nearly one million workers engaged in 1,377 actions, including 280 strikes, during 2011, the largest number of actions with nearly twice as many participants as any year of the previous decade."[51] Furthermore, such contentious actions increased as the transition continued. There were 1,969 collective actions by workers in 2012, "more than triple the pre-2011 highs of 614 in 2007 and 609 in 2008."[52]

Tantawi and SCAF spent a lot of effort using the recovering state apparatus to criminalize worker demonstrations. In March 2011, SCAF issued communiqué 34, which leveled heavy fines and jail time for halting production or disrupting a public institution. SCAF generals also repeatedly used rhetoric that cast suspicion on the workers' demands and tried to cast themselves as the guardians of the revolution in order to capture and appropriate it. In the process they tried to discredit the protesters that persisted.

Sallam details the rise in strikes and workplace stoppages and how the media, which developed close links to SCAF, began to describe the protests as *fi'awī*, or "special interest," almost as soon as Mubarak was forced to leave office. By the time I arrived in mid-March 2011 for my first field research trip after the January uprising, the term *fi'awī* was being used to describe any ongoing protest. This designation attempted to divorce them from the larger movement pushing for deeper change and expanding rights. As Sallam argues, *fi'awī* came to describe "any demonstration, strike, or sit-in advancing demands that related to distribution of wealth, whether the protesters are blue or white-collar employees and whether they are calling for higher wages, greater benefits, improved working conditions or replacement of corrupt management personnel."[53] Field Marshal Tantawi, who frequently stated that "the wheels of production" had to continue moving, declared *fi'awī* protests illegitimate because they threatened Egypt's economy and security.[54]

Although the designation of labor protests as *fi'awī* was new, such protests themselves were not, having increased nearly every year following the installation of Ahmad Nazif's government in 2004. Labor demands would be met in some instances and not in others. But after the uprising, there was an explosion of collective worker strikes. Any concessions led to a rise in public expenditures that the state could not afford without increasing revenue or the tax base. While the United States and European countries as well as the IMF pledged loans to Egypt, governments and lenders tried to assess just how much damage had been done and what type of government would emerge before they actually wired the money. As the IMF representative to Egypt stated, "The transition was a missed opportunity. The SCAF agreed with the Fund's advice but they took decisions against it. SCAF never met with us and played the transition from behind the curtain. The Brotherhood did similar things by using satellite advisors instead of the cabinet. In a way, it was a repeat of the dysfunctional transition. This [Egypt] is a bucket with holes. The Fund is willing to commit support if the holes were being patched. But we are not an ATM."[55]

SCAF repeatedly said it was not their place to make an agreement with IFIs because they were merely temporary custodians of the state and the transition. The idea was that an elected government would enter into those arrangements. This does not mean SCAF opted to wait when it came to the economy. SCAF used the uprising to eliminate previous competitors, such as through a selective corruption campaign after Mubarak was ejected because protesters were demanding a crackdown on corruption.[56] As Shana Marshall and I have argued, "By jailing big businessmen like Ahmad 'Izz, an intimate of Gamal's, and unpopular officials like the former housing minister, Ibrahim Sulayman, the SCAF channeled the public's demand for justice. Not surprisingly, civilian businessmen with strong links to military companies were passed over by prosecutors—another signal to politicians to accept the military's role in the economy or be shut out completely."[57] Those with links to the military, such as the Sawiris family, were left alone, while those with more traditional business links to the civilian side or NDP cooled off in prison.[58] However, the change became one of actors, not practices.

In the beginning of the transition, when SCAF felt that a transitional pact with the systemic opposition Muslim Brotherhood was possible and the revolutionary fever might be tamed through elections, Military Inc. extended its tentacles into the economy. As Shana Marshall argued, "Actions taken by the EAF [Egyptian Armed Forces] leadership to shape the post-SCAF political system also helped the military maintain and expand its institutional control over critical economic resources."[59] SCAF and Military Inc. became the arbitrators of the Egyptian economy as they became the only game in town. One would think the power would be insurmountable. Yet, at the moment of its economic apex, the military also began to realize that along with the profits, it had inherited the country's problems.

On the eve of 2012 and after nearly a year of increased public expenditure, the Egyptian military gave a LE 1 billion donation to the state coffers.[60] The economy of social revolt deepened during SCAF's stewardship, but their gift was telling. Most interpreted it as a product of the unseen profits of the military's budget. After all, the military had LE 1 billion to donate. Yet it also signaled that sometimes the military needed to use its capital to ward off an economic crisis. This move would be repeated after the coup against the elected president in 2013 and as the regime-making project began.

The Muslim Brotherhood's Moment

While they never publicly discussed their intentions, the Muslim Brotherhood's leadership understood the 2011 uprising as an opportunity to become a legal player within Egypt's political landscape. They upgraded their offices in Cairo's Manyal District and then opened another new office in Muqattum. The Brotherhood also opened a parliamentary headquarters in Lazoughli Square, which is where the Interior Ministry is located. They ran for parliamentary elections and secured 49 percent of the assembly, and in July 2012 their back-up candidate, Muhammad Mursi, won the presidential election. Brotherhood delegations toured capitals in North America and Europe while Mursi gave long-winded presidential addresses in which he frequently expressed his faith in the security establishment, reassuring its elite that order was more important than satisfying the demands of the revolutionary protesters. The Brotherhood was in unchartered territory in the movement's history, which stretches back to 1928.

Banned in 1954 but tolerated since the days of Sadat, the Brotherhood had previously seen its peak moment in formal politics during the 2005 parliamentary elections. After winning 20 percent of parliamentary seats (88 out of 444), the bloc challenged, and occasionally embarrassed, the ruling NDP, whose approach to parliamentary business could be described as lazy.[61] In many respects, the Brotherhood was the only true political party in Egypt in the sense that it had a professional middle-class constituency and did not rely on personal patronage networks, bribes, or intimidation by the security forces to run electorally viable candidates. When the state determined that it needed to rein in the Brotherhood's political gains, it used the organization's illegal status to crack down on it.[62] Nevertheless, the Brotherhood and the Egyptian state often worked together, especially to provide social services before the uprisings, as Steven Brooke has meticulously detailed,[63] as well as to calm sectarianism in the uprising's wake.[64]

Initially skeptical of the prospects of the January 25 protests, Brotherhood leaders infamously declared they would not participate in the action. After they realized that the Mubarak regime was teetering on its heels by January 28, however, the organization jumped into the fray, tilting the balance of power toward the revolutionaries before using the shifting landscape to negotiate a place for themselves. The legitimacy of elections internationally seemed to be the cornerstone of their and SCAF's post-Mubarak strategy. But their new status and assumption of political power also required them to change their approach. Khayrat al-Shatir, a senior Brotherhood member who had spent twelve of the nineteen years prior to 2011 in prison, explained, "The group recognizes that times have changed. We cannot manage our meetings and information in the way that we had. But this was never a function of secrecy, as analysts said. It was because of the oppressive climate in which we had to operate."[65] The strategy of participating in elections was essentially to appease the generals and use repeated electoral contests to make a military intervention impossible. The Brotherhood was always a calculating actor and one that many antisystemic revolutionaries became deeply resentful toward because of its willingness to work closely with SCAF and to prioritize its own interests before those of the wider population. As former deputy general guide Muhammed Habib argued during 2011, "After they smelled freedom, they ran behind the council [SCAF]."[66]

The Brotherhood's leadership understood themselves as trapped in a long-term battle with SCAF. Some analysts even wrongly thought that, over the long term, the Brotherhood held the advantage over SCAF.[67] Their leadership did not appear to think a military coup was possible. In fact, when discussing post-Mubarak Egypt, President Mursi's team often invoked "the Turkish model," a reference to how in Turkey political Islamists gradually outflanked the country's politically active military before preventing them from more interventions. During a visit to the Wilson Center in Washington, DC, presidential adviser Issam al-Haddad explained that a democratic transition underpinned by an economic vision for stability was underway in Egypt. "The transition has already removed the military from the process," he stated.[68]

Husayn al-Qazzaz, who served as Mursi's sustainable development adviser, was even more explicit about how Mursi might pursue economic development as a way to consolidate control over the state (and by default the military). First, he noted that the Mursi administration had to balance the budget and was clear that the IMF's help was needed to stabilize the economy. As he stated, "We need to do serious structural adjustment."[69] He argued that it was difficult to meet the many expectations of a large population wanting change because of the cost it entailed. He also blamed the size of the bureaucracy for this budget predicament. For example, he compared Egypt's 5.6 million state employees (it actually was employing about a million more at the time) to the much smaller state bureaucracies of Turkey, Japan, and Germany. The massive size of Egypt's bureaucracy, he argued, allowed for there to be "structured corruption." Al-Qazzaz advocated "managing the economic side of the bureaucracy," and in particular ending "corruption," which had gotten worse since the 2011 uprising. He also implied that subsidies would have to be removed. While these discourses of anticorruption and budget cuts tended to be normal over decades when discussing Egypt's economy, cuts to the state bureaucracy and to subsidies have always been sensitive areas.

When Mursi's presidential advisers made such statements to domestic and foreign audiences, it terrified the Egyptian public, and people began to speak fearfully of "the Brotherhoodization of the state" (*ikhwanat al-dawla*).[70] In the public's view this seemed to mean that austerity would be a vehicle by which the Brotherhood administration would replace non-Brotherhood members with its members into positions within the state. This, in turn, would change the character, composition, and orientation of Egypt's state.

Additionally, the prospect of austerity measures that would cut the number of public sector jobs was immediately met with resistance from state employees involved in the day-to-day operations of central sectors, such as the workers who control the stamps in Cairo's central administrative building (the Mugama'a) and those that oversee the country's electrical grids. At the same time, moving up the hierarchy of the state, senior figures also began to speculate that the Brotherhood sought to sideline them.[71] As Mursi's team began to isolate major institutions such as the foreign ministry and the judiciary, the bureaucrats the Brotherhood depended upon to run the state became suspicious of its aims.

Austerity discourse and appeals to secure IMF loans came to be understood as an initiative of a weak but dangerous president. In hindsight, it seems far-fetched that the Mursi administration could have either cut state jobs entirely or done massive layoffs, only to make Brotherhood loyalists new bureaucrats. Perhaps the military also felt that they might be targeted in a Turkish-model approach to governance, although it seems improbable given the levers and pressure points the military continued to control in the bureaucracy and economy. In any case, public sector employees as well as the general population came to view the Brotherhood's plan as the beginning of a new and unfamiliar type of cronyism. Reem Abou-El-Fadl captured this dynamic, writing, "Mubarak's ruling National Democratic Party was notorious for its corruption and cronyism—packing all positions of influence in public institutions with loyalists. This cronyism has reappeared under Morsi . . . as successive ministries and advisory positions have become occupied by Brotherhood figures or sympathizers, while dissenters are marginalized or coopted."[72]

The newly elected president became known as "Muhammad Mursi Mubarak." As Abou-El-Fadl argued, "Mubarak's rule was reviled for many reasons, multiplying down the class scale. The language of the call to protest on 25 January 2011 gives the best indication: it was declared against 'torture, poverty, corruption, and unemployment.' . . . And yet, since the accession to the presidency of Muslim Brother Mohamed Morsi in summer 2012, each one of these political grievances has been refueled and reloaded."[73] This perception of Mursi being worse than Mubarak, as well as the economic problems getting worse for many, became the final straw of his short presidency. With each new government announcement or initiative—such as ration cards for gas cooking tanks or asking Egyptians to limit electricity use by staying at home and not using lights—ridicule increased as people lost confidence in his leadership.[74]

The population worried about whether Mursi and his cronies sought to return Egypt to the "dark ages," an accusation Mubarak loyalist Ahmad Shafiq had leveled during his presidential election campaign.[75] The more criticism Mursi and his administration received, the more they became obsessed with a "deep state" that frustrated and blocked their initiatives. This obsession had basis in reality, even if it is also true that the Brotherhood were genuinely unpopular and deluded about their mandate. The term "deep state" was thrown around a lot in Egypt after Mubarak was ejected. Just exactly what the Brotherhood and others meant by it seems nicely defined by Hesham Sallam.[76] The deep state became shorthand for the Brotherhood whenever they failed to communicate their policies. It led to a simplistic analysis and explanations of more complicated political dynamics. Just as the population viewed Mursi's presidency as an attempt to "Brotherhoodize" the state, the Brotherhood explained all politics in terms of the deep state that haunted its every move. Essentially, the Brotherhood mishandled and misunderstood their lack of popularity because they so frequently invoked the deep state. To offset the deep state variable, Brotherhood administration figures consistently reminded everyone that "this was voted on," as though elections endowed them with absolute authority. Over the course of Mursi's time in office, it appeared that the Brotherhood grew increasingly paranoid and turned increasingly inward.[77] The more they tried to get things done away from the prying eyes of the state apparatus, the more easily agents of the status quo and those loyal to the military were able build and execute a discursive and actual conspiracy against Mursi.

On balance, Mursi was not actually capable of inducing mass changes to Egypt's state, much less pursuing an unbridled campaign of neoliberal economic reform. Any changes he could have made would have been superficial. An IMF official expressed in an interview that a loan was unlikely to solve Egypt's macroeconomic problems. As he claimed, "Economics is a simple business. A country has to spend less than they make. Today, what has to happen in Egypt needs to happen with or without the Fund."[78] At the time, the IMF seemed to understand it needed to provide financial assistance to ease gradual austerity. What this suggests though is that socially empowering political transitions are just not conducive to economic austerity. Yet the IMF official blamed the character of Egypt's transition. As he noted, there was never a transformation in which the old order was replaced by the new one. Rather, both SCAF and then Mursi sought to increase the top income tax, create more permanent and temporary public sector jobs, and increase wages. As he argued, "Nothing has happened. It was a lost opportunity."[79] The IMF refused to sign an agreement with SCAF and Mursi as long as they were unable or unwilling to pursue the IMF's prescribed macroeconomic adjustments, preferring instead to wait until someone that was capable of policing these types of painful social measures came into power.

By April 2013, Mursi and his government were still balking at undertaking austerity in exchange for a $4.8 billion IMF loan.[80] At the time, the speculation was that Mursi's administration did not have the clout to seal the deal because the group was also hampered in dealing with loan donors because there was no legislature. While the Brotherhood had proven adept at performing well in elections, the group did not possess the control over the state or coercive apparatus necessary to enforce austerity measures. Thus, despite discourse to the contrary, the Brotherhood, like SCAF and Mubarak before them, seemed content to crisis spend rather than implement neoliberal reforms. This preference reflects a continuity, rather than a break, with the post-1952 state.

The major difference is that Mursi failed not only to cut state spending but also to increase it. As the economic situation continued to worsen and no outside financial help materialized, Egypt's transition hobbled along. People felt their standard of living further decline, and electricity cuts around the country as well as gas shortages became increasingly frequent.[81] Mursi did not have the ability to resolve the shortages and, consequently, assumed the blame. As Saber Mohammed Saber, a 30-year-old chauffeur, told the Associated Press, "It certainly is state mismanagement. The president is not competent."[82]

As protests continued against Mursi and the Brotherhood, SCAF's generals initially seemed to wager, along with the president's men, that the military's informal pact with the Brotherhood would outlast the mobilizations. But this belief was a recipe for the continued fragmentation of a political order, not the rebirth of a nation. The military elites had the option to sacrifice Mursi and the transition rather than capitulate to popular demands for freedom, economic growth, and social equality. When the informal pact began to strain, and with the likelihood of Gulf states dangling aid, the military moved with alacrity to align with the anti-Brotherhood forces and organize a rebellion against the elected Mursi.[83] In late June, on the eve of the one-year anniversary of his assumption of the office, the military gave Mursi an ultimatum: resign from the presidency or be removed by arrest. Mursi refused, and on July

3, 2013, the military, led by General al-Sisi, deposed and detained him in a coup d'état.

The Rent Injection: The 2013 Military Coup

The military coup that ended Egypt's post-Mubarak experiment was not rooted solely in the political economy. Rather, it reflected a political problem caused by ongoing mobilization and the failing informal pact between the Brotherhood and the country's leading generals. The generals based their intervention on public support for ending Mursi's tenure, leaving pundits and participants to debate whether what happened could be called a coup. Often the numbers cited were improbable. There were unsubstantiated claims that the Tamarrud group collected twenty-two million signatures between late April and late June on petitions calling for Mursi to step down and new presidential elections to be held. The sizes of the crowds at protests were similarly exaggerated. Prominent business mogul and military intervention advocate Naguib Sawiris tweeted that the BBC claimed "the number of people protesting today [June 30, 2013] is the largest number in a political event in the history of mankind."[84] Even revolutionary socialists agreed. As Gigi Ibrahim tweeted, "I think this might be the largest protest in terms of numbers in history and definitely in Egypt ever."[85] Numbers as high as thirty-three million were reported multiple times by Egyptian private and public channels. While the coup was underway, former general Samih Sayf al-Yazal told CNN, "This is not a military coup at all. It is the will of the Egyptians who are supported by the army. We have not seen in the past—even in modern history, any country in the world driving 33 million people in the street for four days asking the president for an early presidential election."[86] That the 2013 military coup was primarily political, however, does not mean that there were no connections to Egypt's political economy. After all, the economic indicators during Mursi's presidency reveal the worst crisis spending situation since 1981. And the aftermath of the political problem immediately uncovered political economy imperatives. Regional aid provided postcoup Egypt a buffer against further economic decline. The fiscal year 2013–14 saw Egypt's economic indicators level off for a year, the least amount of decline of any of the tumultuous years after the uprising. In other words, the economic crisis-spending situation did not get worse in the year following the coup, but merely stayed the same. What caused the economy to pause on its downward cycle? The answer lies in the external rent injections lavished onto the post-Mursi government, a seeming reward from foreign governments for ending both Egypt's fledging democratic experiment and the normalization of the Brotherhood in the region's politics.

Although on July 3, 2013, the generals arrested the elected president, secured the major roads and bridges around the country, and took control over the radio and television building (and also, some have speculated, ordered an end to the electricity cuts and gas shortages), the coup did not initially produce a government run by al-Sisi and the generals. With people from different representative groups of citizens standing behind him and indicating they supported him, al-Sisi announced a new roadmap for transition. Within a day of Mursi's ouster, a judge named 'Adli Mansur was installed as an interim president. He had served as head of the Supreme Constitutional Court for about five days before being appointed the republic's interim president. For most Egyptians, Mansur was an unknown figure.

Mansur, in turn, appointed Hazim al-Bablawi to be the interim prime minister. A former economist prominent in international academic circles, al-Bablawi had previously served as finance minister under the first SCAF transition in 2011. He had a record of being critical of the Gamal Mubarak succession and enjoyed an aura of being neither an old-guard apparatchik nor a "yes man" to the generals, who were governing from behind a paper-thin veneer of civilian politics. Ironically, al-Bablawi's chief contribution to the academy had been his theory on rentier states.[87] His central argument was that the more rents a state has access to, the fewer incentives it has to be accountable to its citizens. The result is a "no taxation, no representation" arrangement between state and society, and a "rentier mentality" among government elite. In his research, al-Bablawi spoke mostly of hydrocarbons and oil. But other types of income such as foreign aid, tourism, and the remittances of migrant workers also constitute rents. While Egypt had always been bolstered by these types of rents, al-Bablawi came to office amid a windfall of rent in the form of foreign aid.

He indicated that the crisis spending could not continue. As he argued on the eve of Mursi's ouster, "The canceling of subsidies requires sacrifices from the public and therefore necessitates their acceptance. It is crucial that they understand the scope of the danger that the current size of subsidies imposes on Egypt's economy, and they must also feel that rationing is done in a way that guarantees social justice."[88] As the rent came in, however, there was little sign that Egypt was reversing course. Indeed, in the year following the coup the economic indicators stayed relatively constant before the gap between expenditures and revenues widened again, indicating a further decline of the state's fiscal health. The rent windfall had merely given the new transitional team some time to strategize, and even that brief period of respite was not without some international drama about aid.

The United States, which sponsored exchange programs between the US and Egyptian militaries and had given Egypt over $60 billion in military and social and economic aid since the signing of the Camp David Accords with Israel in 1979, faced a dilemma.[89] Specifically, US laws forbid the government from providing aid to any country that had overthrown a democratically elected government by coup.[90] Throughout the tensest moments of Mursi's presidency, such as the December 2012 referendum on the new constitution, the Obama administration had maintained a position that they wanted to see the elected Mursi government serve its term.[91] In the day before the intervention, US agencies moved toward action, threatening to suspend US aid to Egypt, which would primarily affect the Egyptian military.[92] Defense Secretary Chuck Hagel reassured al-Sisi, but he cautioned against a coup.[93] Sisi and the military could have cared less.

Following the coup, a chorus of voices demanded the United States comply with its laws and cut aid to its bulwark ally. The debate within the Obama administration was fierce but never drifted into a space where it would label the general's intervention a coup.[94] The State Department's daily briefings became filled with word play as it tried to avoid calling what took place in Egypt a coup. Even *The Daily Show with Jon Stewart* skewered the department's semantics.[95] With the pressure mounting to refer to Mursi's ousting as a coup, the administration deferred indefinitely.

As State Department spokesperson Jen Psaki said, the government conducted "a review of what is applicable under the law, abiding by the law. We're continuing to work with Congress. This is ongoing. Obviously, our relationship with Egypt and the aid we provide and decisions over that is an ongoing process." In response to the question of whether the Obama administration or the State Department would ever produce a definitive statement on what transpired in Egypt, she replied, "The law does not require us to make a formal determination as to whether a coup took place, and it is not in our national interest to make such a determination."[96] After the Obama administration decided it would not be making a determination, thereby allowing aid to continue to flow, Egypt responded.

Al-Sisi said that the United States had turned its back on Egyptians. The US government doubled down on its support. Secretary of State John Kerry responded by trying to close the diplomatic nonrift. In Pakistan of all places, Kerry argued that Egypt's generals were "restoring democracy" and stated, "The military was asked to intervene by millions and millions of people. The military did not take over to the best of our judgment—so far."[97] About two weeks later, al-Sisi helped coordinate the largest massacre by a state of its citizens since at least 1989, when Chinese troops opened fire on protesters in Tiananmen Square.[98]

While the US government creatively and disingenuously sought to keep its aid flowing to Egypt's military, Gulf countries rushed in to save the day with supplemental cash injections. Whereas Qatar had provided nearly $8 billion in aid to Mursi's government during its year in power, Saudi Arabia, the United Arab Emirates, and Kuwait donated a combined $12 billion for 2013 to the "civilian" interim government in Cairo.[99] Thus were Egypt's generals thrown a lifeline in their time of need, as the transition continued to wear on the state's cohesion and capacity. Rather than pivot toward a new economic trajectory, however, the military-backed postcoup government doubled down on the only kind of spending Egyptian elites since Nasser have known.

Some could have speculated that the gloves had come off and now the military would solely protect its economic interests and insert itself as the primary beneficiary of Egypt's economy. Yet the military's control over Egypt's economy did not translate into singular dominance. Instead,

Egypt's generals entered the great game of trying to govern a society that had lived in a political economy of social revolt for decades. This political economy was spiraling out of control, with expenditures outpacing revenues by an ever-widening amount. The generals might have been understood to be next in line to rule Egypt because the military was the only state institution that survived the 2011 uprising intact, but the story that began to unfold after the coup was one of further state fragmentation, not consolidation.

Military Inc. Tries to Build a Regime?

In Egypt after the uprising, military generals thought they possessed a state rather than serving as one part of it. After the coup and their destruction of Egypt's largest systemic and antisystemic groups, this thought became a reality. Egypt is not unique in this respect. In her rich book about the role of Pakistan's military in the country's economy, Ayesha Siddiqa examines how military elites use capital to safeguard their positions within the state's political economy.[100] She refers to the confluence of the participation of the generals in the economy and politics as "Milbus." There is much to learn from the experience of Pakistan and other countries—such as Turkey, Indonesia, and Burma/Myanmar (to name some exemplary, albeit different, cases)—where the military uses its political power to protect and enhance its economic position. After the uprising Egypt's military elites started to resemble Pakistan's in terms of their access to state and economic power, but this has changed as a regime is being built around 'Abdel Fattah al-Sisi. Egypt's military-economic nexus is powerful but not without emerging challenges. This suggests that while there are similarities to what Siddiqa describes in Pakistan, there are also important different inherited constraints, such as the size of Egypt's large state bureaucracy.

The Egyptian civil service is so large and organized that even the most pliant of parliaments refused to pass legislation that would allow the president to reform and shrink it.[101] Apparently, these powerless MPs felt doing so would be akin to political suicide. This refusal continues even after the Egyptian government signed a $12-billion loan agreement with the IMF in November 2016 that required it to rein in state expenditures on subsidies and the public sector. The cuts amounted to a war on the poor. As Zeinab Abul-Magd argues, "The Egyptian army has used the agreement to punish the lower classes while maximizing its commercial gains."[102] To reform economically means to place an even larger number of people in an even more precarious situation than what millions have already endured for decades. How many people is too many before the levee breaks?

The former field marshal that now governs Egypt oversees a far more narrowly based, more violent, and less robust state than any apparatus that Mubarak governed.[103] While there are important continuities—rents in the form of Suez Canal remittances, tourism dollars, and foreign aid still make up the bulk of the state's revenue, which continues to be outpaced by expenditures—differences between the al-Sisi and Mubarak governments abound. Mubarak engaged in crisis spending to hold together a regime coalition—made up of state employees, workers, neoliberal businessman, security types, and the military's companies—that was mostly harmonious even if competition existed and society protested declines in the standard of living. By contrast, al-Sisi is currently in the process of building a regime. A narrow sector of elites wields state violence and cracks down on any dissent in order to prop up al-Sisi and his clique. Al-Sisi's own intolerance for dissent sinks to the level of getting state TV anchors suspended for criticizing the government's response to flooding in Alexandria.[104] Crushing the protests against the coup, jailing activists who helped organize the January 25 uprising, reining in civil society, and fighting a war against an Islamic State affiliate in Sinai has not left al-Sisi with much time to build outwardly.

Rather al-Sisi, much like Muhammad Mursi before him, began his term by relying on a trusted constituency to try and build a regime. One of the first things al-Sisi did was expand military intelligence (MI), which is where he hails from institutionally. During Mubarak's tenure, MI had a tense but workable relationship with the General Intelligence Services (GIS) as well as state security; now, an officer from MI runs GIS. Al-Sisi's own son is rising in the ranks of GIS as well. MI appears to be colonizing and replicating itself in the other intelligence agencies. This new age of the generals, it seemed, would see even less friction than Nasser's early years.[105] As Tom Stevenson reported in the *London Review of Books*, "A series of promotions for other loyalists and military intelligence veterans . . . enabled Sisi—himself a former head of military intelligence—to consolidate his control over first the military and then the other organs of the security state. Sisi has concentrated the power of the regime in the presidency and a small entourage of senior generals."[106] Egypt was thought to be on the path to the "Algerianization" of the state. Recent protests in Algeria reveal that a government shadow-run by the military generals is also susceptible to a mass protest movement.[107] Whether al-Sisi and his team can consolidate a regime, however, remains to be determined. After all, regime building costs money.

Most of the recent literature on the Egyptian military's economic holdings focuses on how the military is becoming more deeply entrenched within the everyday workings of Egyptian economic life. Marshall, for instance, argues, "The consolidation of the new military regime has facilitated the EAF's capacity to channel state funds into projects in which it has an interest." While "subsidizing military enterprises through state-owned banks and parceling out coveted contracts to the firms of retired generals is an old practice," she predicts that "it is likely to escalate in intensity given the military's new grip on power."[108] Abul-Magd is even more forceful in this interpretation.[109] While it may be true on some level that the military is simply escalating or deepening long-standing practices, there is also evidence of a transformation in the military's behavior as al-Sisi's government increases crisis spending just to keep pace.

Since becoming president, al-Sisi has embarked on a number of large and fanciful projects to revitalize an economy awash in aid from the UAE, Kuwait, and Saudi Arabia as well as IFI loans. The type of projects that Military Inc. is undertaking under al-Sisi, however, are not profit generating. Rather, they are incurring losses, which the military is willing to concede for the sake of regime building around al-Sisi. In many ways, Military Inc. is trading its previous autonomy for a greater role in distributing—or withholding—economic rewards. Instead of maximizing profits, they are spending Military Inc.'s accumulated capital to fortify and broaden their existing constituencies of state employees, unaligned businessmen, and aggrieved laborers.

For example, the military is initiating labor-intensive infrastructure projects—such as the New Suez Canal project, the Electric Power plan, and the Million-Unit Housing project—that require foreign investors to use Egyptian labor and materials. In the words of Abdel-Fattah Barayez, "These initiatives . . . can be better understood as efforts to enhance the legitimacy and popularity of the current regime." Military Inc. aims to build the al-Sisi regime by building alliances with business partners, guaranteeing employment for Egyptians, and ensuring power cuts become a thing of the past. The Suez Canal project, for instance, involved over seventy private sector companies in a deliberate manner. As Barayez argued, "Rather than crowding out private competition, then, the military ceded part of its share—and thus potential economic return—to the private sector."[110] In this sense, Military Inc. is putting its money behind al-Sisi's political order as opposed to predatorily using its position to generate a return.

Notably, as Military Inc. gives up some of its autonomy and profits in order to help build a regime around al-Sisi, it has started to marginalize the private Egyptian businessmen that previously served as the middlemen for foreign capital. Nowhere is this more visible than with the National Service Projects Organization (NSPO) and the Armed Forces Land Project Organization (AFLPO). Created in the 1970s and early 1980s, respectively, to offset declining expenditures on defense, both organizations established legal entities for the military to cooperate with and benefit from foreign and Egyptian businessmen. They were also supposed to help with national development. The military is the largest landowner. Through NSPO, it would sell land at below market costs to Egyptian business interests that, in turn, would develop tourism ventures with foreign capital. This has changed after the military intervention in 2013. Whereas before most foreign investment went through the private sector, now NSPO and AFLPA, which allow the military to establish commercial companies, are being used to connect foreign capital to the military directly.[111] A new legal framework is permitting foreign investors to directly deal with military companies, which is producing a new kind of collusion of power and wealth. In the words of Adly, "This reconfigures crony networks. Because of the ability of the military to allocate land, now they are directly benefiting and profiting. The well-armed and resource-rich formal empire did not dominate the economy before the revolution. Now, these changes will crowd people out as the informal aspects of their empire become more prominent."[112]

Yet none of these changes address the bigger structural problems of a bloated civil service, volatile rents, and ballooning deficit. The deficit in the first half of the 2015–16 fiscal year was larger than in any six-month period since the uprising.[113] Furthermore, between February 2016 and April 2017 the Egyptian pound depreciated from LE 7.75 per dollar to LE 18.17 per dollar—its lowest value ever. Expenditures continue to exceed revenues and are higher than they were compared to the political economy under Mubarak. Thus, while Military Inc. has adapted its approach to help construct al-Sisi's regime, it has failed to tackle the primary economic factor that produces the conditions for social revolt—the crisis spending that happens when expenditures are higher than revenues over a number of years, leading to a gradual decline in living standards and social provisions. The decline is so incremental that as it deteriorates, it becomes normalized. Al-Sisi may be trying to create a regime, but Egypt's economy and political arena have never been less sturdy.

The continuous crush of state violence and the security crackdown are driving most political dissent underground. While some emigrate or depress their activity, others react to state violence with decentralized violent responses such as bombings. This keeps Egypt's security specialists at the fore of any budgetary considerations as the state continues its war against the insurgency of the self-proclaimed Islamic State in Sinai or so-called Islamist sympathizers up and down the Nile Valley and Delta. The more state capital is invested in security, the less money is available to address the grievances of a society that already led an uprising that nearly broke Egypt's once formidable state.

The other complicating factor for regime building around al-Sisi is that it is predicated on Suez Canal revenues, tourism, and foreign aid from the oil-rich Gulf states. Rentier economies are notoriously vulnerable to swings in the local and international political economy. If an insurgent attack on one of the cargo ships that traverse the canal were successful, it could render the passage unusable for weeks. Al-Sisi's government is keen to protect the canal and has set up a new police force tasked with stopping attacks on cargo ships transiting the passage.[114] A sudden unexpected drop in rent would severely damage the state's ability to operate.

Tourism rents are likewise susceptible to drops in the wake of a terrorist attack, such as after the bombing of the Russian Metrojet in October 2015. If tourists quit going to Sinai, thereby keeping foreign currency out of the country, the Egyptian economy could experience a setback. Yet, any setback would occur against the backdrop of a more desperate economic situation. As *Rebel Economy* suggested, "Unlike the 1990s, Egypt's economy is in a much more precarious position."[115] Furthermore, foreign currency reserves continue to sit at $16 billion.[116] They did not move in five years. Since mid-2017, the currency reserves have increased to $42.5 billion.[117] This is largely due to the amount of aid and loans coming in from outside the country.

Lastly, foreign aid is always political and hence contingent. In the wake of the 2013 coup, Saudi Arabia, the UAE, and Kuwait rushed to provide al-Sisi's regime with cash, public relations help in Washington, DC, and political cover to fortify its base. Over eight years after the coup, Egypt remains as dependent on Gulf aid as ever. Given that Gulf monarchies also spend generously on their own societies to ward off discontent and uprisings, there is no guarantee that they can fund al-Sisi's counterrevolutionary regime-making experiment forever. Furthermore, the coffers of the Gulf monarchies are dependent on international oil prices. A downturn in the price of oil will put an unprecedented squeeze on the Gulf states' accelerated spending on their societies as well as on wars in Yemen and Syria or counterrevolution in Sudan. Egypt's stability will be secondary to their own. Egypt's elites have sold the idea that Egypt is too big to fail. So far, this line has worked. Yet it seems untenable to maintain given the contingent factors that can disrupt the streams of rent. Egypt's regime-in-formation is vulnerable on a number of fronts, and its political economy resides in a perpetual state of social revolt.

Egypt's Political Economy Colonizes Its Military

The politicians that represent the military's business empire—like the ex-military and civilian politicians before them—have relied on foreign aid and other rents while continuing the policy of fiscally exhaustive crisis spending. Along with their predecessors since Sadat, the generals appeal to international donors and financial institutions for bailouts and then do the bare minimum to meet the conditions of the loans. They also use the military's war chest and transnational partners to try to construct a new regime under the general-turned-president al-Sisi. In the process, the military has gone from an autonomous economic actor to the most recent subsidizer of Egypt's post-1952 state.

Any current or future government in Egypt will have to wrestle with the legacy of the postindependence state. It can try to sustain the political economy that formed during the Nasser years. It can continue to employ over 6.5 million people in its bureaucracy, maintain its overdeveloped security establishment, pay concessions to the millions of underpaid factory workers, and patch up the infrastructure that routinely fails across the country.[118] It can continue to appeal to the patriotism of Egyptians, whether they are poor agricultural workers or middle-class parents that feel the financial pinch as private tutors are needed to supplement public school education. It can continue to speak to international financial institutions about the importance of taxation without actually being able to increase the financial burden on a population that is already strapped beyond capacity. But this political economy, which siphons more money for state expenditures than it earns, is a system that all but foretells a perpetual economic crisis keeping Egypt on the brink of a revolutionary unknown. Under the current configuration, Egyptian leaders will never pay less to govern than they do today.

The alternative is to listen to the IMF and World Bank. In fact, since taking the IMF loan of $12 billion in November 2016, the options available to them are limited. They can implement economic austerity measures in exchange for cash now. They can increase the assault on workers' rights. They can eliminate subsidies that drag on the state's revenue as they weather the resistance from the middle and below.[119] They can redesign the state and issue redundancy notices to millions in their employ. Yet pursuing such policies will only accelerate the velocity of the neoliberal train as it heads toward an unraveling endgame. Both the Nasserist and neoliberal chalices are filled with a poison tonic.

There is evidence that recent austerity measures have already accelerated the situation. The one constituency that al-Sisi and his regime-makers cannot trick are Egyptians themselves. As Teti, Abbott, and Cavatorta show through their research, youth unemployment—a driver of the uprising—increased from 16 percent in 2010 to 42 percent by 2014.[120] When Egyptians were asked about the major challenges facing the country in 2011, respondents—who were allowed to choose up to six areas—felt that the economic situation was the most important area named. In 2011, 81.5 percent of respondents named the economic situation as the most important problem. By 2014, 90.3 percent of respondents felt the economic situation was of paramount importance.[121] Egyptians are far from satisfied with the regime-in-formation or don't believe such challenges are being addressed. Other daily signs reinforce that they are seeing the situation with clarity.

The Egyptian pound began to collapse in March 2016 and then saw a further steep drop after November, when the state agreed to the conditions of the IMF loan—an indicator that is significant on its own. The IMF also recommended other spending cuts as well as introducing a value-added tax, which was enacted in September 2016; by June 2017 it had resulted in a rise of core inflation by 32 percent, according to the government.[122] The prices of other items like food, fuel, and electricity are much higher. As Neil Ketchley and Thoraya El-Rayyes note, "Egyptians have seen the cost of bread and cooking gas go up by nearly 60 percent. To put this into perspective, in the year leading up to the 2011 Arab Spring, food prices in Egypt were subject to an annual increase of around 15 percent."[123] The subsequent economic protests, unlike the previous political ones, have not been met with overwhelming state violence. Most notably, immediately after the state cut the ration cards for bread, Egypt saw its largest protest since the coup. Rather than be beaten, arrested, and detained, however, "protestors involved in small scale blockages of local supply offices were left to continue their sit-ins with only minimal interference from security forces."[124] The government also responded to the protesters' grievances. It said it would investigate corruption within state-registered bakeries. It rushed to increase the amount of subsidized bread, which it described as a right for all citizens, and al-Sisi promised not to cut bread quotas again. This episode shows the real contradictions of the state's political economy.

To neoliberalize is to undermine the state's capacity to govern. To maintain state spending courts fiscal exhaustion. Whether al-Sisi stays and consolidates something that resembles a regime or that task falls to the next person in line for the job of president, Egypt's current fiscal state and Military Inc. offer instructive examples other states will eagerly watch. For the time being, observers can anticipate that al-Sisi, like his predecessors, will try what Khalil and Dill call "statist neoliberalism."[125]

After the euphoric revolutionary attempt that almost overran the state, all signs pointed to the military becoming the uncontestable power for years to come. The generals eliminated their main political rival by inviting the Muslim Brotherhood into a pact that would destroy them. SCAF had lawyers present political rivals with only bad options. The senior generals won all the constitutional concessions they sought. They put themselves above the law and beyond parliamentary oversight. They had the ability to organize and eventually mobilize nationally. No other national group had as much economic power or was as cohesive or as well armed as the military's empire. There was no group that could negotiate with it.

Yet after five years of al-Sisi's presidency, the military is funding the abyss that is Egypt's ever-increasing state expenditures. It is one thing to dictate outcomes behind the scenes and another thing to govern in the open, with constituencies that one must appease. Even the most savvy and unconstrained leader probably could not overcome the political economy of Egypt's postindependence state, much less correct it. In many ways, it would be preferable if such a leader could start from scratch. But even for a field marshal with the most enthusiastic of cults, this is not on the menu of possibilities. The declining fiscal health of Egypt's state, whether absent or in concert with neoliberalism, will continue to fuel a political economy of social revolt for those trapped under its weight.

Conclusion

No Going Back

> Fākir bukra illī māgāsh (Remember tomorrow that didn't come yet)
> —Street art by Keizer in downtown Cairo,
> days after Mubarak's resignation in 2011

The situation in Egypt might feel like people lived through and observed a trip back to the future. For so long under Nasser, Sadat, and Mubarak, tomorrow's promise of a better, more democratic future never came. Then it did. For nearly thirty months after the January 2011 uprising began, the politics of Egypt wandered around unfamiliar territory. For a government and society so used to the established routine of a political regime, the situation drifted into uncertainty as Mubarak was deposed and the regime he oversaw collapsed. Politics moved, but the end point was unclear. The atmosphere was revolutionary, even as leading military generals, opposition relations, elections, competing forces within the state apparatus, and support from foreign governments and companies blocked a path to more inclusive political change. Despite this unsettled field, regime change did not occur with the uprising in 2011 or with Mursi's election in 2012. Regime change did, however, occur in July 2013 with the military coup d'état. Since that moment, Egypt's military body, SCAF, has tried to make a regime on the ruins of a democratic transition it sabotaged. Egypt's uprising and transition produced a more fragile state, a more violent political system, the destruction of oppositional relations, a more trying economic situation, and a loss of faith in procedurally fair elections. Many Egyptians likely feel as if they were victims of a watermelon transition, as the anecdote in the preface to this book describes. The more troubling aspect is many move forward thinking that democracy is likewise a waste of time. As Teti, Abbot, and Cavatorta show, not only are Egyptians watching democracy decline in practice but also in their political dreams.[1] While this belief would shatter if a revolutionary atmosphere reemerged, the lack of hope to pursue democracy may contribute to delays in such rare moments occurring. Furthermore, the next revolutionary moment in Egypt will look utterly different than the one in 2011 because of the changes that have taken place.

After the presidential election, Mursi was trapped between his party, the military, and the state apparatus. He could not just resign. Too many people around the country believed, campaigned, donated money, and put in sweat equity to get him elected. Stepping down likely would have produced so much strife inside the Brotherhood, the group would have been permanently damaged as an organization. Many of its more right-wing members had already been flirting with emerging Salafist groups operating in Egypt since the uprising. More liberal Brotherhood members had drifted toward 'Abd al-Mun'im Abu al-Futuh when he broke with the Brotherhood and ran for president in 2012. Mursi's resignation on al-Sisi's dictate not only would have exacerbated these splits in both directions but also would have likely produced an exodus of more centrist Brotherhood members that would be frustrated by such prostrate acquiescence. The office of the presidency was Mursi's *Titanic* and, as captain, he went down with the ship. His decision to reject al-Sisi's ultimatum was the calculation of someone who had recognized they had already lost the political battle. It is entirely plausible, but hard to imagine, any Brotherhood leader having a good option while ruling next to the unelected SCAF generals.

The 2013 military coup was a watershed event. It was also an event with recent and distant historical antecedents. Egypt's January 25 uprising was built on a history of divisions between systemic and antisystemic opposition groups. When the uprising happened, these groups could not overcome their suspicions of one another, or this nurtured history. The speed of the uprising also complicated the horizontal organizing approach through which the antisystemic opposition attempted to produce more lasting political change. These feeble linkages and this challenge of organizing horizontally came after decades of contested but fabricated elections together with the international discourses that stress the importance of free and fair elections in democratizing societies. When the uprising was launched, there was a sense that state violence and repression could not get worse because of the capricious and increasing police brutality under Mubarak. There was also a sense that the economy and its growing wealth gap could not get worse because people lived for decades in a political economy of impending social revolt, which had become normalized.

After the uprising started, the mistakes and concessions citizens made—letting SCAF's constitutional declarations pass without resistance, trusting the institution of the military too much, and voting in the transitional elections even when there was no candidate that many wanted—enabled a regime-making experiment when the 2013 coup placed the military in control. Yet regime-making is not an absolute win for the supposed victors. It just determines the parameters for the next phase of political and social struggle. This struggle is defined by the al-Sisi-led state's attempt to establish a new regime over society. While a honeymoon period between the ruling military generals and the public could be anticipated, politics is always about deliverables over the long term to those who are governed. The military did not possess the power to convince people deprived of political or economic rights of its altruism. Nor could it prevent or reverse the gradual fragmentation of the state, in terms of its ability to encourage a population's disgruntled but passive acceptance of a worsening status quo. The amount of state violence the military unleashed after the coup and the assassination of Prosecutor Hisham Barakat reveals the continuation of the state's atrophying condition and its lack of authority without coercive force. As in any failing political situation, the 2013 coup could not produce a decisive victory. Dislodging the Brotherhood from power and the group's unwillingness to accept it meant the military had to lead a campaign that would violently disorganize the group for decades to come in order to maintain control over a contracting state and a polarizing society.

The mid-summer 2013 mobilization that removed the flawed but elected Mursi and authorized the al-Sisi-led coup ended the revolutionary aspirations of millions and signaled the beginning of a different, narrower, and more repressive political orientation. The army's boot dropped on the neck of both the revolutionaries and the Muslim Brotherhood. The Muslim Brotherhood that so many had belonged to, worked for, and studied across the decades starting in the 1960s ceased to exist as it was crushed through killings, arrests, and exile. The future of the Brotherhood will, once again as in the 1960s and 1970s, emerge out of the cages inside prisons. While the military installed a former judge to lead the interim government, all paths led to and from al-Sisi as the military's representative and the actual source of the state's diminishing political authority and administrative capacity.

Some scholars make the argument that the transition failed and Egypt returned to the days of authoritarian rule.[2] Others, such as Bruce Rutherford, try to conceptually clarify this dynamic as one of "new authoritarianism," whereby the calculations of the state elites have shifted from a patronage-laden provisional pact under Mubarak to a protectionist pact where the leaders are charged with eliminating and neutralizing domestic and international enemies under al-Sisi.[3] This argument is not incorrect. The revolution is also said to have died with the transition.[4] The end of the revolution and the failure of the transition were not cast as inevitable, but it seems overdetermined. After all, the outcome of a new autocratic regime remains the expectation when a revolutionary atmosphere takes hold. Yet, outcome-based analysis hides the multilayered ways in which new autocrats achieve their goals or even begin regime-making.

While we should expect the side with access to the state apparatus, weapons, cash, and transnational diplomatic support to outmaneuver the masses, these factors explain Egypt's authoritarian reentrenchment only in its most basic terms. Likewise, while it is also not wrong to claim that Egypt's transition led to a return of authoritarianism,[5] it is not the same kind of autocratic state that existed before the 2011 uprising. In Trotsky's words, "There is no way back."[6] Calling it a return to authoritarianism fails to capture some of the greater changes that took place, or the path traveled to arrive at this new autocracy. Field Marshal al-Sisi's eventual 2014 election as president and the military's ascendance to the top of Egypt's state have not produced a clean or cohesive regime. Building a new regime with an embattled state over a reconfigured society requires an enormous amount of effort, coordination, money, penetration across the country, and structured domestic and transnational support. These factors leave open a future that no one can predict.

There is an axiom that states betray their own weakness when they use extreme violence to quash dissent. In the words of Nazih Ayubi, "That the Arab state is an authoritarian state, and that it is so averse to democracy and resistance to its pressures should not, of course, be taken as a measure of the strength of the state—indeed, quite the reverse."[7] Egypt's leading and often publicly unknown generals should feel vulnerable even if the machinery of propaganda tells everyone otherwise. The national security state never dissolved, but this does not mean al-Sisi or the military generals control the security forces either. Emboldened by popular support, which in turn is boosted by the swagger of the military's civilian lackeys in the Egyptian media, Egypt's generals govern an illusion. The so-called "stability" of the government is a house of cards, and the facade is exposed after each attack on state buildings or other social institutions, each fake election, each arrest of a person of conscience, or anytime an overwhelming majority of Egyptians peer into their wallets. We also see this in the state's attempts to use violence against its opponents. The government's strategy relies on baiting supporters of the Muslim Brotherhood and others into using violence against the state and citizens. The Islamists have obliged with political assassinations and a rash of sectarian attacks on churches, Christian orphanages, Sufi mosques, and schools. These attacks, of course, only invite and authorize more state repression. This increase in social and state violence shows that al-Sisi has failed to create a truly stable government. Furthermore, he has been unable to cobble together a coherent regime, much less demonstrate an ability to rebuild a state that can penetrate society and produce less visibly violent autocracy. Al-Sisi sits atop an Egyptian state that is but a shell of the clanking steamroller that Mubarak had run into the ground. During the course of this book, I have described the post-2013 order as one of regime-making on the ruins of an older regime and a turbulent transition. In what ways do people experience an unconsolidated regime? The existing dynamics in Egypt are telling but unlikely to reveal all the tools at the hands of ambitious autocrats.

The Illusion of Stability

An authoritarian regime may be unpopular, even loathed, but at least it has rules. The rules may bear little resemblance to the law, but relations between state officials and society come to have a predictable rhythm. People understand where the red lines are, and they can choose to stay within them or to step across. Egypt does not work this way under the field marshal who became president. On a short research trip nearly three years after the coup, I encountered a reality in which not only are the red lines blurred, but the unconsolidated regime itself is so fuzzily defined that Egyptians doubt it is one coherent entity. The country's multiple security agencies seem to have slipped the leash of the executive branch. As one journalist told me in Cairo, "You never know which security branch it is any more. The only thing that's clear is that Sisi does not control them. It's unpredictable and unsettled. That's what makes everything dangerous."[8]

The 2011 uprising brought countless Egyptians to political activism, but the period since the July 2013 coup has been the single most repressive one in modern Egyptian history. Whether one is counting the dead, imprisoned or tortured activists, or people chased into exile, the toll is staggering. International NGOs, such as Human Rights Watch, are also documenting similar trends.[9] Some seeking to leave the country found they have been barred from doing so, even for short trips abroad. This movement restriction is also haphazard—the dark joke making the rounds is that you have to be at the Cairo Airport's passport control to know whether you can travel. To cope, some have dropped their political lives in favor of completely unrelated careers.[10] Few take these measures out of fear alone. It is just too painful to contemplate what has happened. Some are so depressed they avoid friends and stay home. Others turn to pharmaceuticals like Tramadol to dull the pain of the memories or to cope with being forced to live in contemporary Egypt.[11] There are also stories of organizers who are so angry about the course of events that they refuse to practice their craft. As one activist worried, "We are not going to be ready next time. Everyone is paralyzed. Some days, I wished I would have died."[12]

Yet all the pronouncements that the transition away from authoritarianism failed, all the clichés about spring turning to winter, also miss the mark because mobilizations and activism continue. It is just not in public squares. The overall level of dissent is much higher than in the final days of Mubarak before the uprising. On average there have been five times as many collective labor actions and other protests per day under al-Sisi than there were in the 2008–10 period.[13] The country is in dire straits.

The 2011 uprising did not create the mess—the decisions of powerful actors did. Pining for the status quo ante, the elites failed to meet the most basic popular demands; now they are trying to contain the lingering tensions while building a new regime amid intense competition among old regime figures and newer entrants. These struggles, in addition to the structural fiscal weakness of the state and the poor economy, generate fears of a polity coming undone and explain the viciousness of the backlash.

Many Egyptians say that no amount of aid from the Gulf, US diplomatic cover, or police brutality can keep the state running. More than one person openly told me that al-Sisi might be overthrown, despite the huge investments and grand spectacles that went into putting him on the wobbling throne, and despite his attempts to place his sons high up in intelligence agencies.[14] It is a bold prognostication. Yet one need only read the newspapers and be in Cairo to see the outlines of such a narrative. The posters, chocolates, and women's underwear bearing al-Sisi's visage that popped up in the immediate wake of the coup are all gone. The stray tattered al-Sisi signs on the city walls look like someone forgot to take them down. And when on February 24, 2016, al-Sisi delivered the longest speech of his presidency, the jokes started before the speech ended. In his usual colloquial Arabic, he warned detractors, "Please, don't listen to anyone but me. I am dead serious. Be careful. No one should try my patience or exploit my good manners in attempts to tear down the state. I swear to God that anyone who comes near the state, I will remove from the face of the earth. I am telling you this as the whole of Egypt is listening. What do you think you are doing? Who are you?"[15] At a social gathering in a Cairo apartment, Egyptian and foreign journalists debated whether al-Sisi is "baby Saddam" or "baby Qaddafi," before someone chimed in that al-Sisi can only wish he had the authority of either doomed dictator. During an address about his vision for 2030, the president said he would sell himself, if he could, for the good of the country. Less than two hours later, an Egyptian in the United States listed al-Sisi for sale on eBay. One former protester told me, "Don't call it a regime because it's not. This country is a joke, a parody, a satire. We don't have to be in opposition. We just need to sit and wait."[16]

The jocularity coexists with palpable anger. On February 18, 2016, the week before al-Sisi's speech, a police officer got into the cab of Muhammad Sayyid in the Cairene district of Darb al-Ahmar and asked the driver to transport some furniture. An argument broke out between the officer and the twenty-four-year-old cabbie, known in the neighborhood as Darbaka, over the agreed-upon fare. The officer ended the argument by killing Darbaka with a shot to the head. The response of residents was to beat the policeman senseless. At first, the government said, "The bullet mistakenly came out of the gun." The following day, over a thousand protested outside the Interior Ministry. When protesters invoke the name of the driver in Darb al-Ahmar, they also mention 'Afifi Husni of Isma'iliyya and Tal'at Shabib of Luxor, two others who were tortured and murdered by police that winter and whose killings sparked protests.[17] Al-Sisi and the interior minister, Magdi 'Abd al-Ghaffar, scrambled to quiet the furor, placing the blame on a few bad apples in the police ranks. In response, seven men calling themselves the Coalition of Low-Ranking Police Officers headed to a satellite TV studio to air their discontent. They were arrested before the interview began. The next day, scores of police demonstrated in front of the Security Directorate in the Sharqiyya Governorate to demand their release.

Another flashpoint is the relationship between the police and groups like middle-class professionals, which has become increasingly tense with the growing incidence of police brutality since the coup. One example is medical doctors. In late January 2016, two officers appeared at Matariyya General Hospital, which is near one of the deadliest police stations in the country.[18] One had minor cuts but wanted a report with a doctor's signature that exaggerated his condition. When the physician, Mu'min 'Abd al-'Azim, said no, the officer punched him. Another doctor intervened to help his colleague, and the officers called for backup. Eight more police showed up and dragged the two doctors outside for a further beating. The doctors tried to press charges at the police station and were threatened with jail time if they insisted. On February 12, nearly ten thousand doctors gathered in front of their professional syndicate building. The physicians issued a set of demands calling for accountability for violent police and fundamental reform in hospital security, including a firearm ban and installation of video cameras. The rallying cry was "the rule of law."

Those working for the embattled state want to intimidate Egyptians who monitor and publicize abuses like those in Matariyya. The same week as Darbaka was murdered and the two doctors assaulted, police showed up at al-Nadim Center, which provided psychological and other support to torture victims beginning in 1993 until the government issued a closure order for the NGO. The Health Ministry claimed that the center had exceeded its mandate to treat victims and entered the realm of advocacy with its well-researched reports. As 'Aida Seif al-Dawla said at that time, "As long as they keep torturing, the reports will continue to be issued. The only way those reports are not issued is if they stop torture practices."[19] Al-Nadim Center was closed one year later, in February 2017, and in October 2017 Seif al-Dawla was banned from traveling. On February 22, 2016, Hossam Bahgat, perhaps the country's leading investigative journalist, was barred from traveling to Jordan for a UN conference on justice in the Arab world. The previous November, Bahgat had been summoned and detained by military intelligence because of an article he had published about the secret conviction of twenty-six army officers on charges of conspiring to oust al-Sisi.[20] He had, however, been allowed to leave Egypt twice since that time, so the February 2016 ban came as a surprise. He joins a growing no-fly list that includes human rights activist Gamal Eid.

The crackdown extends to the arts. On February 20, 2016, two days before Bahgat was banned from travel outside the country, a Cairo court sentenced novelist Ahmad Naji to two years in prison for offending "public morality" because his latest offering, *Istikhdam al-Hayat* (*The Use of Life*), features scenes of sex and drug use.[21] The case was particularly egregious: Naji was acquitted in a lower court and the draconian sentence was imposed after the prosecutor appealed. The novelist's jailing provoked outrage from many corners in civil society, and even al-Sisi's culture minister, Hilmi al-Namnam, attended a solidarity press conference.[22]

Some of these individual cases may quiet as sustained criticism and campaigns dwindle as time passes. Yet only a fool would be unfazed by the frequency of the travesties of justice. As one journalist said, rattling off the previous week's litany of bad news, "You don't get over one tragedy, and then another one happens."[23] The list of incidents they rattled off sounded like the week of Darbaka, Naji, al-Nadim, and Bahgat, only with different names and details. Yet, it is not just the names of individuals caught up in the public web of the security forces or the faceless thousands lingering in newly built prisons; there are also changes to the capital's iconic locations. The state authorities are transforming central Cairo into spaces where they try to erase the past and expand surveillance.

The spirit of 2011 is no longer audible in chants resounding from Tahrir Square or visible in graffiti covering the walls downtown. For a time after the uprising, the torched headquarters of Mubarak's National Democratic Party was left standing—a reminder of people power. It has now been demolished. On Qasr al-'Ayni Street, the main artery leading south from the iconic plaza, a steel gate painted like an Egyptian flag opens and shuts to regulate access. As one researcher told me, "That whole area was closed because that is where the dissent used to gather."[24] Such sweeping orders have emptied downtown Cairo of much of its leisure activity as well. The coffee shops no longer bustle on the pedestrian mall near the stock exchange, and art galleries have been closed. A pair of Egyptian journalists agreed: "Oh, we never go downtown anymore. There is too much security, and no one wants to have a run-in."[25]

Indeed, the area is crawling with police, both men in uniform and plainclothes officers who blend into the crowd. Closed-circuit video cameras protrude from balcony after balcony. Blast walls encircle government buildings such as the Foreign Ministry, the Central Bank, the Court of Cassation, and Parliament. The effect is that state security agencies seem to be everywhere and nowhere at the same time. Local journalists regard it as "crazy" to snap pictures downtown.

The security presence might be even heavier in Garden City, southeast of Tahrir Square along the Nile, which is home to the US, British, Canadian, and Italian Embassies, among others. The Italian Mission was busy in February 2016 between the press attention to the murder of researcher Giulio Regeni (almost certainly by security forces) and the deal cut by Italian energy conglomerate Eni to develop the "supergiant" natural gas field off Egypt's Mediterranean shore. Blast walls surround many embassies as well.

Two organizations the government dislikes, the Egyptian Initiative for Personal Rights and the independent newspaper *Mada Masr,* were also located in Garden City at the time of this visit in February 2016. Both are churning out hard-hitting research and reporting, in both Arabic and English, and both receive regular, thinly veiled threats from anonymous security officers. "They call and say, 'We know about your personal life. We know you don't mean to ruin the reputation of the country.' Stuff like that," says one contact.[26] *Mada Masr* moved into new offices in Dokki in an effort to get away from the security forces' intense gaze, which Garden City's embassies and high-end hotels facilitate.

The swanky island district of Zamalek feels less closely watched. Egyptians mingle more freely with foreigners there, and speaking a foreign language arouses less suspicion. The island has its own unnerving sights, though, such as convoys of black Jeep Wranglers bearing heavily armed paramilitaries in gray-and-black camouflage and, sometimes, black masks. The jeeps are adorned with a decal that reads "the People's Police" (*shurṭat al-sha'b*). But no one can remember when this new force appeared and few seem overly concerned. As one journalist said, "I don't even notice them anymore. I think they are mostly performative. They do a lot of driving around at night and pointing their guns—only in upper-class neighborhoods, though."[27] Another reporter concurred, "It is still plainclothes security that comes to your house and arrests you at 4 a.m. They are the ones that carry out the disappearances."[28] Since the days of Gamal Abdel Nasser's presidency, these arrests in the middle of the night have been called "Zawir al-Fagr" or "Dawn Visitors." Now, like then, these have become commonplace.

An Isolated Economic Empire

Besides trepidation about the aggression of the security agencies, the common refrain in Egypt is worry about the economy. By February 2016, purchasing dollars was almost impossible, even at the airport, and the official exchange rate was LE 7.6 to US$1, and the black market paid LE 9.5 to US$1. Everyone was expecting another devaluation of the pound, and indeed in November 2016, its value dropped by 32.3 percent to LE 13 to US$1. By April 2019, it was LE 17.32 to US$1. This rapid devaluation produced inflation and strained household budgets even further. Another significant devaluation could cause the pension system to collapse.

The military, despite its vaunted economic empire, may not be able to keep the wolf from its own door, let alone Egypt's. After Mubarak was overthrown, the army strove to enshrine its interests in the constitution and various laws, for instance shielding its budget from parliamentary oversight. But these moves did not give the army access to even greater wealth. "They now subsidize the treasury," says one analyst, "not the other way around."[29] As previously mentioned, the military has donated money from its reserves to the state. Military Inc. is also said to be paying the subsidies on the population's electricity bills. Such actions send a message to foreign capital that the economy is at risk. As one Egyptian academic argued, "Sure, the military gained influence, but they are paying for a civil bureaucracy that cannot be counted on politically. They cannot reform the bureaucracy, so they pay them, while also spending money for development and investment opportunities. It's lose-lose. It's a Greek tragedy that is not sustainable."[30]

The dilemma is not a new one for Egypt's rulers. As rents like foreign aid and Suez Canal transit fees shrank as a percentage of the economy, the state had less revenue to work with. The state reduced social expenditures to prevent foreign debt from spiraling upward. Yet alongside the cuts, the civil service burgeoned to more than five million employees, and no one dared to touch the most important subsidies on gas and electricity. This tepid neoliberalism makes the state try to have it both ways: to cut enough to please the international financial institutions, but not so much that the austerity sparks popular discontent. It was neither a command economy nor neoliberalism that led Egypt to erupt in protest in the late Mubarak years. It was the state's attempt to maintain both contradicting systems at once. As Heba Khalil and Brian Dill have argued, Egypt's military masters are trying to reproduce a political economy "through a strategic wedding of seemingly contradictory state types, to create a hybrid we call 'statist neoliberalism.'"[31]

As quality of life and purchasing power eroded and hundreds of thousands of families suffered tremendous hardship, the population started to rebel. The state had no systemic response but to double down on repression. Yet the more money Mubarak funneled into the Interior Ministry, the less was available for affordable housing, hospitals, schools, universities, public transportation, and recreational space, and such existing infrastructure slipped into unusable condition. Households stretched their fixed incomes to accommodate rising food costs, private tutors, and clinic visits. Savings vanished, and millions were thrown into the informal economy to earn a little extra cash. Luxury housing developments served a tiny fraction of the population, while everyone else worked two or more jobs just to get by.

Military Inc. was relatively protected from both the economic malaise and the public anger about it. Everyone knew the military had its perks, but they were mostly hidden from view. Then the 2013 coup thrust al-Sisi and the generals into the spotlight. It is lonely at the top: al-Sisi has no party patronage machine like Mubarak did. But he does have to contend with the same assertive public sector, which is now the largest it has been since 1952. By the calculations of the Central Agency for Regulation and Administration, the state employed 5.6 million workers in 2010. According to media reports, another 900,000 employees have been added to the rolls since the uprising.[32]

One of al-Sisi's first gambits was to issue a presidential decree (there was no Parliament when he took office) altering the civil service payment system. Previously, 80 percent of pay was made up of bonuses awarded by seniority and the rest was fixed salary. The edict switched the percentages, tied bonuses to performance, and capped their size. The civil service unions objected that the changes amounted to pay cuts. In January 2016, a new Parliament was seated and charged with passing all of al-Sisi's 342 decrees into permanent law. The assembly was widely expected to have a wet noodle for a spine, and indeed approved most of the executive orders, but MPs struck down the civil service decree by a count of 332 to 150, with 7 abstentions.[33] According to the Finance Ministry, the public-sector wage bill increased wages by 8.4 percent from July to December 2015, even with the decree in effect.[34] The increases in the state budget are like pressure building on a levee, and few know what the failure threshold is.

Additionally, al-Sisi decided to raise Egypt's minimum wage from LE 1,200/month (US$70) to LE 2,000/month (US$115)[35] just before society passed, by a reported 88 percent, constitutional amendments that allow al-Sisi to remain president (if reelected) until 2030. The amendments also close more activist loopholes to resist.[36] Should he make it to 2030, al-Sisi would have been in power for sixteen years. The major problem is the Egyptian pound has devalued so much since 2016 that today's minimum-wage increase looks more sizable than it actually is, and doesn't provide Egyptians a chance to purchase beyond their basic necessities. State employees are also receiving a 7 percent raise, which will cost the state another LE 30.5 billion (or $1.765 billion). Salaries on the public sector will cost Egypt LE 300 billion ($17 billion) in 2019–20.

Al-Sisi thus confronts the same catch-22 that Mubarak did.[37] Indeed, in the first week of March 2016, a wave of strikes, mostly by public-sector workers upset about stagnant wages, rolled across the country.[38] Meanwhile, there is friction between the military and those in big business, almost the only Egyptians to prosper under Mubarak. After the uprising, Military Inc. might have expected to profit from the exile of select Mubarak cronies and the prosecution of others. Yet when the army took over the state, problems started. There is evidence that Military Inc. is pursuing two major policies that rest on an inherent contradiction. First, as political economist Abdel-Fattah Barayez has shown, the armed forces are reaching out to civilian big business to pursue the grand national prestige projects over which al-Sisi presides.[39]

This development is stoking animosity between the military and business elites but also fusing state power and wealth. As Amr Adly argued, "This is reconfiguring all the crony networks. The same people that allocate the land are now directly profiting. They become more powerful, are armed and have resources."[40] These two policies build tensions between the military and private business people, which periodically surface. For example, during November 2015, the state froze the assets of press mogul Salah Diab after he was charged with appropriating state land.[41] They are also visible in the anemic performance of the Long Live Egypt fund, a presidentially supervised charity that al-Sisi hoped would attract billions of pounds in citizen donations. Despite the thicket of billboards that advertise upscale residences across the capital, it is not business as usual. The military's economic empire is powerful but, ironically, it is more isolated now that it is more fully integrated into the state.

In private, or out of earshot of the lone informer sitting in the corner, nearly every Egyptian observer says that neither the political system nor the economy is working. More recently, protests over bread have returned to Egypt.[42] No one uses the word "stability," unlike under Mubarak, when many gave it lip service though most thought it was a fantasy. No one defends al-Sisi or his policies, though charitable sorts might say, "It's not him. It's his people"—the Interior Ministry, army, parliamentarians, judges, and media personalities. If Egyptians once gave al-Sisi a chance, their patience is now wearing thin.

It is one thing to dictate outcomes behind the scenes and another thing to govern, in the open, with constituencies that one has to appease. In just nine short years, the military's private economic empire has transformed into a new domestic subsidizer of the state. Pencil-pushing bureaucrats, sweaty laborers, and fed-up consumers, as well as rehabilitated crony capitalists of the Mubarak era, are bringing Military Inc. and its public faces to heel.

While the dust settles in this multisided melee around regime-making, the only certainty is more protest, whereby ordinary Egyptians try to preserve their bare-bones prerogatives in a capricious system that will arrest and torture anyone who does not have several layers of protection. If al-Sisi survives to fashion a regime as falsely stable as what reigned in the bad old days of Mubarak, he will be a magician. At present, he resembles a quasi-comical warm-up act, albeit one with an army, while everyone awaits the next chapter of Egypt's tumultuous story.

Regime-Making on the Ruins

The case of Egypt and the various twists and turns since 2011 unveil a process. From the false stability of the late Mubarak years to the hopeful revolutionary atmosphere of 2011 to an electionized transition fraught by divisions among systemic and antisystemic opposition groups to increases in state violence and deteriorating political economy, all of these aspects (as well as transnational support) allowed central unaccountable elites to guide a transition that looked democratic but was empty of any content. Average citizens—from the impoverished and uneducated to hipster social media denizens and those in white-collar professions—could see and understand how the transition was being limited with respect to empowering the people. The protesters organized for more equality and social justice. Instead, SCAF delivered a watermelon democracy. Many continued to protest and agitate as a result. Seeing that the various spectacles of elections with real choice, the threat of mass state violence, or crisis spending on the public sector failed to convince the protesters to stand down, the generals, who were fearful of another uncontrolled protest movement, sprang into action reluctantly. Since the moment of their 2013 intervention, al-Sisi and the other SCAF generals have tried to build a regime. Only time and future maneuvers will tell if they eventually consolidate one.

This process, however, exposes the limitations about what researchers know about political transitions. Currently, whether one looks at the early or late transitions literature, which think very differently about the collapse of autocratic regimes, the research question boils down to this: "Is the outcome of the transition a democracy or autocracy?" Whether one thinks about pacts that lead to democracy or we examine the afterlives of popular protests, elections, state violence, or the state's fiscal weakness that cut down an established autocratic regime, there remains a popular and academic fascination with how political systems change. Even if democracy does not emerge after an attempted revolutionary uprising, a state does not remain similarly autocratic as before a mass attempt to change the political system. Yet, how do we collectively move past the politics of naming an outcome either democracy or autocracy?

An uprising that disrupts a state or collapses a long-standing regime requires either a new democratic or a new autocratic order to be created. Both processes involve strategy, labor, resources, governing tools, and ultimately rest on the unpredictable historical contingencies of social struggle.

Any research that neatly emphasizes an outcome over a process renders important aspects invisible. An autocracy that emerges after an uprising or transition requires political elites to create a new kind of regime—which includes both new actors and institutions, like a ruling party—as well as develop new quotidian practices and relationships with society. This is regime-making. In Cairo, this regime-making process is incomplete as the current occupants of the state's highest offices remain haunted by the specters of the past uprising as well as imagined ones yet to materialize.

The systematic study of politics bolsters a rich theoretical literature about transitions that includes revolutions, regime change, and political liberalization; such studies should have been helpful for understanding this seismic event and its aftermath in Egypt. Even if the most likely result is the reemergence of autocracy, the literature comments on, among other things, incumbent regime-opposition dynamics, elections, violence, and political economy. This book attempts to change this conversation to one about uneven and combined factors that unknowingly worked in concert to keep Egypt's state from disintegrating but also led to military types governing and trying to construct a new regime after their intervention.

Despite the enormous amounts of research on revolutions, protests, and political transitions, the arc of revolutionary life cycles remains undertheorized. Mark Beissinger's work not only shows us how infrequently revolutions happen but also how especially rare a democratic revolution is. He is interested in fleshing out a theory of this wider arc.[43] There is no puzzle to solve by naming a case's transition either democratic or autocratic. The expectation shows that the counterrevolutionary autocracy is the norm. In addition to the research on transitions in contemporary states since 1989, this also holds historically.[44] As Kurt Weyland's research show, counterrevolutionary actors pursued policies to stop movements toward progressive change in 1848, which led to new autocratic regimes being established.[45]

This body of research indicates that political scientists are progressing on building better theories about revolutions, regime change, and transitions. Yet, any broader theory will be built on researching the individual processes of many cases. This book tries to detail the process of a revolutionary life cycle by examining the case of Egypt to understand the arc of the 2011 revolutionary moment and its aftermath. We can anticipate some of the topics covered in this book will factor into the processes in other cases. We can also anticipate that other cases will shed new light on why revolutions usually get deferred to another time.

Area studies have always tried to be a reality check against social sciences that center universalized outcomes, especially in the fields of democratization and transitology.[46] Since area studies became a field of study in American universities in the 1940s, regionalists have had a fraught relationship with universal social scientists because the former group sought to understand other regions on their own terms. Area specialists speak back and frequently undermine universalized theories that assume the mythologized experience of the United States is the norm. Area specialists used frameworks developed by social scientists and then revealed how regional history and developments produced different lived experiences. As Timothy Mitchell argued in 2003, "Each of these frameworks provides a way of incorporating the non-West into a universal story, whose narrative is always that of global history, which means the history of the West. The consequence of this relationship between the discipline and world region, then, is that the object of study remains defined and grasped only in terms of its relationship to the West, and only in terms of its place in a narrative defined in terms of the global history of the West."[47] Applying a label of a transitional outcome to the process that transpired and continues to unfold in Egypt only replicates this error. Research that builds a case about returned or new authoritarianism is not inaccurate, but also it does little to illuminate, much less explain, the complexity and nuance of a revolutionary arc.

For generations, scholars have learned languages, lived in the societies they studied, and conducted research projects with both inductive and deductive designs to explain political transitions as an outcome. Whether in the study of pact-transitions, mobilization-induced regime change, or electoral transitions, the literature's goal of greater epistemic scientific knowledge seems impossible. Likewise, these theories also produce findings about the political economic foundations of uprisings, or the amount of violence unleashed by the uncertainty of a transition, while failing to understand them as part of a wider historical process. As a result, while the project that social scientists are engaged in can produce provocative findings and heated debates, it ultimately produces a literature obsessed with the most important reason or variable to explain the outcome because it fails to understand the wider character and multiple influences on an unfolding historical process.

This book, however, does not prescribe a universally applicable corrective. There have been few claims that add to an understanding of transitions that apply to all, or even most, cases. Instead, this book assesses the literature in relation to what happened in Egypt. It emerged out of a decades-long immersion in such literature and a commitment to studying the politics of Egypt in solidarity with Egyptians. When Egypt's uprising began, I, like many others, chased the lessons of other regional and nonregional scholars to make sense of what many of us experienced virtually and in person. A couple of conclusions became evident. Egypt teaches us that taking one aspect of a transition as explanatory of an unfolding historic process does not work. Revolutions, uprisings, and regime changes are simply too broad and complex to have separable, isolated causes. The various elements of Egypt's revolutionary and counterrevolutionary arcs had to be studied on their own terms with a careful eye on process rather than outcome and history rather than focus on the exciting events of a crucial moment. Even then, describing an outcome produces an incomplete narrative and closes off future ways of knowing and understanding events in a particular place. Eliminating the search for a singular cause that definitively produced an outcome was frustrating. Yet it was also liberating—and necessary if we wish to draw lessons from Egypt's turbulent transition.

Egypt's uprising may likely be the intellectual pinnacle for researchers that study the politics of Egypt. It is hard to imagine replicating the sense of intellectual wonder, energy, and excitement of Egypt's uprising and its people's attempted revolution. At the same time, the tragedy of the military coup and the current circumstances of regime-making have been a deep well of concern, disappointment, and depression. While democratic revolutions are possible, many contingencies underpin them and make them special historical moments. Witnessing such a process deepened my awe of, and commitment to, Egyptians. Yet as was also witnessed, revolutionary atmospheres do not always culminate in a revolution. The willingness of people to believe in the hope of protests when living in a repressive state where representation theoretically exists on paper but never materializes in practice, while only a tiny fraction benefits economically, seems like the stuff of legend. And yet it happened in 2011 and will happen again. As the graffiti from Keizer suggests in this chapter's epigraph, tomorrow has yet to be written. While the practice of democracy is under threat daily around the world's states as rights seem to evaporate without producing unified resistance, Egyptians gifted us their experiences as a precautionary tale. Will we learn these lessons about how power works, the limitations of elections, oppositional compromise, countering the effects of state violence, and political life in less robust states as less money circulates? At the moment, Algerians, Sudanese, Iraqis, and Lebanese are struggling with these lessons after another round of incumbent ejections.

Nazih Ayubi once observed that Arab states were not strong, they were fierce. As he argued, "The strong state is complementary, not contradictory, to society, and its strength is not demonstrated by its subjugation of the society but by its ability to work with and through centers of power in society."[48] This is also why the generals resorted to reactive or preservationist state violence to hold a regime in place. In this formulation, Ayubi didn't want people to see Arab states as strong because of the ferocity. Today, there is no mistaking Egypt's state or regime-making project as strong. Egypt's regime-makers might remain fierce, and they definitely do not possess a cohesive regime, but now they reside in a "brittle" state.[49] In the words of Teti, Abbott, and Cavatorta, we should understand such postuprising states as "precarious autocracies."[50] This aptly describes the military elites at the top of Egypt's tired state both in terms of political vitality and economy health. All they have left is to continue to build a regime on the ruins of the discredited and destroyed one. Time and resilient pressure from above might eventually produce a regime for al-Sisi and his supporters. But, then again, time and pressure also produce the diamond of revolution. All those possibilities and more remain in play in the struggle over the politics of Egypt.

Egyptians have repeatedly shown scholars interested in their country that without empathy and a willingness to suspend our theories in favor of creating close studies of what is happening on the ground, we can only, at best, contribute in a limited way to our collective scholarly knowledge. Egyptians gave scholars an opportunity to deepen their understanding of transitions when they launched their uprising. This book has tried to show who and what was complicit in producing this crime of autocratic regime-making by looking at different aspects of the political transition. This book's commitment started and remains with people not as objects of study but as partners. Time will tell if academic researchers learn the lessons Egyptians produced before the uprising, during its execution, through a troubled transition, and after the coup. Or, will we continue safeguarding our bodies of knowledge by ignoring inconvenient experiences that diverge from our expectations? The consequences of an individual academic contributing another flop to a body of knowledge are minor. But, collectively, there is very real harm done by scholars producing knowledge about Egypt because such knowledge underpins much of the international support provided to Egypt's state. This has serious consequences for people that now chafe under repressive military rulers in a violent state. Egyptians wanted democracy and ended up living in unstable autocracy, or watermelon democracy, where unqualified generals try to build a regime. Everyone should resist that and push for more liberating politics in the future.

Notes

Bibliography

Index

Notes

Preface

1. Mark R. Beissinger, "Work in Progress: The Urban Advantage in Revolution," https://scholar.princeton.edu/mbeissinger/home.

2. Mark R. Beissinger, "The Semblance of Democratic Revolution: Coalitions in Ukraine's Orange Revolution," *American Political Science Review* 107, no. 3 (August 2013): 574.

3. A state is "the permanent organizations of bureaucracy, the military and police forces, the legislature, taxation structures, economic regulation agencies, communication agencies (e.g. postal services and railways), penal institutions, and so forth." A regime, by contrast, is "a set of rules for determining how key public offices are filled. These rules are determined by governments—through bargaining and struggle with opposition groups, societal interest groups, and even international actors, including foreign governments. Regimes can be democratic, semi-democratic, or non-democratic." See Mona El-Ghobashy, "Governments and Oppositions," in *Politics and Society in the Contemporary Middle East*, ed. Michele Penner Angrist (Boulder, CO: Lynne Rienner, 2010): 30.

Introduction

1. I am indebted to Charles Kurzman for this phrase. Charles Kurzman, *The Unthinkable Revolution in Iran* (Cambridge: Harvard Univ. Press, 2004).

2. Andrea Teti and Gennaro Gervasio, "The Unbearable Lightness of Authoritarianism: Lessons from the Arab Uprisings," *Mediterranean Politics*, 16, no. 2 (July 2011): 321.

3. During 2005, three items drew a lot of press attention: the Kifaya movement, which protested on a near weekly basis; President Husni Mubarak's call in February for an amendment to constitutional article 76 to change how the president was chosen from a single candidate popular referendum to a multicandidate election (Mubarak subsequently won the election over his nearest competitor, Ayman Nur, in September of that year); and, lastly, the surprise electoral victories by the Muslim Brotherhood, which won an unprecedented 20 percent of the parliamentary seats.

4. Nathalie Bernard-Maugiron, "The 2007 Constitutional Amendments in Egypt and Their Implications on the Balance of Power," *Arab Law Quarterly* 22, no. 4 (2008): 397–417.

5. Samer Shehata, "After Mubarak, Mubarak?" *Current History* 107, no. 713 (December 2008): 418–24.

6. Mona El-Ghobashy, "The Liquidation of Egypt's Illiberal Experiment," *Middle East Report Online*, December 29, 2010, http://www.merip.org/mero/mero122910.

7. "Obama Interview: The Transcript," BBC, June 2, 2009, http://www.bbc.co.uk/worldservice/news/2009/06/090602_obama_transcript.shtml.

8. Jeff Zeleny, "For Obama's Speech, Cairo Streets Empty," *New York Times*, June 4, 2009, https://thelede.blogs.nytimes.com/2009/06/04/before-obamas-address-cairo-streets-empty/.

9. For example, in February 2002, US Ambassador to Egypt David Welch responded to a question about democracy in Egypt by telling the audience at the American University in Cairo, "The United States considers Egypt to be a friend and we don't put pressure on our friends."

10. Asmaa Mahfouz, "Meet Asmaa Mahfouz and the Vlog that Helped Spark the Revolution (Fixed Subs)," streamed live on February 2, 2011, YouTube video, 4:36, https://www.youtube.com/watch?v=eBg7O48vhLY.

11. "Egypt Protesters Clash with Police," *Al Jazeera*, January 25, 2011, http://www.aljazeera.com/news/middleeast/2011/01/201112511362207742.html.

12. Mona El-Ghobashy, "The Praxis of the Egyptian Revolution," *Middle East Report* 258 (Spring 2011): 3. El-Ghobashy adopts a framework developed by Charles Tilly. Tilly makes the case that a revolution happens when sovereignty splits because two or more groups lay claim to authority. It ends when one of the parties is able to assert authority over the government. For Tilly, the distribution of resources affects a state's ability to deploy coercion, and when protesters change the balance of power regarding the use of coercion, the government's ability to effectively use force to maintain regime practices and hierarchy decreases. As he argues, "The increase in the coercive resources of the alternative bloc is equivalent to the contraction of the government's own coercive resources. The efficiency of governmental coercion is likely to decline, at least in the short run, when the character, organization, and daily routines of the population to be controlled change rapidly; this appears to be one of the most direct effects of large-scale structural change on the likelihood of revolution." See Charles Tilly, "Does Modernization Breed Revolution?" *Comparative Politics* 5, no. 3 (April 1973): 443.

13. Rabab El Mahdi and Philip Marfleet, eds., *Egypt: Moment of Change* (London: Zed Books, 2009): 9–11, 153–55.

14. Theda Skocpol, *States and Social Revolutions: A Comparative Analysis of France, Russia, and China* (Cambridge: Cambridge Univ. Press, 1979), 4.

15. Jack A Goldstone, *Revolutions: A Very Short Introduction* (New York, Oxford Univ. Press, 2014): 3.

16. Hussein A.H. Omar, "The Arab Spring of 1919," *LRB Blog*, April 4, 2019, https://www.lrb.co.uk/blog/2019/april/the-arab-spring-of-1919.

17. Leon Trotsky, "Five Days," in *The History of the Russian Revolution* (New York: Simon & Schuster, 1936), 131.

18. Issandr El Amrani, "Sightings of the Egyptian Deep State," *Middle East Report Online*, January 1, 2012, https://merip.org/2012/01/sightings-of-the-egyptian-deep-state/.

19. Beissinger, "Semblance of Democratic Revolution," 574.

20. Beissinger, "Semblance of Democratic Revolution," 574.

21. Francisco Serrano, "Egypt's Sisi has Established Brutal Authority, but Not a Secure Regime," *World Politics Review*, December 27, 2018, https://www.worldpolitics review.com/articles/27072/egypt-s-sisi-has-established-brutal-authority-but-not-a-secure -regime.

22. "From War Room to Boardroom: Military Firms Flourish in Sisi's Egypt," Reuters, May 16, 2018, https://www.reuters.com/investigates/special-report/egypt-economy -military/.

23. Amy Hawthorne and Andrew Miller, "Worse than Mubarak," *Foreign Policy*, February 27, 2019, https://foreignpolicy.com/2019/02/27/worse-than-mubarak/.

24. Marc Lynch claimed credit naming the uprisings "the Arab Spring," a reference to the failed democratic revolutions of Europe after 1848. See Marc Lynch, *The Arab Uprisings: The Unfinished Revolutions of the New Middle East* (New York: Public Affairs, 2012), 9.

25. David D. Kirkpatrick, *Into the Hands of the Soldiers: Freedom and Chaos in Egypt and the Middle East* (New York: Viking, 2018); H. A. Hellyer, *A Revolution Undone: Egypt's Road beyond Revolt* (London. Hurst, 2016).

26. Nermin Allam, *Women and the Egyptian Revolution: Engagement and Activism during the 2011 Arab Uprisings* (Cambridge: Cambridge Univ. Press, 2017).

27. Maha Abdelrahman, *Egypt's Long Revolution: Protest Movements and Uprisings* (London: Routledge, 2016).

28. Neil Ketchley, *Egypt in a Time of Revolution: Contentious Politics and the Arab Spring* (Cambridge: Cambridge Univ. Press, 2017).

29. Joel Beinin, *Workers and Thieves: Labor Movements and Popular Uprisings in Tunisia and Egypt* (Stanford, CA: Stanford Univ. Press, 2015).

30. Hazim Kandil, *Soldiers, Spies, and Statesmen: Egypt's Road to Revolt* (London: Verso, 2013).

31. Jack Shenker, *The Egyptians: A Radical Story* (New York: New Press, 2016).

32. Ashraf Khalil, *Liberation Square: Inside the Egyptian Revolution and the Rebirth of a Nation* (New York: St. Martin's, 2012).

33. M. Cherif Bassiouni, *Chronicles of the Egyptian Revolution and Its Aftermath: 2011–2016* (Cambridge: Cambridge Univ. Press, 2016).

34. Eric Trager, *Arab Fall: How the Muslim Brotherhood Won and Lost Egypt in 891 Days* (Washington, DC: Georgetown Univ. Press, 2016).

35. Thanassis Cambanis, *Once Upon a Revolution* (New York: Simon & Schuster, 2015).

36. Steven A. Cook, *False Dawn: Protest, Democracy, and Violence in the New Middle East* (Oxford: Oxford Univ. Press, 2017), 145–48.

37. Zeinab Abul-Magd, *Militarizing the Nation: The Army, Business, and Revolution in Egypt* (New York: Columbia Univ. Press, 2017).

38. Alfred Stepan and Juan J. Linz, "Democratization Theory and the 'Arab Spring,'" *Journal of Democracy* 24, no. 2 (April 2013): 27–29.

39. Stepan and Linz, "Democratization Theory," 27–29.

40. Nathan Brown, "Egypt's Failed Transition," *Journal of Democracy* 24, no. 4 (October 2013): 52–53.

41. Jason Brownlee, Tarek Masoud, and Andrew Reynolds, *The Arab Spring: Pathways of Repression and Reform* (New York: Oxford Univ. Press, 2015), 11.

42. Brownlee, Masoud, and Reynolds, *Arab Spring*, 39.

43. Brownlee, Masoud, and Reynolds, *Arab Spring*, 13–14.

44. Robert Springborg, *Egypt* (Cambridge, MA: Polity Press, 2018), 19.

45. *Time*, July 22, 2013 (cover).

46. Max Fisher, "'The Square' Is a Beautiful Documentary: But Its Politics Are Dangerous," *Washington Post*, January 17, 2014, https://www.washingtonpost.com/news/worldviews/wp/2014/01/17/the-dangerously-one-sided-politics-of-oscar-nominated-documentary-the-square/.

47. Eric Trager, "Egypt's Heroic Protesters Bear Responsibility for the Mess That Followed: The Incoherence of Tahrir Square's Activists," *New Republic*, January 6, 2014, https://newrepublic.com/article/116111/square-egypts-protesters-bear-some-blame-mess-followed.

48. Hugh Roberts, "The Revolution That Wasn't," *London Review of Books*, September 12, 2013, 3–9.

49. International Crisis Group, "Reforming Egypt: In Search of a Strategy," *Middle East/North Africa Report*, no. 46, October 4, 2005, https://d2071andvip0wj.cloudfront.net/46-reforming-egypt-in-search-of-a-strategy.pdf.

50. John Chalcraft, "Horizontalism in the Egyptian Revolutionary Process," *Middle East Report* 262 (Spring 2012): 7.

51. Asef Bayat, *Revolution without Revolutionaries: Making Sense of the Arab Spring* (Stanford: Stanford Univ. Press, 2017), 13.

52. William I. Robinson, *Transnational Conflicts: Central America, Social Change, and Globalization* (London: Verso, 2003).

53. Bayat, *Revolution without Revolutionaries*, 11.

54. Bayat, *Revolution without Revolutionaries*, 18.

55. Bayat, *Revolution without Revolutionaries*, 19.

56. Bayat, *Revolution without Revolutionaries*, 23.

57. Nadine Marroushi, "US Expert: Leadership of 'Military Inc.' Is Running Egypt," *Egypt Independent*, October 26, 2011, http://www.egyptindependent.com/us-expert-leadership-military-inc-running-egypt/.

1. Retiring Mubarak

1. "Founder of Egypt's April 6 Movement Weighs In," NPR, February 14, 2011, https://www.npr.org/2011/02/14/133756340/Founder-Of-Egypts-April-6-Movement-Weighs-In.

2. Remarks of Egyptian Vice President Omar Suleiman, CNN, February 10, 2011, https://web.archive.org/web/20110211072558/https://www.cnn.com/2011/WORLD/africa/02/10/egypt.suleiman.transcript/index.html.

3. One recent example is Jack A. Goldstone, *Revolutions: A Very Short Introduction* (New York: Oxford Univ. Press, 2014), 26–32.

4. I. William Zartman, "Opposition as Support of the State," in *The Arab State*, ed. Giacomo Luciani (Berkeley: Univ. of California Press, 1990): 220–46.

5. Edward Aspinall, *Opposing Suharto: Compromise, Resistance, and Regime Change in Indonesia* (Stanford, CA: Stanford Univ. Press, 2005).

6. Aspinall, *Opposing Suharto*, 256. Aspinall's work on Indonesia after Suharto also reveals a dynamic similar to what Egypt experienced. He notes that the state elites dumped Suharto and reconstituted the regime by working with opposition groups that accepted his regime but formally resisted his "New Order" government. He argues, "The organizational weakness and disunity in opposition allowed the bulk of the old governing elite to abandon Suharto, as a concession to the societal upsurge, yet retain power" (270).

7. Holger Albrecht, "How Can Opposition Support Authoritarianism? Lessons from Egypt," *Democratization* 12, no. 3 (2005): 378–97; Samer Shehata and Joshua Stacher, "The Brotherhood Goes to Parliament," *Middle East Report* 240 (Fall 2006): 32–39.

8. Holger Albrecht and Dorothy Ohl, "Exit, Resistance, Loyalty: Military Behavior during Unrest in Authoritarian Regimes," *Perspectives on Politics* 14, no. 1 (March 2016): 38–52; Holger Albrecht, "Does Coup-Proofing Work? Political-Military Relations in Authoritarian Regimes amid the Arab Uprisings," *Mediterranean Politics* 20, no. 1 (2015): 36–54; Kevin Koehler, "Political Militaries in Popular Uprisings: A Comparative Perspective on the Arab Spring," *International Political Science Review* 38, no. 3 (May 2016): 363–77; and Phillip Droz-Vincent, "The Military amidst Uprisings and Transitions in the Arab World," in *The New Middle East: Protest and Revolution in the Arab World*, ed. Fawaz Gerges (Cambridge: Cambridge Univ. Press, 2014), 180–208.

9. Holger Albrecht, "Authoritarian Transformation or Transition from Authoritarianism? Insights on Regime Change in Egypt," in *Arab Spring in Egypt: Revolution and*

Beyond, ed. Bahgat Korany and Rabab El-Mahdi (Cairo: American Univ. of Cairo Press, 2012), 252.

10. Joshua Stacher, "Blame the SCAF for Egypt's Problems," *Foreign Policy*, October 11, 2011, http://foreignpolicy.com/2011/10/11/blame-the-scaf-for-egypts-problems/; Amy Austin Holmes, "Egyptians Blame Military for Failures of Transition Period," *Ahram Online*, June 28, 2012, http://english.ahram.org.eg/NewsContent/1/64/46401/Egypt/Politics-/Egyptians-blame-military-for-failures-of-transitio.aspx; and Joshua Stacher, *Countries at the Crossroads 2012: Egypt* (Washington, DC: Freedom House, 2012), https://freedomhouse.org/sites/default/files/Egypt%20-%20FINAL.pdf.

11. Popular protests of over ten thousand people or more have removed forty-two leaders since 1980. See Beissinger, "Semblance of Democratic Revolution," 574.

12. Guillermo O'Donnell, Phillippe C. Schmitter, and Laurence Whitehead, vol. 4 of *Transitions from Authoritarian Rule: Tentative Conclusions about Uncertain Democracies*, (Baltimore: Johns Hopkins Univ. Press, 1986), 26–28.

13. Daniel H. Levine, "Paradigm Lost: Dependency to Democracy," *World Politics* 40, no. 3 (April 1998): 389–91.

14. Michael McFaul, "The Fourth Wave of Democracy and Dictatorship: Noncooperative Transitions in the Postcommunist World," *World Politics* 54, no. 2 (2002): 220–25; and Valerie Bunce, "Rethinking Recent Democratization: Lessons from the Postcommunist Experience," *World Politics* 55, no. 2 (January 2003): 171–79.

15. McFaul, "Fourth Wave," 226.

16. Bunce, "Rethinking Recent Democratization," 172.

17. Thomas Carothers, "The End of the Transition Paradigm," *Journal of Democracy* 13, no. 1 (January 2002): 6.

18. Carothers, "End of Transition Paradigm," 6–7.

19. Larry Diamond, "Thinking about Hybrid Regimes," *Journal of Democracy* 13, no. 2 (April 2002): 21–35; Marsha Pripstein Posusney, "Multi-party Elections in the Arab World: Institutional Engineering and Oppositional Strategies," *Studies in Comparative International Development* 26, no. 4 (2002): 34–62; Staffan I. Lindberg, *Democracy and Elections in Africa* (Baltimore: Johns Hopkins Univ. Press, 2006); Staffan I. Lindberg, *Democratization by Elections: A New Mode of Transition* (Baltimore: Johns Hopkins Univ. Press, 2009); Andreas Schedler, *Electoral Authoritarianism: The Dynamics of Unfree Competition* (Boulder, CO: Lynne Rienner, 2006); Lisa Blaydes, *Elections and Distributive Politics in Mubarak's Egypt* (Cambridge: Cambridge Univ. Press, 2011); Ellen Lust-Okar, "Elections under Authoritarianism: Preliminary Lessons from Jordan," *Democratization* 13, no. 3 (2006): 455–70; Jennifer Gandhi and Ellen Lust-Okar, "Elections under Authoritarianism," *Annual Review of Political Science* 12 (2009): 403–22; and Valerie Bunce and Sharon Wolchik, *Defeating Authoritarian Leaders in Postcommunist Countries* (Cambridge: Cambridge Univ. Press, 2010).

20. There are some notable exceptions. See Mark Beissinger, *Nationalist Mobilization and the Collapse of the Soviet State* (Cambridge: Cambridge Univ. Press, 2002); and Vincent Boudreau, *Resisting Dictatorship: Repression and Protest in Southeast Asia* (Cambridge: Cambridge Univ. Press 2004).

21. On included and excluded oppositions, see Ellen Lust-Okar, *Structuring Conflict in the Arab World* (Cambridge: Cambridge Univ. Press, 2005). For works that consider the opposition a unified bloc, see Bunce, "Rethinking Recent Democratization," 172.

22. See, for example, Andreas Schedler, "Nested Game of Democratization by Elections," *International Political Science Review* 23, no. 1 (2002): 103–22. Critiques of this perspective can be found in Lust-Okar, *Structuring Conflict*; Gandhi and Lust-Okar, "Elections under Authoritarianism," 403–22; and Lust, "Competitive Clientelism in the Middle East," *Journal of Democracy* 20, no. 3 (2009): 122–35.

23. Mona El-Ghobashy, "Egypt's Summer of Discontent," *Middle East Report Online*, September 18, 2013, http://merip.org/mero/mero091803; Mona El-Ghobashy, "Egypt Looks Ahead to Portentous Year," *Middle East Report Online*, February 2, 2005, http://merip.org/mero/mero020205; Manar Shorbagy, "Understanding Kefaya: The New Politics in Egypt," *Arab Studies Quarterly* 29, no. 1 (Winter 2007): 39–60.

24. For a comprehensive survey of these movements, see Dina Shahata, *'Awdat al-Siyasiyya: Al-Harakat al-Ihtijajat al-Jadida fi Misr* (Cairo: Center for Political and Strategic Studies, 2010).

25. Chalcraft, "Horizontalism," 6–11.

26. International Crisis Group, "Reforming Egypt."

27. Rabab El-Mahdi, "Enough! Egypt's Quest for Democracy," *Comparative Political Studies* 42, no. 8 (2009): 1011–39.

28. Joshua Stacher, "Parties Over: The Demise of Egypt's Opposition Parties," *British Journal of Middle Eastern Studies* 31, no. 2 (November 2004): 215–33.

29. International Crisis Group, "Reforming Egypt," 15.

30. It may appear confusing that the Muslim Brotherhood was the best organized opposition group in Egypt, which exposed its leaders and members to routine arrests and jail time (often at the hands of military court verdicts), but also was supportive of the regime's norms. Yet, both of these aspects are true. The Muslim Brotherhood would alert Mubarak's security forces about any planned mass mobilizations, police their members to keep their actions predictable, and run for elections. Many, inside the Brotherhood as well as in the press, used to joke that parliamentary elections were also the season of arrests. Jason Brownlee, "The Muslim Brothers: Egypt's Most Influential Pressure Group," *History Compass* 8, no. 5 (2010): 419–30. Steven Brooke's work on the Brotherhood's security cooperation with the regime, which began in the 1970s as it distributed health-care services, is another example of the group being systemic opposition. See Brooke, *Winning Hearts and Votes: Social Services and the Islamist Political Advantage* (Ithaca, NY: Cornell Univ. Press, 2019): 39–46.

31. Asef Bayat, "Revolution without Movement, Movement without Revolution: Comparing Islamic Activism in Iran and Egypt," *Comparative Studies in Society and History* 40, no. 1 (January 1998): 138–69.

32. Bayat, "Revolution without Movement," 169.

33. Dan Murphy, "Egypt Keeps Muslim Brotherhood Boxed In," *Christian Science Monitor*, June 7, 2005, https://www.csmonitor.com/2005/0607/p01s04-wome.html.

34. In addition to establishing new groups, there were also a number of books published in Arabic that were heavily anti-Mubarak, antiregime, and antisystemic opposition. See 'Abd al-Halim Qandil, *Didd al-Ra'is: Akhtar Hamlat Maqalat didd Hukm al-'A'ila* (Cairo: Dar Mirit, 2005); 'Abd al-Halim Qandil, *Al-Ayam al-Akhira* (Cairo: Dar al-Thaqafa al-Jadid, 2008); Ibrahim 'Issa, *Ladayya Aqwal Ukhra* (Cairo: Maktabat Madbuli, 2009); and Muhammad al-Sayyid Sa'id, *al-Intiqal al-Dimuqrati al-Muhtajaz* (Cairo: Dar Mirit, 2006).

35. Field notes, Cairo, July 20, 2005.

36. Maha Abdelrahman, "'With the Islamists?—Sometimes. With the State?—Never': Cooperation between the Left and Islamists in Egypt," *British Journal of Middle Eastern Studies* 36, no. 1 (April 2009): 37–54.

37. Joel Beinin and Hossam el-Hamalawy, "Strikes in Egypt Spread from Center of Gravity," *Middle East Report Online*, May 9, 2007, http://www.merip.org/mero/mero050907.

38. World Bank, "Most Improved Business Reformers in DB 2010," *Doing Business 2010*, http://www.doingbusiness.org/reforms/top-reformers-2010. It is also worth noting that the IMF also lauded Tunisia just prior to their revolution beginning. https://www.doingbusiness.org/en/reforms/top-reformers-2010.

39. Margaret Scobey, "Scenesetter for General Petraeus' Visit to Egypt," WikiLeaks, June 24, 2009, https://wikileaks.org/plusd/cables/09CAIRO1185_a.html.

40. Marsha Pripstein Posusney, *Labor and the State in Egypt* (New York: Columbia Univ. Press, 1997).

41. Beinin, *Workers and Thieves*, 7.

42. Joel Beinin, "A Worker's Social Movement on the Margins of the Global Neoliberal Order," in *Social Movements, Mobilization, and Contestation in the Middle East and North Africa*, ed. Joel Beinin and Frédéric Vairel (Stanford, CA: Stanford Univ. Press, 2011), 183.

43. Beinin, "Worker's Social Movement," 198–201.

44. El-Ghobashy, "Praxis."

45. Ketchley, *Egypt*, 49–57.

46. Robert Springborg, "Game Over: The Chance for Democracy in Egypt Is Lost," *Foreign Policy*, February 2, 2011, http://foreignpolicy.com/2011/02/02/game-over-the-chance-for-democracy-in-egypt-is-lost/.

47. "Brothers: We Will Not Participate in the January 25 Demonstrations," *al-Wafd*, January 20, 2011, https://alwafd.news/السياسي-الشارع/12821-الاخوان-لن-نشارك-فى-تظاهرات-25-يناير.

48. Tamim Elyan, "Parties Distance Themselves from Jan 25 Demos as Preparations Announced," *Daily News Egypt*, January 21, 2011, https://dailynewsegypt.com/2011/01/21/parties-distance-themselves-from-jan-25-demos-as-preparations-announced/.

49. Shahata, 'Awdat al-Siyasiyya.

50. El-Ghobashy, "Praxis."

51. Hazem Kandil, "The Muslim Brotherhood Failed in Egypt Because It Was Inept, Incompetent and Out of Touch," *The Conversation*, February 27, 2014, http://theconversation.com/the-muslim-brotherhood-failed-in-egypt-because-it-was-inept-incompetent-and-out-of-touch-23738.

52. Steve Coll, "Mubarak and the Generals," *New Yorker*, January 28, 2011, https://www.newyorker.com/news/news-desk/mubarak-and-the-generals.

53. "Husni Mubarak's Speech: Full Text," *Guardian*, February 1, 2011, https://www.theguardian.com/world/2011/feb/02/president-hosni-mubarak-egypt-speech.

54. "And Now, 'Omar Suleiman Posters," *Middle East Institute Editor's Blog*, September 2, 2010, http://mideasti.blogspot.com/2010/09/and-now-omar-suleiman-posters.html.

55. Ambassador Francis J. Ricciardone, "Presidential Succession in Egypt," WikiLeaks, May 14, 2007, https://wikileaks.org/plusd/cables/07CAIRO1417_a.html.

56. Ian Black, "Omar Suleiman, Mubarak Deputy Who May Be Key to Resolving Egypt Protests," *Guardian*, February 1, 2011, https://www.theguardian.com/world/2011/feb/01/omar-suleiman-mubarak-egypt-protests?intcmp=239.

57. Nadia Idle and Alex Nunns, eds., *Tweets from Tahrir* (New York: OR Books, 2011), 70.

58. Ahmed Kadry, "Egypt: The Story So Far," *Daily News Egypt*, February 7, 2011, https://dailynewsegypt.com/2011/02/07/egypt-the-story-so-far/.

59. "Clinton Calls Suleiman, Urges Probe of Violence," Reuters, February 2, 2011, http://af.reuters.com/article/egyptNews/idAFN0226375820110202; and Office of the Vice President, "Readout of the Vice President's Call with Egyptian Vice President Omar Soliman," press release, February 8, 2011, http://www.whitehouse.gov/the-press-office/2011/02/08/readout-vice-presidents-call-egyptian-vice-president-omar-soliman.

60. The elders were a collection of independent, respectable social figures that went to the square and talked to the demonstrators. The self-appointed group assumed they had a credibility to negotiate on behalf of the protesters that they did not in fact have.

61. This also marked the first time that regime figures met with Brotherhood members publicly since the group's reintroduction to the political sphere in the 1970s under Sadat.

62. Samer Shehata, "Dialogue of the Deaf," *Foreign Policy*, February 8, 2011, http://foreignpolicy.com/2011/02/08/dialogue-of-the-deaf-2/.

63. Jack Shenker and Brian Whitaker, "The Muslim Brotherhood Uncovered," *Guardian*, February 8, 2011, https://www.theguardian.com/world/2011/feb/08/egypt-muslim-brotherhood-uncovered.

64. "Brotherhood Engaged in Secret Deals with Ousted Regime," *Al-Masri Al-Youm*, March 31, 2011, http://web.archive.org/web/20110403052423/http://www.almasryalyoum.com/en/node/381513.

65. Muhammad Habib, interview by author, Cairo, March 23, 2011.

66. Joel Beinin, "Egypt's Workers Rise Up," *Nation*, February 17, 2011, https://www.thenation.com/article/egypts-workers-rise/.

67. Beinin, *Workers and Thieves*, 109.

68. Bunce, "Rethinking Recent Democratization," 189.

69. Hesham Sallam, "Elections in the Midst of Revolution," *Jadaliyya*, November 28, 2011, http://www.jadaliyya.com/pages/index/3304/elections-in-the-midst-of-revolution.

70. Jason Brownlee, "Egypt's Incomplete Revolution: The Challenge of Post-Mubarak Authoritarianism," *Jadaliyya*, July 5, 2011, http://www.jadaliyya.com/pages/index/2059/egypts-incomplete-revolution_the-challenge-of-post.

71. Hesham Sallam, "Striking Back at Egyptian Workers," *Middle East Report* 259 (Summer 2011): 20–25.

72. Ketchley, *Egypt*, 111–13.

73. Hesham Sallam, "Morsy, the Coup and the Revolution: Reading between the Red Lines," *Jadaliyya*, August 15, 2012, http://www.jadaliyya.com/Details/26882.

74. "Inqath Masr min al-halak wa al-damar Lan ya'tee al-abathad al-Geish wa al-Sha'b," *Al-Destor*, August 11, 2012, https://web.archive.org/web/20120821034014/http://onaeg.com/wp-content/uploads/2012/08/اليوم-مصادراتها-تم-التي-الدستور-جريدة-من-الأولى-الصفحة.jpg.

75. Dina Ezzat, "Egypt's SCAF Holding Meetings in President's Absence: Military Sources," *Ahram Online*, February 20, 2013, http://english.ahram.org.eg/NewsContent/1/64/65226/Egypt/Politics-/Egypts-SCAF-holding-meetings-in-presidents-absence.aspx.

76. Egyptian Armed Forces, Facebook, https://www.facebook.com/Egyptian.Armed.Forces. This site has since been removed from Facebook.

77. Ayman Mohyeldin (@aymanM), "The post denying a 'coup' is on FB page that appears close to Egypt's Military but not the official Armed Forces Spokesman's page @NBCNews," Twitter, February 25, 2013, 9:51 a.m., https://twitter.com/AymanM/status/306053798500130816.

78. Korva Coleman, "As Egypt Grows More Lawless, Army Chief Warns against 'State Collapse,'" NPR, January 29, 2013, https://www.npr.org/sections/thetwo-way/2013/01/29/170546905/as-egypt-grows-more-lawless-army-chief-warns-against-state-collapse.

79. "Profile: Egypt's Tamarod Protest Movement," BBC, July 1, 2013, https://www.bbc.com/news/world-middle-east-23131953.

80. Salma Abdullah, "Tamarod Surpasses 22 Million Signatures," *Daily News Egypt*, June 29, 2013, https://dailynewsegypt.com/2013/06/29/tamarod-surpasses-22-million-signatures/.

81. "Egypt Opinion Polls Reveal Dissatisfaction with Morsi," *Ahram Online*, July 2, 2013, http://english.ahram.org.eg/NewsContent/1/152/75491/Egypt/Morsi,-one-year-on/Egypt-opinion-polls-reveal-dissatisfaction-with-Mo.aspx.

82. Ketchley, *Egypt*, 104.

83. "Profile: Egypt's Tamarod Protest Movement," BBC.

84. Yasmine Saleh and Paul Taylor, "Mahmoud Badr, Tamarod Protest Leader, 'Owns the Streets' in Egypt," Reuters, July 7, 2013, http://www.huffingtonpost.com/2013/07/08/mahmoud-badr-tamarod-protest-leader-egypt_n_3559487.html.

85. Mike Giglio, "A Cairo Conspiracy," *Daily Beast*, July 12, 2013, http://www.thedailybeast.com/a-cairo-conspiracy.

86. "Egypt's Tamarod Co-founder Detained 15 Days for Joining 'Outlawed Group,'" *Ahram Online*, January 11, 2016, http://english.ahram.org.eg/NewsContent/1/64/180704/Egypt/Politics-/Egypts-Tamarod-cofounder-detained--days-for-joinin.aspx.

87. Kirkpatrick, *Into the Hands*, 162–64.

88. Joshua Stacher, "Establishment Mursi," *Middle East Report* 265 (Winter 2012): 10–11.

89. "Obama: 'Everyone Must Show Restraint' in Egypt," *Ahram Online*, July 1, 2013, http://english.ahram.org.eg/NewsContent/1/64/75416/Egypt/Politics-/Obama-Everybody-must-show-restraint-in-Egypt.aspx.

90. Shaimaa Fayed and Yasmine Saleh, "Millions Flood Egypt's Streets to Demand Mursi Quit," Reuters, June 29, 2013, https://www.reuters.com/article/us-egypt-protests/millions-flood-egypts-streets-to-demand-mursi-quit-idUSBRE95Q0NO20130630.

91. Jack Brown, "On Those Protest Numbers in Egypt," *Counterpunch*, July 18, 2013, https://www.counterpunch.org/2013/07/18/on-those-protest-numbers-in-egypt/.

92. "CNN Egypt Reporter Ben Wedeman Sees Broadcast Cut Short as Military Confiscates Camera," streamed live on July 5, 2013, YouTube video, 0:46, https://www.youtube.com/watch?v=OnuDk7D6wbA.

93. SCAF issued a statement on July 1, 2013, that "the Armed Forces repeats its call to respond to the people's demands and gives everyone a 48-hour deadline to carry the burden of these historic circumstances." See "Armed Forces Warns of Intervention in 48 Hours," *Mada Masr*, July 1, 2013, https://www.madamasr.com/en/2013/07/01/news/u/armed-forces-warns-of-intervention-in-48-hours/.

94. Hesham Sallam, "Down with Military Rule . . . Again?" *Mada Masr*, July 2, 2013, https://www.madamasr.com/en/2013/07/02/feature/politics/down-with-military-rule-again/.

95. Michael O'Hanlon and Tamara Wittes, "A Popular Impeachment in Egypt," *USA Today*, July 4, 2013, https://www.usatoday.com/story/opinion/2013/07/04/michael-ohanlon-and-tamara-wittes-on-what-next-in-egypt/2489419/.

96. The Brotherhood's actions continued to reinforce SCAF after the fall of Mubarak. The group's decision-making body, the Guidance Council, became a reliable supporter of SCAF. The Brotherhood's communiqués have been filled with praise for SCAF's announcements. The Brotherhood also sprang into action when sectarianism turned violent. For example, when Muslims attacked the Saint Mina and George Coptic Church in the village of Soul, south of Cairo, in March 2011, the Brotherhood dispatched teams to lead reconciliation talks between Copts and Muslims in the area. They also supported the army's goal of "national unity" through outreach to the Coptic Church hierarchy and meetings with Christian youth. The general guide, Muhammad Badi', sent his regards to the Coptic pope after the pontiff's brief treatment in a hospital. All these instances reveal the Brotherhood being a stabilizing force after the uprising disrupted the state's institutions.

2. Electoral Recalibration?

1. SCAF "electionized" the transition process by calling the population to national polls five times in fifteen months. They used elections to guide the transition and thereby forced the citizens to engage through voting.

2. The Carter Center, *Preliminary Report on All Three Phases of the People's Assembly Elections*, January 24, 2012, https://www.cartercenter.org/resources/pdfs/news/peace_publications/election_reports/egypt-peoples-assembly-elections.pdf.

3. See Mona El-Ghobashy, "Egypt's Paradoxical Elections," *Middle East Report* 238 (Spring 2005), http://merip.org/mer/mer238/egypts-paradoxical-elections; Jason Brownlee, *Authoritarianism in the Age of Democratization* (Cambridge: Cambridge Univ. Press, 2007); Brownlee, "Executive Elections in the Arab World: When and How Do They Matter?" *Comparative Political Studies* 44, no. 7 (2011): 807–28; Samer Shehata, "Inside an Egyptian Parliamentary Campaign," in *Political Participation in the Middle East*, ed. Ellen Lust-Okar and Saloua Zerhouni (Boulder, CO: Lynne Rienner, 2008); Mona El-Ghobashy, "The Dynamics of Egypt's Elections," *Middle East Report Online*, September 29, 2010, http://merip.org/mero/mero092910; El-Ghobashy, "Liquidation"; and Tarek Masoud, *Making Islam Count: Religion and Party Politics in the Arab World* (Cambridge: Cambridge Univ. Press, 2013).

4. Shenker, *Egyptians*, 5.

5. Sallam, "Elections."

6. Sheila Carapico has explored elections as theatrical performance in her most recent book. See Sheila Carapico, *Political Aid and Arab Activism: Democracy Promotion, Justice, and Representation* (Cambridge: Cambridge Univ. Press, 2013): 63–75.

7. Mouin Rabbani, "Year Three," *Jadaliyya*, December 18, 2012, http://www.jadaliyya.com/Details/27646/Year-Three.

8. Middle-range theory aims at "being general and parsimonious but that appreciates the need to confront empirical complexity." See Daniel Ziblatt, "Of Course

Generalize, but How? Returning to Middle-Range Theory in Comparative Politics," *APSA-CP Symposium* 17, no. 2 (2006): 8–11.

9. Exemplary of this body of literature is Gandhi and Lust-Okar, "Elections under Authoritarianism." Other works beyond those mentioned elsewhere in this chapter include Daron Acemoglu and James A. Robinson, *Economic Origins of Dictatorship and Democracy* (Cambridge: Cambridge Univ. Press, 2005); Lindberg, *Democracy and Elections*; Lindberg, *Democratization by Elections*; Lust-Okar, *Structuring Conflict*; Carles Boix and Milan Svolik, "The Foundations of Limited Authoritarian Government: Institutions and Power-Sharing in Dictatorships," *Social Science Research Network*, September 24, 2011, https://papers.ssrn.com/sol3/papers.cfm?abstract_id=1352065; Jennifer Gandhi and Adam Przeworski, "Cooperation, Cooptation, and Rebellion under Dictatorship," *Economics and Politics* 18, no. 1 (2006): 1–26; Jennifer Gandhi, *Political Institutions under Dictatorship* (Cambridge: Cambridge Univ. Press, 2008); Bunce and Wolchik, *Defeating Authoritarian Leaders*; Schedler, *Electoral Authoritarianism*; and Beatriz Magaloni, *Voting for Autocracy: Hegemonic Party Survival and Its Demise in Mexico* (Cambridge: Cambridge Univ. Press, 2008).

10. Jillian Schwedler, *Faith in Moderation: Islamist Parties in Jordan and Yemen* (Cambridge: Cambridge Univ. Press, 2007), 34–67; also see articles by Graham Usher, Ranjit Singh, Jillian Schwedler and Laryssa Chomiak, Mona El-Ghobashy, and Joshua Stacher in *Middle East Report* 238 (Spring 2005).

11. Posusney, "Multiparty Elections," 94; Brownlee, "Executive Elections," 807–28; Brownlee, *Authoritarianism*; Blaydes, *Elections and Distributive Politics*; Lust, "Competitive Clientelism," 123; Lisa Wedeen, *Peripheral Visions: Publics, Power, and Performance in Yemen* (Chicago: Univ. of Chicago Press, 2008), 69–81.

12. Lust, "Competitive Clientelism," 124, 126.

13. Lindberg, *Democratization by Elections*, xxi.

14. Lindberg, *Democratization by Elections*, 9. Italics in original.

15. Amel Ahmed, *Democracy and the Politics of Electoral System Choice: Engineering Electoral Dominance* (Cambridge: Cambridge Univ. Press, 2012): 64–88.

16. Lindberg, *Democratization by Elections*, 13. He notes that Zimbabwe, Ethiopia, Russia, and "perhaps" Venezuela are cases where elections produced autocratization.

17. Lindberg, *Democratization by Elections*, 13.

18. Bunce and Wolchik, *Defeating Authoritarian Leaders*, 95.

19. Otpor was the beneficiary of $2.8 million from the National Endowment of Democracy between 1998 and 2000. Other groups and foreign governments supplied additional grants and resources to the Serbian opposition. Most notably, the Open Society Institute, Rockefeller Brothers, Mott, and the US and EU governments provided assistance. See Bunce and Wolchik, *Defeating Authoritarian Leaders*.

20. Bunce and Wolchik, *Defeating Authoritarian Leaders*, 101.

21. Bunce and Wolchik, *Defeating Authoritarian Leaders*, 109.

22. Bunce and Wolchik, *Defeating Authoritarian Leaders*, 110.

23. Dorothy Solinger, "Ending One-Party Dominance: Korea, Taiwan, Mexico," *Journal of Democracy* 12, no. 1 (2001): 30.

24. Solinger, "Ending One-Party Dominance," 31.

25. Andreas Schedler, "Mexico's Victory: The Democratic Revelation," *Journal of Democracy* 11, no. 4 (2000): 6.

26. Solinger, "Ending One-Party Dominance," 39. Italics in original.

27. McFaul, "Fourth Wave," 222–25.

28. Although voters had more of a choice and the polls were free of state interference, turnout was low in the Shura Council elections. Some argued that voters suffered from "elections fatigue." See 'Abd al-Mun'im Sa'id, "al-Arhaq al-Intikhabi," *al-Ahram*, February 4, 2012.

29. Voter turnout under Mubarak was abysmally low even by standards of an autocracy in the developing world. For example, Springborg wrote that in an Alexandrian by-election in 1984, less than 10 percent of registered voters turned out. See Robert Springborg, *Mubarak's Egypt: The Fragmentation of the Political Order* (Boulder, CO: Westview, 1989), 163. In more recent elections, the official turnout in the first multicandidate presidential election in 2005 was 23.5 percent, which would still be one of the lowest turnout rates in the world if the figure is true. In the final parliamentary election of Mubarak's tenure in December 2010, it is estimated that around 5 percent of the population voted despite the state claiming that 27.5 percent did. See Reuters, "Rights Groups Contest Egypt Official Vote Turnout," *Khaleej Times*, November 29, 2010, https://www.khaleejtimes.com/article/20101129/ARTICLE/311299952/1016.

30. Joshua Stacher, "The Anatomy of Succession: Egypt's Presidential Election," *Review of African Political Economy* 35, no. 116 (2008): 301–2.

31. One example among many is reported in Joshua Stacher, "Damanhour by Hook or by Crook," *Middle East Report* 238 (2006): 26–27. Elections routinely invited the deployment of state-hired "thugs" and systematic violence. See "Egypt's Elections 'Fraudulent,' Says Rights Group," *Egypt Independent*, November 29, 2010.

32. El-Ghobashy, "Liquidation."

33. Aspinall, *Opposing Suharto*, 272; and Mona El-Ghobashy, "The Metamorphosis of the Egyptian Muslim Brothers," *International Journal of Middle East Studies* 37, no. 3 (2005): 373–95.

34. 'Isam al-'Aryan, "Limadha Asawwit bi-'Na'm' li-l-Ta'dilat al-Dasturiyya," *al-Sharuq*, March 12, 2011, http://www.shorouknews.com/columns/view.aspx?cdate=12032011&id=9f395480-2766-4a0e-8c12-6febbab43e6f.

35. I was the recipient of such an SMS-text while on a research trip during the March 2011 referendum.

36. Amr Hamzawy ['Amr Hamzawi], "Istifta' al-Ghad," *al-Sharuq*, March 18, 2011, http://www.shorouknews.com/columns/view.aspx?cdate=18032011&id=cb5530c4-dfd1-49d3-80be-6d4c5fc92e04.

37. Khalid Fahmy, interview by author, Cairo, March 17, 2011.

38. Fahmi Huwaidi, "al-Istifta' Kashif Azmat al-Nukhba al-Masriyya," *al-Sharuq*, March 22, 2011, http://www.shorouknews.com/columns/view.aspx?cdate=22032011&id=80835593-35b4-482b-bd0f-ea6967119bbe.

39. Ahmad Salama, "Raba'a al-Dimuqratiyya," *al-Sharuq*, March 21, 2011, http://www.shorouknews.com/columns/view.aspx?cdate=21032011&id=006349f0-7137-44f2-ab42-2acbf9733b05.

40. Wa'il Qandil, "La . . . La . . . La," *al-Sharuq*, March 17, 2011, http://www.shorouknews.com/columns/view.aspx?cdate=17032011&id=9885c664-1688-4c4b-886a-da139f215e50.

41. Maggie Michael, "Constitutional Amendments Approved in Egypt Referendum," *Star*, March 20, 2011, https://www.thestar.com/news/world/2011/03/20/constitutional_amendments_approved_in_egypt_referendum.html.

42. This was distinctly apparent in Cairo's Bulaq al-Dakrur, where citizens thanked the army for securing the vote and for being "one hand" with the people.

43. Joshua Stacher, "Egypt without Mubarak," *Middle East Report Online*, April 7, 2011, http://www.merip.org/mero/mero040711.

44. Wael Eskandar, interview by author (Skype), November 11, 2012.

45. The fine for an offense was $83,000 and included the possibility of jail time.

46. Sallam, "Striking Back."

47. There are not exact numbers for how many military trials were used against civilians during Mubarak's presidency. Therefore, only estimates based on reporting can be made. According to data I collected, there were between 2,000 and 2,500 military trials against civilians under Mubarak. If this is accurate, SCAF's first ten months of leading the transition represents nearly a sixfold increase in military trials against civilians compared to Mubarak's nearly thirty-year tenure as president.

48. Joshua Stacher, *Countries at the Crossroads 2012: Egypt* (Washington, DC: Freedom House, 2012), https://freedomhouse.org/sites/default/files/Egypt%20-%20FINAL.pdf.

49. Wael Eskandar, "Year of the SCAF: A Time-line of Mounting Repression," *Ahram Online*, February 11, 2012, http://english.ahram.org.eg/NewsContent/1/64/34046/Egypt/Politics-/Year-of-the-SCAF-a-timeline-of-mounting-repression.aspx.

50. Field observations from Tahrir Square, Cairo, July 8, 2011.

51. Egypt used a proportional representation (PR) system in the 1984 legislative elections as well as a split PR-individual candidacy system for the 1987 legislative elections. The Supreme Constitutional Court struck down the constitutionality of both systems in separate rulings. Since 1990, legislative elections have been entirely based on individual candidacy. On September 20, 2011, SCAF amended the People's Assembly law (Law 28/1972), reinstituting a split PR-individual candidacy system. Then, five days later, they reamended the law with two-thirds of the seats to be determined by PR and one-third to be based on individual candidacy. There were 508 seats at stake. SCAF retained

Mubarak's old prerogative of appointing ten figures. Of the 498 seats on offer, 332 were be determined by PR, and the remaining 166 came from individual candidacy.

52. Zeinab El-Gundy, "Political Parties and Powers to Approve El-Selmi Document, on Condition It Is Amended," *Ahram Online*, November 16, 2011, http://english.ahram.org.eg/NewsContent/1/64/26754/Egypt/Politics-/Political-parties-and-powers-to-approve-ElSelmi-do.aspx.

53. Dunya Sallam, Mustafa Hashim, and Ranya Rabi'a, "Khilaf bayn al-Ahzab 'ala Wathiqat al-Silmi wa-l-Musharaka fi Milyuniyya Taslim al-Sulta," *al-Sharuq*, November 14, 2011, http://www.shorouknews.com/news/view.aspx?cdate=14112011&id=fa843ebc-58ef-4672-a5de-fca65daa948c.

54. Eskandar, interview.

55. Hesham Sallam, "Post-Elections Egypt: Revolution or Pact?" *Jadaliyya*, February 10, 2012, http://www.jadaliyya.com/Details/25249/Post-Elections-Egypt-Revolution-or-Pact.

56. Eskandar, interview.

57. Anthony Shadid, "Egypt Military Tries to Woo Wider Public to Keep Power," *New York Times*, November 25, 2011, http://www.nytimes.com/2011/11/26/world/middleeast/egypt-military-tries-to-woo-wider-public-beyond-protesters.html.

58. Ellis Goldberg, "The Missing Ikhwan and an Electorate Split in Three," *Nasr al-Nasr* (blog), June 3, 2012, http://nisralnasr.blogspot.com/2012/06/presidential-elections-case-of-missing.html.

59. Wahid 'Abd al-Magid, "al-Intikhabat al-Barlmaniyya . . . wa-l-Fursa al-Akhira," *al-Ahram*, November 14, 2011, http://www.ahram.org.eg/archive/Issues-Views/News/112944.aspx (article no longer available).

60. Fahmi Huwaidi, "al-Intikhabat Hiya al-Hal," *al-Sharuq*, November 23, 2011, http://www.shorouknews.com/columns/view.aspx?cdate=23112011&id=73be389f-3b87-49f2-9e6b-1cdcb75e9ed4.

61. 'Amr al-Shubki, "Bitanat al-Intikhabat," *al-Masri al-Yum*, November 20, 2011, http://www.almasryalyoum.com/news/details/211622.

62. Sallam, "Post-Elections Egypt."

63. Shadid, "Egypt Military."

64. "Turnout for Shura Council Polls Remains Weak," *Egypt Independent*, February 15, 2012, http://www.egyptindependent.com/turnout-shura-council-polls-remains-weak/.

65. In August 2008, an electrical shortage caused a fire to break out in the Shura Council. As plumes of smoke rose from the building, dozens of fire trucks and military helicopters battled the flames. People passing by along the street stopped and watched. Riot police separated them from the fire. Hundreds gathered and took photos. One Egyptian told the media, "I'm just sorry Parliament wasn't in session." Maggie Michael, "Egypt Parliament Fire Fuels Scorn of Government," Associated Press, August 22, 2008.

66. Sa‘id, “al-Arhaq al-Intikhabi.”

67. ‘Amr Khafaga, “al-‘Abur ila al-Jumhuriyya al-Thaniya,” *al-Sharuq*, May 20, 2012, http://www.shorouknews.com/columns/view.aspx?cdate=20052012&id=ee7c46e7-5c08-4f0d-b4f2-09677e227957.

68. Samir al-Sayid, “al-Aswani: Arfad Shafiq wa-Mursi . . . wa-l-Qabul bi-‘Nasf al-‘Ama’ Sinhi al-Thawra,” *al-Ahram*, June 2, 2012, http://gate.ahram.org.eg/News/215011.aspx.

69. Usama al-Ghazali Harb, “Fi Intizar al-Ra’is,” *al-Ahram*, May 16, 2012, http://www.ahram.org.eg/archive/Issues-Views/News/149541.aspx (article no longer available).

70. Goldberg, “Missing Ikhwan.”

71. Wa’il Qandil, “al-Sumit Taswit didd al-Thawra,” *al-Sharuq*, June 2, 2012, http://www.shorouknews.com/columns/view.aspx?cdate=02062012&id=e817ec6e-b8fa-464a-9557-ac4febe6eb0d.

72. Fahmi Huwaidi, “Akbar Ghalat,” *al-Sharuq*, June 17, 2012, http://www.shorouknews.com/columns/view.aspx?cdate=16062012&id=654314a1-3d86-4871-8b91-0e601ae84129.

73. Al-Sayid, “al-Aswany”; Muhammad Shuman, “Fi Mushru‘iyya al-Muqata‘a,” *al-Yum al-Sab‘a*, June 10, 2012, http://www.youm7.com/story/2012/6/10/فى-مشروعية-المقاطعة/701602; and Nasir ‘Iraq, “al-Muqata‘a . . . Hiya al-Hal,” *al-Yum al-Sab‘a*, June 12, 2012, http://www.youm7.com/story/2012/6/12/المقاطعة-هى-الحل/701602.

74. Ashraf Khalil (journalist), interview by author, Cairo, June 12, 2012.

75. Ahmed Shafiq rally attended by author, Cairo, June 13, 2012.

76. Justice Minister ‘Abd al-‘Abd al-Hamid issued a decree on June 4, just four days after the state of emergency, which had been in effect for thirty-one years, was lifted. Decree No. 4991 was published on June 13 and claimed that military police and intelligence officers could have “judicial arresting authority for crimes commuted by non-military personnel.” See “Egypt: Military Power Grab Creates Conditions for Abuse,” Human Rights Watch, June 21, 2012, https://www.hrw.org/news/2012/06/21/egypt-military-power-grab-creates-conditions-abuse.

77. Roberts, “Revolution That Wasn’t.”

78. This was particularly contradictory because one Muslim Brotherhood candidate (Khayrat al-Shatir) was barred from the presidential election because he had been convicted during Mubarak’s presidency.

79. The parliamentary elections of 2011 were under a mixed proportional representation and individual candidacy model. Two-thirds were reserved for party lists and one-third for individual candidates. This type of model had been declared unconstitutional following the 1990 elections. All parliamentary elections since 1995 followed an individual candidacy model.

80. Shafiq campaign coordinator in Gharbiyya, interview by author, Mahalla al-Kubra, June 14, 2012.

81. "Relive Vote Count in 1st Round of Egypt Presidential Race: How Morsi and Shafiq Moved On," *Ahram Online*, May 25, 2012, http://english.ahram.org.eg/News/42755.aspx.

82. Brotherhood member of parliament and Mursi campaign coordinator in Minufiyya, interview by author, Shibin al-Kum, June 14, 2012.

83. Author witnessed this exchange, Talla, Minufiyya, June 17, 2012.

84. Author witnessed this exchange, Talla, Minufiyya, June 17, 2012.

85. "The Carter Center Releases Preliminary Statement on Second Round of Egypt's Presidential Election," press release, Carter Center, June 18, 2012, https://www.cartercenter.org/news/pr/egypt-prelim-061912.html.

86. Jason Brownlee, "2012 Egyptian Presidential Post-Election Report: President Asterisk," *Monkey Cage*, June 25, 2012, http://themonkeycage.org/2012/06/2012-egyptian-presidential-post-election-report-president-asterisk/.

87. Mursi took 13,230,131 votes (51.3 percent) to Shafiq's 12,347,380 votes (48.27 percent). Despite a boycott effort by some segments of the revolutionary movements, 843,252 (3 percent) of the ballots were invalid. Usually spoiled ballots account for 1 percent.

88. Marwa Awad and Edmund Blair, "Military Man Shafiq Has Egypt Presidency in Sights," *al-Arabiya News*, June 15, 2012, https://www.alarabiya.net/articles/2012/06/15/220786.html.

89. David Kirkpatrick, "Egypt Is Counting on Worries of Elites," *New York Times*, May 27, 2012, http://www.nytimes.com/2012/05/28/world/middleeast/ahmed-shafik-counting-on-egyptian-elites-fears.html.

90. Kandil, *Soldiers, Spies*, 235.

91. Raymond Hinnebusch, *Egyptian Politics under Sadat: The Post-populist Development of an Authoritarian-Modernizing State* (Cambridge: Cambridge Univ. Press, 1985), 120–28.

92. Eskandar, "Year of the SCAF."

93. This process of more deeply entrenching the military into the fabric of Egyptian politics continues nearly nine years after the uprising. In February 2019, Parliament introduced amendments to protect the role of the armed forces as the "guardian and protector" of the Egyptian state. The new proposed amendments to the constitution also continue to allow the military to try civilians in military courts and enshrine SCAF's "veto" power in the president's ability to appoint a minister of defense. See "A Look at Proposed Amendments to Egypt's Constitution," Associated Press, February 14, 2019, https://apnews.com/0496eac8134840e89295dabbfbf50bfa.

94. William R. Liddle, "Indonesia's Democratic Opening," *Government and Opposition* 34, no. 1 (January 1999): 94–116.

95. Aspinall, *Opposing Suharto*; and Bunce and Wolchik, *Defeating Authoritarian Leaders*.

96. Ayesha Siddiqa, *Military Inc.: Inside Pakistan's Military Economy* (London: Pluto Press, 2007).

97. Hesham Sallam, "Egypt: Transition in the Midst of Revolution," in *Elections and Democratization in the Middle East: The Tenacious Search for Freedom, Justice, and Dignity*, ed. Mahmoud Hamad and Khalil al-Anani (London: Palgrave Macmillan, 2014): 35–66.

98. Sallam, "Post-Elections Egypt."

99. "Jimmy Carter Warns Egypt 'Stands on the Precipice,'" *Guardian*, May 17, 2014, https://www.theguardian.com/world/2014/may/17/jimmy-carter-egypt-election-sisi-president-precipice.

100. Hossam Bahgat, "Anatomy of an Election," *Mada Masr*, March 14, 2016, https://www.madamasr.com/en/2016/03/14/feature/politics/anatomy-of-an-election/.

101. In April 2019, Parliament initiated changes to the constitution to allow a president to completely bypass two four-year term limits. Al-Sisi's 596-member Parliament extended two presidential terms from four to six years. Then, Parliament applied that change to al-Sisi's current term, which meant that it will end in 2024, not 2022. Given the change, al-Sisi was also green-lighted to run for another term in 2024. Should al-Sisi follow through on this, he will be Egypt's president for sixteen years, with his presidency ending in 2030. Opposition might not have been mobilized in the streets, but online sites offered a space to debate. In response, the state in Egypt blocked more than thirty-four thousand websites in an attempt to counter the #Void campaign against the amendments. The public saw the amendments for the first time on a Tuesday (April 16, 2019) when Parliament voted on them. They were put to a national referendum days later on April 19–21, 2019. Official turnout produced a "yes" vote of 88.83 percent, with 44 percent of the electorate participating (twenty-seven million). Few believe this figure. Perhaps the biggest takeaway was that invisible opposition produced three million "no" votes. See "Egypt Filters 34,000 Domains in a Bid to Block Opposition Campaign Platform," Netblocks, April 15 2019, https://netblocks.org/reports/egypt-filters-34000-domains-in-bid-to-block-opposition-campaign-platform-7eA1blBp.

102. Shahira Amin, "Proposal to Extend Sisi's Term Sparks Controversy in Egypt," *Al-Monitor*, August 17, 2017, https://www.al-monitor.com/pulse/originals/2017/08/egypt-parliament-proposal-amend-extend-sisi-term-controversy.html.

103. Shahira Amin, "Slew of Strange Bills Brings More Controversy for Egypt's Parliament," *Al-Monitor*, May 24, 2017, http://www.al-monitor.com/pulse/originals/2017/05/egypt-parliament-controversy-bills-effective-economy-poor.html.

3. State Violence as Life

1. *Egypt Independent*, December 19, 2011, http://www.almasryalyoum.com/en/node/557636 (article no longer available).

2. Mayy El Sheikh, "Egypt's Military Leader Promises a Fair Election," *New York Times*, May 16, 2012, https://www.nytimes.com/2012/05/17/world/middleeast/egypt-military-leader-tantawi-promises-fair-vote.html.

3. Videos and images of the January 25 uprising and its aftermath are stored on a digital archive called the 858 Archive. Please see this website for crowdsourced videos of different events: https://858.ma/grid/title.

4. Jennifer Earl, "Tanks, Tear Gas, and Taxes: Toward a Theory of Movement Repression," *Sociological Theory* 21, no. 1 (March 2003): 44–68.

5. Laleh Khalili, "Thinking about Violence," *International Journal of Middle Eastern Studies* 45, no. 4 (2013): 791; and Laleh Khalili and Jillian Schwedler, eds., *Policing and Prisons in the Middle East: Formations of Coercion* (London: Hurst, 2010).

6. An illuminating example of this kind of scholarship is Daniel Neep's work, which shows how violence forged state making in Syria. Daniel Neep, *Occupying Syria under the French Mandate* (Cambridge: Cambridge Univ. Press, 2014). His research joins Charles Tilly's work about how violence aids the process of state building. Charles Tilly, "War Making and State Making as Organized Crime," in *Bringing the State Back*, ed. Peter Evans, Dietrich Rueschemeyer, and Theda Skocpol (Cambridge: Cambridge Univ. Press, 1985), 167–87.

7. Nicola Pratt and Dina Rezk, "Securitizing the Muslim Brotherhood: State Violence and Authoritarianism in Egypt after the Arab Spring," *Security Dialogue* 50, no. 3 (2019): 1–18, https://doi.org/10.1177/0967010619830043.

8. Christian Davenport, "State Repression and Political Order," *Annual Review of Political Science* 10, no. 1 (2007): 1–23.

9. In the words of Hannah Arendt, "No one engaged in thought about history and politics can remain unaware of the enormous role violence has always played in human affairs, and it is at first glance rather surprising that violence has been singled out so seldom for special consideration." Arendt, *On Violence* (New York: Harcourt, 1969), 8.

10. Nazih Ayubi, *Overstating the Arab State: Politics and Society in the Middle East*, (London: Tauris, 1995), 23.

11. According to Freedom House rankings, states in the Middle East and North Africa region include twenty-one countries and 395 million people, but the region is only 2 percent free. The next lowest-ranking region is sub-Saharan Africa, which includes thirty states, 901 million people, and is 13 percent free. See "Middle East and North Africa," Freedom House, https://freedomhouse.org/regions/middle-east-and-north-africa.

12. Arendt, *On Violence*, 56.

13. James Ron, *Frontiers and Ghettos: State Violence in Serbia and Israel* (Berkeley: Univ. of California Press, 2003): 15.

14. Joshua Stacher, *Adaptable Autocrats: Regime Power in Egypt and Syria* (Stanford: Stanford Univ. Press, 2012): 44.

15. Charles Tilly, *The Politics of Collective Violence* (Cambridge: Cambridge Univ. Press, 2003), 27.

16. Wedeen, *Peripheral Visions*, 67–102.

17. Eva Bellin, "The Robustness of Authoritarianism in the Middle East: Exceptionalism in Comparative Perspective," *Comparative Politics* 36, no. 2 (January 2004): 144–45.

18. "Egyptian Revolution Cost at Least 846 Lives," CBS News, April 19, 2011, https://www.cbsnews.com/news/egyptian-revolution-cost-at-least-846-lives/.

19. George Derpanopoulos, Erica Frantz, Barbara Geddes, and Joseph Wright, "Are Coups Good for Democracy?" *Research and Politics* 3, no. 1 (January–March 2016): 4–6.

20. Egyptian Initiative for Personal Rights, *The Weeks of Killing: State Violence, Communal Fighting, and Sectarian Attacks in the Summer of 2013*, June 2014, https://eipr.org/sites/default/files/reports/pdf/weeks_of_killing-en.pdf; and Human Rights Watch, *All According to Plan: The Rab'a Massacre and Mass Killings of Protesters in Egypt*, August 12, 2014, http://www.hrw.org/reports/2014/08/12/all-according-plan-0.

21. Vincent Boudreau, "State Building and Repression in Authoritarian Onset," *Southeast Asian Studies* 39, no. 4 (March 2002): 553.

22. Tilly, "War Making," 181.

23. Sheryl Gay Stolberg, "Shy U.S. Intellectual Created Playbook Used in a Revolution," *New York Times*, February 16, 2011, http://www.nytimes.com/2011/02/17/world/middleeast/17sharp.html.

24. Nixon has used "slow violence" to mean everyday violations such as environmental pollution to constitute a type of violence that society accepts because it is not as visible as a violent event such as a school shooting. Yet over time, slow violence is perhaps deadlier to a society than spectacular events. It can also include limited, everyday levels of repression that physically maim or inflict psychological damage but do not necessarily result in actual or immediate death. Rob Nixon, *Slow Violence and the Environmentalism of the Poor* (Cambridge, MA: Harvard Univ. Press, 2011), 2–3, 6–14.

25. During field research in the spring and summer of 2005, for example, I personally witnessed Kifaya protesters in Egypt beaten and sexually assaulted by security forces or those employed by them. In 2006, a video appeared on YouTube of a taxi driver being sodomized by a broomstick in an Egyptian police station. The purpose of its release was to humiliate the victim.

26. In Egypt, most of the Muslim Brotherhood leaders I had contacts with had spent time in jail.

27. Diane Singerman, *Avenues of Participation* (Princeton, NJ: Princeton Univ. Press, 1996).

28. Asef Bayat, *Life as Politics* (Stanford, CA: Stanford Univ. Press, 2013): 43–64.

29. Mohamed Kamal, interview by Sharon Otterman, "Egypt's Mohamed Kamal: Islamists Should Be Integrated into Egyptian Political Debate," Council on Foreign

Relations, December 1, 2005, https://www.cfr.org/interview/egypts-mohamed-kamal-islamists-should-be-integrated-egyptian-political-debate.

30. This was defensive state violence meant to preserve the existing status quo. The deaths happened in a variety of places around the country, suggesting the haphazard, reactive character of state violence.

31. Joshua Stacher, *Countries at the Crossroads 2011: Egypt* (Washington, DC: Freedom House, 2011), http://www.freedomhouse.org/sites/default/files/inline_images/EgyptFinal.pdf.

32. Field notes, 2005.

33. "This Day in History, 25 May 2005: Mubarak Thugs Sexually Assault Journalist Nawal Ali," *Egypt Independent*, May 25, 2013, http://www.egyptindependent.com/news/day-history-25-may-2005-mubarak-thugs-sexually-assault-journalist-nawal-ali. On torture, see Human Rights Watch, "Egypt's Torture Epidemic," February 25, 2004, https://www.hrw.org/report/2004/02/25/egypts-torture-epidemic. An example of the kind of targeted harassment activists faced can be seen in the case of the late Ahmad Sayf al-Islam. On two occasions in 2004 and 2005, Sayf al-Islam had his house broken into and his computer stolen. He blamed the security forces, while the police chalked it up to random thieves, even though nothing else besides his computer was stolen (Sayf al-Islam, interview by author, February 22, 2005).

34. Ahmed Abdalla, "The Armed Forces and the Democratic Process in Egypt," *Third World Quarterly* 10, no. 4 (October 1988): 1452–66. Also see Robert Springborg, "The President and the Field Marshal: Civil-Military Relations in Egypt Today," *Middle East Report* 147 (July–August 1987): 7.

35. Hinnebusch, *Egyptian Politics*, 120–28.

36. Roger Owen, *The Rise and Fall of Arab Presidents for Life* (Cambridge, MA: Harvard Univ. Press, 2012): 44–48.

37. Hossam Hamalawy, "The General's Budget," *3arabawy* (blog), November 29, 2006, http://www.arabawy.org/2006/11/29/adlys-budget.

38. For Kifaya protests, see El-Mahdi and Marfleet, *Moment of Change*, 87–102; and Holger Albrecht, *Raging against the Machine: Political Opposition under Authoritarianism in Egypt* (Syracuse, NY: Syracuse Univ. Press, 2013), 72–77. For labor protests, see Beinin, "A Workers' Social Movement," 181–201.

39. There is evidence of regime extrajudicial killings when it battled the al-Gama'a al-Islamiyya insurgency in the 1990s. For example, when an al-Gama'a al-Islamiyya spokesperson ('Ala Mohieddin) was shot in the streets of Giza in 1990, the Egyptian Organization for Human Rights stated that it "seriously suspects the possibility" that the assassination occurred "at the hands of the state security forces." See Kim Murphy, "Egypt's No. 2 Official Slain in Cairo Attack," *LA Times*, October 13, 1990, http://articles.latimes.com/1990-10-13/news/mn-1930_1_cairo-attack.

40. Amro Ali, "Saeeds of Revolution: De-Mythologizing Khaled Saeed," *Jadaliyya*, June 5, 2012, http://www.jadaliyya.com/pages/index/5845/saeeds-of-revolution_de-mythologizing-khaled-saeed.

41. Lina Attalah, "Alexandria Policemen Beat Young Man to Death, Says Rights Group," *Egypt Independent*, June 11, 2010, http://www.egyptindependent.com/news/alexandria-policemen-beat-young-man-death-says-rights-group.

42. Kareem Fahim, "Death in Police Encounter Stirs Calls for Change in Egypt," *New York Times*, July 18, 2010, http://www.nytimes.com/2010/07/19/world/middleeast/19abuse.html.

43. Joel Beinin, "Revolution and Repression on the Banks of the Suez Canal," *Jadaliyya*, July 12, 2011, http://www.jadaliyya.com/pages/index/2116/revolution-and-repression-on-the-banks-of-the-suez.

44. Hesham Sallam, Joshua Stacher, and Chris Toensing, "Into Egypt's Uncharted Territory," *Middle East Report Online*, February 1, 2011, http://www.merip.org/mero/mero020111.

45. Jason Brownlee and Joshua Stacher, "Change of Leader, Continuity of System: Nascent Liberalization in Post-Mubarak Egypt," *APSA Comparative Democratization Newsletter* 9, no. 2 (May 2011): 1, 4–9.

46. Roberts, "Revolution That Wasn't."

47. Ellis Goldberg, "Mubarakism without Mubarak: Why Egypt's Military Will Not Embrace Democracy," *Foreign Affairs*, February 11, 2011, http://www.foreignaffairs.com/articles/67416/ellis-goldberg/mubarakism-without-mubarak.

48. Yezid Sayigh, "Egypt's Real 'New' Rulers," Carnegie Middle East Center, July 25, 2013, http://carnegie-mec.org/2013/07/25/egypt-s-real-rulers/ggou. (Originally published in Arabic on *al-Hayat*.)

49. Shana Marshall and Joshua Stacher, "Egypt's Generals and Transnational Capital," *Middle East Report* 262 (Spring 2012): 12–19, http://www.merip.org/mer/mer262/egypts-generals-transnational-capital.

50. Abdel-Fattah Barayez, "More than Money on Their Minds: The Generals and the Economy in Egypt Revisited," *Jadaliyya*, July 2, 2015, http://www.jadaliyya.com/pages/index/22023/more-than-money-on-their-minds_the-generals-and-th.

51. Roberts, "Revolution That Wasn't."

52. Stacher, "Egypt without Mubarak." Also, see Wael Eskandar, "Brothers and Officers: A History of Pacts," *Jadaliyya*, January 25, 2013, http://www.jadaliyya.com/pages/index/9765/brothers-and-officers_a-history-of-pacts.

53. Human Rights Watch, "Egypt: Retry or Free 12,000 after Unfair Military Trials," September 10, 2011, https://www.hrw.org/news/2011/09/10/egypt-retry-or-free-12000-after-unfair-military-trials.

54. Stacher, *Countries at the Crossroads: 2012*.

55. Joshua Stacher, "Brotherly Intentions? Egypt's Muslim Brothers and the Politics of a Debate," *History Compass* 8, no. 4 (March 2010): 345–57.

56. Joshua Stacher, "SCAF and the Muslim Brotherhood," Middle East Institute, April 14, 2013, http://www.mei.edu/content/scaf%C2%A0and%C2%A0the%C2%A0muslim-brotherhood.

57. Reza Sayah, "Pro-democracy Activists Allege Torture by Egyptian Soldiers," CNN, March 18, 2011, http://www.cnn.com/2011/WORLD/meast/03/17/egypt.activists/index.html; and Amin Shahira, "Egyptian General Admits 'Virginity Checks' Conducted on Protesters," CNN, May 31, 2011, http://www.cnn.com/2011/WORLD/meast/05/31/egypt.virginity.tests/index.html.

58. "Egypt Health Ministry: 590 Injured in Tahrir and Balloon Theater Clashes," *Egypt Independent*, June 29, 2011, http://www.egyptindependent.com/health-ministry-590-injured-tahrir-and-balloon-theater-clashes/.

59. Yasmine Fathi, "Protest against Persecution of Copts in Egypt Attacked with Bloody Force," *Ahram Online*, October 9, 2011, http://english.ahram.org.eg/NewsContent/1/64/23714/Egypt/Politics-/Protest-against-persecution-of-Copts-in-Egypt-atta.aspx.

60. "Egypt: The Legacy of Mohammed Mahmoud Street," BBC, November 19, 2012, http://www.bbc.com/news/world-middle-east-20395260.

61. "Details Emerge over Latest Cabinet Attack," *Ahram Online*, December 16, 2011, http://english.ahram.org.eg/NewsContent/1/64/29483/Egypt/Politics-/Details-emerge-over-latest-cabinet-attack.aspx.

62. Mohamed Fadel, "One Dead, Dozens Injured in Fifth Day of Egypt Clashes," CNN, February 6, 2012, https://www.cnn.com/2012/02/06/world/africa/egypt-unrest/index.html.

63. Patrick Werr and Marwa Awad, "Army Imposes Curfew in Cairo District after Clashes," Reuters, May 4, 2012, http://www.reuters.com/article/2012/05/04/us-egypt-protest-idUSBRE8430P520120504.

64. Mohamed Fadel Fahmy and Ian Lee, "Anger Flares in Egypt after 79 Die in Soccer Riot," CNN, February 2, 2012, http://edition.cnn.com/2012/02/02/world/africa/egypt-soccer-deaths.

65. "January Death Toll in Egypt's Port Said Reaches 48," *Ahram Online*, March 16, 2013, http://english.ahram.org.eg/NewsContent/1/64/67005/Egypt/Politics-/January-death-toll-in-Egypts-Port-Said-reaches-.aspx.

66. Abdel-Rahman Hussein, "Egyptian Protesters Claim They Were Tortured by Muslim Brotherhood," *Guardian*, December 12, 2012, http://www.theguardian.com/world/2012/dec/12/egyptian-protesters-tortured-muslim-brotherhood.

67. Ayat Al-Tawy, "Egypt's Islamists under Fire over Shia Mob Killings," *Ahram Online*, June 24, 2013, http://english.ahram.org.eg/News/74821.aspx.

68. Andrea Teti, "The Function of Violence in Egypt," *Open Democracy*, August 22, 2013, http://www.opendemocracy.net/andrea-teti/function-of-violence-in-egypt. Italics in original.

69. Patrick Kingsley, "Killing in Cairo: The Full Story of the Republican Guards Club Shooting," *Guardian*, July 18, 2013, http://www.theguardian.com/world/interactive/2013/jul/18/cairo-republican-guard-shooting-full-story.

70. Stuart Hall, Chas Critcher, Tony Jefferson, John Clarke, and Brian Roberts, *Policing the Crisis* (New York: Holmes and Meier, 1978).

71. Hall et al., *Policing the Crisis*, 29.

72. Sarah Carr, "On Sheep and Infidels," *Mada Masr*, July 8, 2013, https://www.madamasr.com/en/2013/07/08/opinion/u/on-sheep-and-infidels/.

73. Diane Singerman has written about the discursive practices and how they enable popularly supported state violence in Egypt in her work about the state's assault on al-Gama'a al-Islamiyya in Cairo's Imbaba district in 1992. See Diane Singerman, "The Siege of Imbaba, Egypt's Internal 'Other,' and the Criminalization of Politics," in *Cairo Contested: Governance, Urban Space and Global Modernity*, ed. Diane Singerman (Cairo: American Univ. in Cairo Press, 2009), 111–44.

74. Even leading progressives, such as Omar Robert Hamilton, openly asked around the time of the coup, "Is it more democratic to elect a fascist ruler, or to topple one?" Omar Robert Hamilton, "Egypt's Latest Revolutionary Act Was Profoundly Democratic," *Guardian*, July 17, 2013, https://www.theguardian.com/commentisfree/2013/jul/17/egypt-revolutionary-act-democratic.

75. Human Rights Watch, "All According to Plan."

76. "Factbox: 189 Killed in Post-30 June Violence," *Egypt Independent*, July 23, 2013, http://www.egyptindependent.com/factbox-189-killed-post-30-june-violence/.

77. David Kirkpatrick, Peter Baker, and Michael Gordon, "How American Hopes for a Deal in Egypt Were Undercut," *New York Times*, August 17, 2013, http://www.nytimes.com/2013/08/18/world/middleeast/pressure-by-us-failed-to-sway-egypts-leaders.html.

78. Human Rights Watch, "All According to Plan."

79. Human Rights Watch, "All According to Plan."

80. Human Rights Watch, "All According to Plan."

81. Human Rights Watch, "All According to Plan."

82. Sharif Abdel Kouddous, "Lecture on Egyptian Uprising," November 7, 2013, Kent State Univ., video, 8:45–9:03, https://video.kent.edu/media/1_0rg97wd0.

83. "Rabaa Massacre Pictures and Images," Getty Images, http://www.gettyimages.com/photos/rabaa-massacre?excludenudity=true&family=editorial&mediatype=photography&phrase=rabaa%20massacre&sort=mostpopular.

84. "Aerial Footage of Cairo on Fire after Morsi Supporters Are Cleared," streamed live on August 14, 2013, YouTube video, 0.44, https://www.youtube.com/watch?v=22tv1hGuoW0.

85. Human Rights Watch, "All According to Plan."

86. Neil Ketchley and Thoraya El-Rayyes, "On the Breadline in Sisi's Egypt," *Middle East Report Online*, March 29, 2017, http://www.merip.org/mero/mero032917.

87. Heba Habib, "Outraged Egyptians Protest Deal That Gave Islands to Saudi Arabia," *Washington Post*, April 15, 2016, https://www.washingtonpost.com/news/worldviews/wp/2016/04/15/outraged-egyptians-protest-deal-that-gave-islands-to-saudi-arabia.

88. The spokesperson for the Forensic Authority, Hesham Abdel Hamid, claimed that al-Sabbagh was "too thin to withstand birdshot." See "Forensic Authority Spokesperson: Shaimaa al-Sabbagh's Death Defies Science," *Mada Masr*, March 22, 2015, https://madamasr.com/en/2015/03/22/news/u/forensic-authority-spokesperson-shaimaa-al-sabbaghs-death-defies-science/. Also see Omar Said, "The Butterfly Effect of Shaimaa Al-Sabbagh's Murder," *Mada Masr*, March 25, 2015, https://madamasr.com/en/2015/03/25/feature/politics/the-butterfly-effect-of-shaimaa-al-sabbaghs-murder/.

89. Human Rights Watch, "'We Do Unreasonable Things Here': Torture and National Security in al-Sisi's Egypt," September 5, 2017, https://www.hrw.org/report/2017/09/05/we-do-unreasonable-things-here/torture-and-national-security-al-sisis-egypt; and Amira Howeidy, "Matariyya, Egypt's New Theater of Dissent," *Middle East Report Online*, June 4, 2015, http://www.merip.org/mero/mero060415.

90. Vivienne Matthies-Boon, "Shattered Worlds: Political Trauma amongst Young Activists in Post-revolutionary Egypt," *Journal of North African Studies* 224, no. 4 (2017): 620–44; and Vivienne Matthies-Boon and Naomi Head, "Trauma as a Counter-revolutionary Colonization: Narratives from (Post) Revolutionary Egypt," *Journal of International Political Theory* 14, no. 3 (2018): 258–79.

91. Markaz al-Nadim li-l-'Ilaj wa-l-Ta'hil al-Nafsi li-Dahaya al-'Unf wa-l-Ta'dhib, *Hisad al-Qahr fi 'Am 2015*, January 2016, https://drive.google.com/file/d/0B2-QqOchi4gFN004cXBxUjBQSnc/view.

92. "'We Do Unreasonable Things Here,'" September 5, 2017, Human Rights Watch, https://www.hrw.org/report/2017/09/05/we-do-unreasonable-things-here/torture-and-national-security-al-sisis-egypt.

93. Heba Afify, "Families of Men Killed in Arish Say They Are Living with Fear and Injustice," *Mada Masr*, January 27, 2017, https://madamasr.com/en/2017/01/27/feature/politics/families-of-men-killed-in-arish-say-they-are-living-with-fear-and-injustice/.

94. "Egypt: 'Officially You Do Not Exist': Disappeared and Tortured in the Name of Counter-Terrorism," Amnesty International, July 13, 2016, https://www.amnesty.org/download/Documents/MDE1243682016ENGLISH.PDF.

95. "Egypt's President El-Sisi Denies Ordering Massacre in Interview His Government Later Tried to Block," *60 Minutes*, January 6, 2019, https://www.cbsnews.com/news/egypt-president-el-sisi-denies-ordering-massacre-in-interview-his-government-later-tried-to-block-60-minutes-2019-01-06/.

96. Muhammed Basil, "al-Sisi: Hunnak Muzalumwn Dakil al-Sigin . . . Wa Watishamlhum Qararat afwa qadima," *al-Shurouk*, July 24, 2015, https://www.shorouknews.com/news/view.aspx?cdate=24062015&id=bee87bc5-aa69-4c1d-9ec2-52707bb22dd8.

97. Before the January 25, 2011, uprising, Egypt had forty-three prisons. The number is now sixty-two. See "Nineteen New Prisons Built in Egypt since 2011: Rights Group," *al-Masry al-Youm*, September 9, 2016, https://www.egyptindependent.com/nineteen-new-prisons-built-egypt-2011-rights-group/.

98. According to the Arabic Network for Human Rights Information, Egypt houses 106,000 inmates in its prisons. Sixty thousand (or 56 percent) are believed to be political prisoners.

99. "There Is Room for Everyone . . . Egypt's Prisons before and after January 25 Revolution," Arabic Network for Human Rights Information, September 6, 2016, http://anhri.net/?p=173532&lang=en.

100. https://wikithawra.wordpress.com.

101. "Egypt: Serious Abuses in Scorpion Prison; Inmates Isolated, Beaten, Denied Food and Medicine," *Human Rights Watch*, September 28, 2016, https://www.hrw.org/news/2016/09/28/egypt-serious-abuses-scorpion-prison.

102. Sherif Mansour, "In Egypt, 'Freedom' Ends Daily at 6pm for Shawkan and Abdelfattah," *Committee to Protect Journalists* (blog), April 2, 2019, https://cpj.org/blog/2019/04/egypt-shawkan-abdelfattah-release-custody.php?fbclid=IwAR1URkSAYvrWBOpMu07i8EpTP42lwsf4lX5ndtNJKGl4k7-tHqGBBueSSik.

103. Mansour, "In Egypt."

104. "Authorities Prevent Hossam Bahgat from Traveling through Cairo Airport," *Mada Masr*, February 23, 2016, https://madamasr.com/en/2016/02/23/news/u/authorities-prevent-hossam-bahgat-from-traveling-through-cairo-airport/.

105. "Egyptian Rights Activist Gamal Eid Banned from Travelling," *Ahram Online*, February 4, 2016, http://english.ahram.org.eg/NewsContent/1/64/186696/Egypt/Politics-/Egyptian-rights-activist-Gamal-Eid-banned-from-tra.aspx.

106. "Egypt. Travel Ban against Aida Seif El-Dawla, Director of el-Nadeem Center for the Rehabilitation of Victim of Torture and Violence," International Federation for Human Rights, November 24, 2016, https://www.fidh.org/en/issues/human-rights-defenders/egypt-travel-ban-against-aida-seif-el-dawla-director-of-el-nadeem.

107. "554 Cases of Banned Entry, Travel Bans in Egypt since 2011," *Mada Masr*, March 9, 2016, https://madamasr.com/en/2016/03/09/news/u/554-cases-of-banned-entry-travel-bans-in-egypt-since-2011/.

108. "Cases of Departure and Entry Ban and Arrests in Egyptian Airports, Based on Activism in the Public Sphere, since 2011," *Daftar Ahwal* (blog), February 2016, https://daftarahwal.wordpress.com/2016/04/18/ban-departure-arrest-airports-full-report/.

109. "Cases of Departure."

110. Michele Dunne and Amr Hamzawy, "Egypt's Political Exiles: Going Anywhere but Home," Carnegie Endowment for International Peace, March 2019, https://carnegieendowment.org/files/Dunne_Hamzawy_EgyptExiles_final.pdf.

111. "Egypt Crackdown on Civil Society," *Human Rights Watch*, February 18, 2019, https://www.hrw.org/tag/egypt-crackdown-civil-society.

112. Declan Walsh, "Why Was an Italian Graduate Student Tortured and Murdered in Egypt?" *New York Times Magazine*, August 15, 2017, https://www.nytimes.com/2017/08/15/magazine/giulio-regeni-italian-graduate-student-tortured-murdered-egypt.html.

113. Amira Howeidy, interview by author, Cairo, February 23, 2016.

114. In July 2015 al-Sisi's cabinet renamed al-Raba'a al-'Adawiyya Square after Hisham Barakat, who served as prosecutor general and was assassinated on June 29, 2015, by a car bombing as he left his home in Cairo's Heliopolis district. As prosecutor general, Barakat oversaw the imprisonment of many dissidents following the coup. Nearly fifty people have been sentenced to death for his killing.

115. Kareem Fahim and Mayy el-Sheikh, "Memory of a Mass Killing Becomes Another Casualty of Egyptian Protests," *New York Times*, November 13, 2013, http://www.nytimes.com/2013/11/14/world/middleeast/memory-egypt-mass-killing.html.

116. Shawkan, like other prisoners of conscience getting released, is only partially free. In many cases, released prisoners are required to report to their local police station and sign in every night for the coming years. In Shawkan's case, he is expected to report each night for the next five years while he is on probation.

117. Amnesty International, "Egypt: Release Photojournalist Immediately," https://www.amnesty.org/en/get-involved/take-action/egypt-email-release-photojournalist-immediately-shawkan/.

118. "Mass Trials and the Death Penalty in Egypt," Reprieve, https://reprieve.org.uk/update/mass-trials-death-penalty-egypt/.

119. "Egypt Inmates Dread Noose as Executions Rise under Sisi," Agence France-Presse, April 13, 2019, https://www.sowetanlive.co.za/news/africa/2019-04-13-egyp-inmates-dread-noose-as-executions-rise-under-sisi/?fbclid=IwAR3CF6stJZM_5rJcp4Gk3CZ_GO5MAH3bzb0bRExUVf2RpaXdLK9u9jsFcuI.

120. "Egypt Inmates."

121. Death Penalty Database, Cornell Center on the Death Penalty Worldwide, http://www.deathpenaltyworldwide.org/country-search-post.cfm?country=egypt.

122. Associated Press, "Egypt Executes 9 Convicted of Assassinating Top Prosecutor," *New York Times*, February 20, 2019, https://www.nytimes.com/2019/02/20/world/middleeast/egypt-executions-hisham-barakat.html.

123. "Egypt Hangs 15 for Sinai Peninsula Violence," *Al Jazeera*, December 26, 2017, https://www.aljazeera.com/news/2017/12/egypt-hangs-15-sinai-peninsula-violence-171226192804875.html.

124. "Egypt: Investigate Allegations of Disappearance, Torture and Extrajudicial Execution of Four Men," Amnesty International, July 6, 2017, https://www.amnesty.org

/en/latest/news/2017/07/egypt-investigate-allegations-of-disappearance-torture-and-extra judicial-execution-of-four-men/.

125. "Egypt Kills Hundreds of Suspected Militants in Disputed Gun Battles," Reuters, April 5, 2019, https://www.reuters.com/investigates/special-report/egypt-killings/?fbclid=IwAR0dKc8MJMt4GdSldS8vk8c7GhV8vMyXpfPBwixrFA8xi_h--EGZl_Gl30o.

126. "Egypt Kills Hundreds."

127. As an example of these posts, please follow these links: October 10, 2019, https://www.facebook.com/MoiEgy/photos/a.181676241876047/2538108092899505/?type=3&theater; September 29, 2019, https://www.facebook.com/MoiEgy/photos/a.181676241876047/2515810425129272/?type=3&theater.

128. "Egypt Kills Hundreds."

129. Domestic and international human rights groups suspect that extrajudicial killings happened during the Egyptian state's war against the al-Gama'a al-Islamiyya insurgency during the 1990s. Yet, there is not a critical mass of cases. According to its 1995 Egypt Report, Human Rights Watch claims the following:

> Since 1990, security forces have been accused of carrying out summary executions of suspected militants, including Dr. Alaa Mohei al-Din, the spokesperson for the Islamic Group who was shot and killed in Cairo in September 1990 under suspicious circumstances. Beginning in February 1994, a series of operations by security forces generated charges that the Ministry of Interior had embarked upon a policy of "shoot-to-kill" in retaliation for its own heavy losses in the ongoing battle with armed militants. In February alone, two separate raids in Cairo left ten suspected "terrorists" dead. At least three of the victims were summarily executed, according to eyewitnesses. Also in February, six suspected militants were killed in one operation in Upper Egypt; local lawyers claim that three of them were in custody at the time, brought to the scene, and summarily executed.

These incidents over years from the 1990s simply do not reflect the number or scale of extrajudicial killing in today's Egypt. See "Human Rights Watch World Report 1995—Egypt," refworld, January 1, 1995, https://www.refworld.org/docid/467fcab41e.html.

130. For example, in *A Grand Delusion*—one of the definitive works on politics in 1990s Egypt—Eberhard Kienle shares statistics about political violence from the Ibn Khaldun Center as well as the Egyptian Organization for Human Rights. Yet, he does not use "extrajudicial killing" or any other variation of state sanctioned murder without a trial to describe this kind of murder. See Eberhard Kienle, *A Grand Delusion: Democracy and Economic Reform in Egypt* (London: Tauris, 2001): 132–40.

131. Jacob Greene and Allison McManus, "Mysterious Deaths and Disappearances: This is Egypt's U.S.-Backed War on Terror," *The Intercept*, (November 11, 2017, https://theintercept.com/2017/11/11/egypt-war-on-terror-extrajudicial-killings/.

132. “Egypt’s Sinai Question,” International Crisis Group, January 30, 2007, https://www.crisisgroup.org/middle-east-north-africa/north-africa/egypt/egypt-s-sinai-question.

133. “Egypt: Mass Arrests and Torture in Sinai,” *Human Rights Watch* 17, no. 3 (February 2005): 1–48, https://www.hrw.org/sites/default/files/reports/egypt0205.pdf.

134. Mohannad Sabry, *Sinai: Egypt’s Linchpin, Gaza’s Lifeline, and Israel’s Nightmare* (Cairo: American Univ. in Cairo Press, 2015).

135. Ellis Goldberg, “Sinai: War in a Distant Province,” *Jadaliyya*, June 30, 2015, http://www.jadaliyya.com/Details/32327/Sinai-War-in-a-Distant-Province.

136. Hebatalla Taha, “Militarisation and Security Challenges in Egypt,” *Adelphi Series* 55: nos. 543–45 (2015): 177–200.

137. “Egypt Says Troops Have Killed 52 Militants in Sinai,” Associated Press, August 5, 2018, https://www.apnews.com/d86b0b82953a4683b67c6f7ff8feadd7?utm_campaign=SocialFlow&utm_source=Twitter&utm_medium=AP.

138. “Sinai Attack Kills at Least 26 Egyptian Soldiers,” dw.com, July 7, 2017, https://www.dw.com/en/sinai-attack-kills-at-least-26-egyptian-soldiers/a-39604697.

139. Heba Afify and Lina Attalah, “Sinai: States of Fear,” *Mada Masr*, February 28, 2015, https://madamasr.com/en/2015/02/28/news/politics/sinai-states-of-fear/.

140. “‘Sinai Is Our Vietnam’: Horror Stories Egyptian Soldiers Tell from the Front Line,” *Middle East Eye*, January 31, 2019, https://www.middleeasteye.net/news/sinai-our-vietnam-horror-stories-egyptian-soldiers-tell-front-line.

141. “Sinai Residents Accuse State of Extrajudicial Killings,” *Al Jazeera*, January 15, 2017, http://www.aljazeera.com/news/2017/01/sinai-residents-accuse-state-extrajudicial-killings-170115201441920.html.

142. “El-Sisi Denies Ordering Massacre.”

143. David D. Kirkpatrick, “Secret Alliance: Israel Carries Out Airstrikes in Egypt, With Cairo’s OK,” *New York Times*, February 3, 2018, https://www.nytimes.com/2018/02/03/world/middleeast/israel-airstrikes-sinai-egypt.html.

144. Sabry, *Sinai*, 239–42.

145. Afify and Attalah, “Sinai: States of Fear.”

4. An Uprising against Neoliberalism?

1. Hamza Hendawi, “Mubarak’s Son Pledges Economic Reform,” NBC News, December 26, 2010, http://www.nbcnews.com/id/40811426/ns/world_news-mideast_n_africa/t/mubaraks-son-pledges-economic-reform/#.Xd2Bsy2ZNUM.

2. Associated Press, “Egypt’s PM: Economy ‘Worse than Anyone Imagines.’” CTV News, December 11, 2011, https://www.ctvnews.ca/egypt-s-pm-economy-worse-than-anyone-imagines-1.738653.

3. Some researchers, such as Yousef Khalil, have argued neoliberalism caused the Arab uprisings. Some view the spike in prices of food commodities during the 2008

global economic crisis as sparking the uprisings in Tunisia, Egypt, and Yemen. Climate change and a decade-long drought in Syria produced migration to cities that had no jobs. According to another study, state budget cuts produced a deteriorating state education system and led to rising unemployment among the educated and the disappearance of disposable income, as household income was diverted to the increasing costs of private tutoring. See Yousef Khalil, "Neoliberalism and the Failure of the Arab Spring," *New Context*, March 4, 2015, http://thenewcontext.milanoschool.org/neoliberalism-and-the-failure-of-the-arab-spring/; "Let Them Eat Baklava," *Economist*, March 17, 2012, http://www.economist.com/node/21550328; Joshua Hammer, "Is a Lack of Water to Blame for the Conflict in Syria?" *Smithsonian Magazine*, June 2013, http://www.smithsonianmag.com/innovation/is-a-lack-of-water-to-blame-for-the-conflict-in-syria-72513729/?no-ist; and Filipe R. Campante and Davin Chor, "Why Was the Arab World Poised for Revolution? Schooling, Economic Opportunities, and the Arab Spring," *Journal of Economic Perspectives* 26, no. 2 (Spring 2012): 167–88.

4. Angela Joya, "The Egyptian Revolution: Crisis of Neoliberalism and the Potential for Democratic Politics," *Review of African Political Economy* 38, no. 129 (2011): 368.

5. K. V. Nagarajan, "Egypt's Political Economy and the Downfall of the Mubarak Regime," *International Journal of Humanities and Social Science* 3, no. 10 (May 2013): 37.

6. Abdelrahman, *Egypt's Long Revolution*, 4.

7. Timothy Mitchell, "Dreamland: The Neoliberalism of Your Desires," *Middle East Report* 210 (Spring 1999): 28–33, http://www.merip.org/mer/mer210/dreamland-neoliberalism-your-desires.

8. Walter Armbrust, "The Revolution against Neoliberalism," *The Dawn of the Arab Uprisings: End of an Old Order?*, ed. Bassam Haddad, Rosie Bsheer, and Ziad Abu-Rish (London: Pluto Press, 2012), 116.

9. Pete W. Moore, "The Fiscal Politics of Rebellious Grievance in the Arab World: Egypt and Jordan in Comparative Perspective," *Journal of Development Studies* 53, no. 10 (2017): 1634–49.

10. Samer Soliman, *The Autumn of the Dictatorship* (Stanford, CA: Stanford Univ. Press, 2011).

11. Ellen Kay Trimberger, *Revolution from Above* (New Brunswick, NJ: Transaction Books, 1978).

12. Amr Adly (political economist), interview by author, Cairo, February 25, 2016.

13. Ayubi, *Overstating the Arab State*, 448.

14. Amr Adly, *The Economics of Egypt's Rising Authoritarian Order* (Cairo: Carnegie Middle East Center, 2014), 14, https://carnegieendowment.org/files/econ_egypt_authoritarian_order.pdf.

15. Soliman, *Autumn of the Dictatorship*, 172.

16. Soliman, *Autumn of the Dictatorship*, 41–43.

17. Soliman, *Autumn of the Dictatorship*, 49.

18. This data was compiled from the Ministry of Finance reports. The citations are as follows: Arab Republic of Egypt, Ministry of Finance, *Financial Monthly* 12, no. 77 (May 2017): xviii–xix, http://www.mof.gov.eg/MOFGallerySource/English/reports/monthly/2005/dec2005/selectionn2-b.htm (petrol and Suez Canal data from 2002 to 2005); http://www.mof.gov.eg/MOFGallerySource/English/reports/monthly/2005/dec2005/selectionn4-A3.htm (aid data from 2002 to 2005); http://www.mof.gov.eg/MOFGallerySource/English/Reports/monthly/2011/Dec2011/t2.pdf (petrol and Suez Canal data from 2006 to 2011); http://www.mof.gov.eg/MOFGallerySource/English/Reports/monthly/2011/Dec2011/t12-b.pdf (aid data from 2006 to 2011); http://www.mof.gov.eg/MOFGallerySource/English/Reports/monthly/2017/October2017/t2.pdf (petrol and Suez Canal data from 2012 to 2016); http://www.mof.gov.eg/MOFGallerySource/English/Reports/monthly/2017/October2017/t12-b.pdf (aid data from 2012 to 2016).

19. Soliman, *Autumn of the Dictatorship*, 63.

20. Siddiqa, *Military Inc.*

21. Soliman, *Autumn of the Dictatorship*, 71.

22. Soliman, *Autumn of the Dictatorship*, 64.

23. Egyptian daily *al-Dustur* reports that the Interior Ministry's budget increased from LE 7.59 billion in 2004–05 to LE 9.579 billion in 2006–07. The budget for housing meanwhile was LE 4.068 billion in 2006–07, a LE 1.4 billion decrease from 2004–05. Hossam El-Hamalawy, "The General's Budget," *3arabawy* (blog), November 29, 2006, http://www.arabawy.org/2006/11/29/adlys-budget.

24. Aida Seif al-Dawla, "Torture: A State Policy," in *Egypt: Moment of Change*, ed. Rabab El-Mahdi and Philip Marfleet (London: Zed Books, 2009), 128.

25. Soliman, *Autumn of the Dictatorship*, 144.

26. Ayubi, *Overstating the Arab State*, 415–17.

27. See, for example, "Most Improved in Doing Business 2008," World Bank Doing Business, http://www.doingbusiness.org/reforms/top-reformers-2008.

28. Panel with Yusuf Butrus Ghali, Gamal Mubarak, and Muhammad Kamal, NDP Conference, Cairo, September 2005. Butrus Ghali argued that these reforms were classic trickle-down economics, but he refused to say how long it might take for wealth to trickle down. He cited the case of Argentina, where he claimed it took twenty years.

29. Paul Amar, "Why Egypt's Progressives Win," *Jadaliyya*, February 8, 2011, http://www.jadaliyya.com/pages/index/586/why-egypts-progressives-win.

30. Beinin, *Workers and Thieves*, 109.

31. Sallam, "Striking Back," 22–23.

32. Beinin, *Workers and Thieves*, 109.

33. Marshall and Stacher, "Egypt's Generals," 17.

34. Sallam, "Striking Back," 25.

35. "The Role of Workers and Labor Unions in the Egyptian Revolution: Video Interview with Hossam El-Hamalawy (Part 1)," *Jadaliyya*, April 9, 2011, video, 16:02, https://www.jadaliyya.com/Details/23879.

36. Jessica Winegar, "Taking Out the Trash," *Middle East Report* 259 (Fall 2011): 35.

37. David D. Kirkpatrick and Dina Salah Amer, "Egypt's Economy Slows to a Crawl: Revolt Is Tested," *New York Times*, June 9, 2011, http://www.nytimes.com/2011/06/10/world/middleeast/10egypt.html?_r=0.

38. Ashraf Hussein, "Do We Really Have Big Government?" *Mada Masr*, October 10, 2015, https://madamasr.com/en/2015/10/09/opinion/economy/do-we-really-have-big-government/.

39. Anthony Shadid, "Suez Canal Workers Join Broad Strikes in Egypt," *New York Times*, February 17, 2011, http://www.nytimes.com/2011/02/18/world/middleeast/18egypt.html.

40. Hussein, "Big Government?"

41. Central Agency for Public Mobilization and Statistics, *al-Kitab al-Ahsa'i al-Sinawi* (Government of Egypt, September 2019), http://www.capmas.gov.eg/Pages/StaticPages.aspx?page_id=5034.

42. Hussein, "Big Government?"

43. "General Economic and Financial Outlook," Ministry of Finance, http://www.mof.gov.eg/MOFGallerySource/English/Reports/monthly/2015/September2015/e.pdf.

44. The data from the IMF comes from here. Put Egypt in the country category: http://data.imf.org/regular.aspx?key=60991462.

45. "Egypt's Costly Revolution," *Russia Today*, January 25, 2012, https://www.rt.com/business/egypt-revolution-economy-impact-657/.

46. Marshall and Stacher, "Egypt's Generals," 14.

47. "Egypt GDP Growth Rate," Trading Economics, https://tradingeconomics.com/egypt/gdp-growth.

48. "Egypt GDP Growth Rate," Trading Economics, http://www.tradingeconomics.com/egypt/gdp-growth.

49. Data was compiled from the Ministry of Finance reports. The citations are as follows: Arab Republic of Egypt, Ministry of Finance, *Financial Monthly* 12, no. 7 (May 2017), xviii–xix, http://www.mof.gov.eg/MOFGallerySource/English/Reports/monthly/2007/December07/t13.pdf (expenditure breakdown from 2002 to 2008); http://www.mof.gov.eg/MOFGallerySource/English/Reports/monthly/2011/Dec2011/t14.pdf; http://www.mof.gov.eg/MOFGallerySource/English/Reports/monthly/2011/Dec2011/t14c.pdf (expenditure breakdown from 2006–07 to 2011–12); http://www.mof.gov.eg/MOFGallerySource/English/Reports/monthly/2017/October2017/t14.pdf; and http://www.mof.gov.eg/MOFGallerySource/English/Reports/monthly/2017/October2017/t14c.pdf (expenditure breakdown from 2011–12 to 2016–17).

50. Mostafa Ali, "Egypt Teachers Strike for First Time since 1951," *Ahram Online*, September 19, 2011, http://english.ahram.org.eg/NewsContent/1/64/21568/Egypt/Politics-/Egypt-teachers-strike-for-the-first-time-since-.aspx.

51. Beinin, *Workers and Thieves*, 111.

52. Beinin, *Workers and Thieves*, 117.

53. Sallam, "Striking Back," 21.

54. It is worth noting this phrase, "keeping the wheels of production turning," is the same language the Muslim Brotherhood adopted when pushing for the constitutional referendum in December 2012. See Marie Vannetzel, "The Muslim Brotherhood's 'Virtuous Society' and State Developmentalism in Egypt: The Politics of 'Goodness,'" in *Development as a Battlefield*, International Development Policy 8 (Geneva: Graduate Institute Publications, 2017), 220–45.

55. IMF representative, interview by author, Washington, DC, March 20, 2013.

56. Marshall and Stacher, "Egypt's Generals," 12–18.

57. Marshall and Stacher, "Egypt's Generals," 17.

58. Marshall and Stacher, "Egypt's Generals," 18.

59. Shana Marshall, *The Egyptian Armed Forces and the Remaking of an Economic Empire* (Washington, DC: Carnegie Middle East Center, 2015), 9, http://carnegie-mec.org/2015/04/15/egyptian-armed-forces-and-remaking-of-economic-empire.

60. David D. Kirkpatrick, "Military to Lend $1 Billion to Bolster Egypt's Currency," *New York Times*, December 28, 2011, http://www.nytimes.com/2011/12/29/world/africa/hosni-mubarak-heads-back-to-court.html?_r=0.

61. Shehata and Stacher, "Brotherhood Goes to Parliament," 32–39.

62. Samer Shehata and Joshua Stacher, "Boxing in the Brothers," *Middle East Report Online*, August 8, 2007, http://merip.org/mero/mero080807.

63. Brooke, *Winning Hearts and Votes*, 39–41.

64. Stacher, "Egypt without Mubarak."

65. Khayat al-Shatir, interview by author, Cairo, March 24, 2011.

66. Muhammed Habib, interview by author, Cairo, March 23, 2011.

67. Robert Springborg, "Egypt's Cobra and Mongoose," *Foreign Policy*, February 27, 2012, http://foreignpolicy.com/2012/02/27/egypts-cobra-and-mongoose/.

68. Issam al-Haddad (presidential adviser), presentation, Wilson Center, Washington, DC, December 3, 2012.

69. Husayn al-Qazzaz (presidential adviser), presentation, Wilson Center, Washington DC, December 3, 2012.

70. Bessma Momani, "In Egypt, 'Deep State' vs. 'Brotherhoodization,'" Brookings Institution, August 21, 2013, https://www.brookings.edu/opinions/in-egypt-deep-state-vs-brotherhoodization/.

71. Muhammad Tawfiq (Egypt ambassador to the United States), interview by author, Washington, DC, December 2012.

72. Reem Abou-El-Fadl, "Mohamed Morsi Mubarak: The Myth of Egypt's Democratic Transition," *Jadaliyya*, February 11, 2013, http://www.jadaliyya.com/Details/28020/Mohamed-Morsi-Mubarak-The-Myth-of-Egypt%60s-Democratic-Transition

73. Abou-El-Fadl, "Mohamed Morsi Mubarak."

74. Farah Halime, "Reinventing Egypt's Energy Subsidies," *Rebel Economy* (blog), May 21, 2013, http://rebeleconomy.com/tag/egypt-ration-cards/.

75. Yasmine Saleh and Edmund Blair, "Egypt's Shafiq: Islamist Rival Heralds 'Dark Ages,'" *Chicago Tribune*, June 3, 2012, http://articles.chicagotribune.com/2012-06-03/news/sns-rt-egypt-electionshafiq-pix-tvl5e8h35bb-20120603_1_muslim-brotherhood-dark-ages-egyptian-presidential-candidate.

76. According to Sallam, the "deep state," "broadly speaking, refers to a diverse set of longstanding, powerful bureaucratic interests entrenched inside the Egyptian state and inherited from the previous political order, including, but not limited to, military institutions and domestic security agencies. While these various bureaucratic interests do not exhibit any ideological or political cohesion, they are all unified by a commitment to resisting any attempts by outside political forces, particularly elected officials, to undermine the financial and institutional autonomy that these organizations have garnered over the course of decades." See Hesham Sallam, "Morsi Past the Point of No Return," *Jadaliyya*, December 8, 2012, http://www.jadaliyya.com/pages/index/8881/morsi-past-the-point-of-no-return.

77. Al-Qazzaz, presentation.

78. IMF representative, interview.

79. IMF representative, interview.

80. Paul Taylor and Tom Perry, "Egypt Stalls on IMF Terms, No Deal Seen: Diplomats," Reuters, April 14, 2013, http://www.reuters.com/article/us-egypt-imf-idUSBRE93D02P20130414.

81. Associated Press, "Power Outages Add to Egypt's Woes," *National* (UAE), May 29, 2013, https://www.thenational.ae/world/africa/power-outages-add-to-egypt-s-woes-1.305254.

82. Associated Press, "Power Outages."

83. As chapter 1 on protests and incumbency discusses, there is evidence that the generals not only left themselves the possibility to defect to prevent another uncontrolled popular uprising but also actively participated in managing the end of Mursi's presidency.

84. Naguib Sawiris, (@NaguibSawiris), "BBC: 'The number of people protesting today is the largest number in a political event in the history of mankind. Keep impressing . . . Egypt,'" Twitter, June 30, 2013, 5:19 p.m., https://twitter.com/NaguibSawiris/status/351449907774754817?s=20.

85. Gigi Ibrahim, (@Gsquare86), "I think this might be the largest protest in terms of numbers in history and definitely in Egypt ever! #Jun30," Twitter, June 30, 2013, 4:15 p.m., https://twitter.com/Gsquare86/status/351433925807177728.

86. Samih Sayf al-Yazal, interview by Jake Tapper, *The Lead with Jake Tapper,* CNN, July 3, 2013, http://transcripts.cnn.com/TRANSCRIPTS/1307/03/cg.01.html.

87. Hazem Beblawi (Hazim al-Bablawi), "The Rentier State in the Arab World," in *The Arab State,* ed. Giacomo Luciana (London: Routledge, 1990), 85–98.

88. Sara Aggour, "Hazem El-Beblawy: Morsi's Overall Economic Performance Was Weak," *Daily News Egypt,* June 29, 2013, https://dailynewsegypt.com/2013/06/29/hazem-el-beblawy-morsis-overall-economic-performance-was-weak/.

89. Jeremy M. Sharp, "Egypt: Background and U.S. Relations," Congressional Research Service, updated March 12, 2019, https://fas.org/sgp/crs/mideast/RL33003.pdf.

90. The Foreign Assistance Act of 1961 restricts aid to the government of any country whose elected head of government is deposed by a coup or decree. Pub. L. No. 161, Stat. 1844, section 608 (1961), https://legcounsel.house.gov/Comps/Foreign%20Assistance%20Act%20Of%201961.pdf.

91. David D. Kirkpatrick, "Obama Walks a Fine Line with Egyptian President," *New York Times,* December 14, 2012, http://www.nytimes.com/2012/12/15/world/middleeast/obama-walks-a-fine-line-with-egyptian-president.html.

92. "US Urges Egyptian Military Not to Overthrow Morsi," UPI, July 2, 2013, http://www.upi.com/US-urges-Egyptian-military-not-to-overthrow-Morsi/12391372745034/.

93. Kirkpatrick, *Into the Hands,* 225–31.

94. Kirkpatrick, *Into the Hands,* 241–44.

95. Dana Hughes, "The Daily Show Takes on Administration's 'Coup or Not' Semantics," ABC News, July 19, 2013, http://abcnews.go.com/blogs/politics/2013/07/the-daily-show-takes-on-administrations-coup-or-not-semantics/.

96. Mark Landler, "Aid to Egypt Can Keep Flowing, despite Overthrow, White House Decides," *New York Times,* July 25, 2013, http://www.nytimes.com/2013/07/26/world/middleeast/aid-to-egypt-can-keep-flowing-despite-overthrow-white-house-decides.html.

97. Michael R. Gordon and Kareem Fahim, "Kerry Says Egypt's Military Was 'Restoring Democracy' in Ousting Morsi," *New York Times,* August 1, 2013, http://www.nytimes.com/2013/08/02/world/middleeast/egypt-warns-morsi-supporters-to-end-protests.html.

98. The US aid to Egypt did change after the al-Raba'a al-'Adawiyya massacre. They funneled more of the military aid into counterterrorism and border security as well as delayed the delivery of ten apache helicopters, which sat unused at Fort Hood military base for about thirteen months.

99. Reuters, "Arab Aid to Egypt Reaches $12 Billion, after Kuwait Pledges $4 Billion," *Egypt Independent,* July 10, 2013, https://www.egyptindependent.com/arab-aid-egypt-reaches-12-billion-after-kuwait-pledges-4-billion/.

100. Siddiqa, *Military Inc.*

101. "Amid Mass Passing of Laws, Egypt's Parliament Rejects Civil Service Law," *Mada Masr,* January 21, 2016, https://madamasr.com/en/2016/01/21/news/u/amid-mass-passing-of-laws-egypts-parliament-rejects-civil-service-law/.

102. Zeinab Abul-Magd, "Egypt's Coming Revolt of the Poor," *Foreign Policy*, March 31, 2017, http://foreignpolicy.com/2017/03/31/egypts-coming-revolt-of-the-poor/.

103. See chapter 3 for a discussion about state violence.

104. In November 2015, 'Azza al-Hinawi, an anchorwoman for state TV channel al-Qahira, was suspended after she criticized al-Sisi for not holding his appointees accountable. See "State TV Anchor Suspended for Criticizing Sisi," *Mada Masr*, November 11, 2015, https://madamasr.com/en/2015/11/11/news/u/state-tv-anchor-suspended-for-criticizing-sisi/.

105. Kandil, *Soldiers, Spies*.

106. Tom Stevenson, "Sisi's Way," *London Review of Books*, February 19, 2015, http://www.lrb.co.uk/v37/n04/tom-stevenson/sisis-way.

107. Hugh Roberts, "Algeria Is a Republic," *LRB Blog*, March 11, 2019, https://www.lrb.co.uk/blog/2019/march/algeria-is-a-republic; and Amir Mohamed Aziz, "Protesting Politics in Algeria," *Middle East Report Online*, March 26, 2019, https://merip.org/2019/03/protesting-politics-in-algeria/.

108. Marshall, *Egyptian Armed Forces*, 14.

109. Abul-Magd, *Militarizing the Nation*.

110. Barayez, "More than Money."

111. Abdel-Fattah Barayez, "'This Land Is Their Land': Egypt's Military and the Economy," *Jadaliyya*, January 26, 2016, http://www.jadaliyya.com/Details/32898/"This-Land-is-their-Land"-Egypt's-Military-and-the-Economy.

112. Adly, interview.

113. "Despite Big Promises, Egypt's Deficit Is Growing," *Mada Masr*, March 7, 2016, https://madamasr.com/en/2016/03/06/news/economy/despite-big-promises-egypts-deficit-is-growing/.

114. "Egypt Setting Up Police Force to Protect Suez," *World Maritime News*, February 19, 2015, http://worldmaritimenews.com/archives/152760/egypt-setting-up-police-force-to-protect-suez/.

115. "How One Bomb Affects Egypt's Economy," *Rebel Economy* (blog), November 9, 2015, http://rebeleconomy.com/economy/how-one-bomb-affects-egypts-economy/.

116. If reserves, which are closely monitored by Egyptian and international authorities, would drop, it would cause the Egyptian pound to be devalued. A particularly extreme devaluation of the pound would effectively destroy the pension system in Egypt.

117. https://tradingeconomics.com/egypt/foreign-exchange-reserves.

118. Walt Curnow, "Deadly Cairo Train Crash Brings to Surface Anger, Discontent in Egypt," *al-Monitor*, March 4, 2019, https://www.al-monitor.com/pulse/originals/2019/03/egypt-fatal-train-crash-government-negligence.html. In August 2017, President al-Sisi questioned why Egypt should invest in fixing the railways when it could put the money in the bank and earn money from the interest instead. See https://www.youtube.com/watch?time_continue=1&v=ipV-kgTcfrg (video no longer available).

119. Amira Howeidy, "Protests against Utility Prices Go Online," *Ahram Weekly*, April 6, 2016, http://english.ahram.org.eg/NewsContentPrint/1/0/198920/Egypt/0/Protests-against-utility-prices-go-online.aspx.

120. Andrea Teti, Pamela Abbott, and Francesco Cavatorta, *The Arab Uprisings in Egypt, Jordan, and Tunisia: Social, Political, and Economic Transformations* (London: Palgrave Macmillan, 2018): 88.

121. Teti, Abbott, and Cavatorta, *Arab Uprisings*, 91.

122. Reuters, "Egypt's Inflation Rises Again, and Is Expected to Keep Going Up," July 10, 2017, https://www.reuters.com/article/us-egypt-economy-inflation/egypts-inflation-rises-again-and-is-expected-to-keep-going-up-idUSKBN19V1I7.

123. Ketchley and El-Rayyes, "On the Breadline."

124. Ketchley and El-Rayyes, "On the Breadline."

125. Heba Khalil and Brian Dill, "Negotiating Statist Neoliberalism: The Political Economy of Post-revolution Egypt," *Review of African Political Economy* 48, no. 158 (2019): 574–91, https://doi.org/10.1080/03056244.2018.1547187.

Conclusion

1. Teti, Abbott, and Cavatorta, *Arab Uprisings*, chapter 3.

2. Brown, "Egypt's Failed Transition," 45–58.

3. Bruce K. Rutherford, "Egypt's New Authoritarianism under Sisi," *Middle East Journal* 72, no. 2 (Spring 2018): 185.

4. Peter Hessler, "Egypt's Failed Revolution," *New Yorker*, January 2, 2017, https://www.newyorker.com/magazine/2017/01/02/egypts-failed-revolution.

5. Beth Van Schaack, "A Return to Authoritarianism in Egypt," *Just Security*, November 10, 2015, https://www.justsecurity.org/27488/return-authoritarianism-egypt.

6. Trotsky, "Five Days," 131.

7. Ayubi, *Overstating the Arab State*, 447.

8. Egyptian journalist, interview by author, Cairo, February 23, 2016.

9. Human Rights Watch, "'We Do Unreasonable Things Here.'"

10. Lina Attalah, "From Revolution to Powerlifting," *Mada Masr*, February 6, 2018, https://madamasr.com/en/2018/01/30/feature/politics/from-revolution-to-powerlifting/.

11. Pesha Magid, "Tramadol: Where Did the Opiate of the Masses Go?" *Mada Masr*, April 17, 2015, https://madamasr.com/en/2015/04/17/feature/society/tramadol-where-did-the-opiate-of-the-masses-go/.

12. Egyptian activist and organizer, interview by author, Cairo, February 22, 2016.

13. Amy Austin Holmes and Hussein Baoumi, "Egypt's Protests by the Numbers," *Sada*, January 29, 2016, http://carnegieendowment.org/sada/?fa=62627.

14. Mahmud al-Sisi serves in the General Intelligence Services and Mustafa al-Sisi heads the Administrative Censorship Office.

15. "Sisi Tells Egyptians: Don't Listen to Anyone but Me," *Al Jazeera*, February 24, 2016, http://www.aljazeera.com/news/2016/02/sisi-tells-egyptians-don-listen-160224181547015.html.

16. Egyptian activist, interview by author, Cairo, February 22, 2016.

17. Kareem Fahim, "Egyptian Officials on Defensive amid Uproar over Police Brutality Cases," *New York Times*, December 3, 2015, https://www.nytimes.com/2015/12/04/world/middleeast/egypt-police-brutality.html?_r=0.

18. Howeidy, "Matariyya."

19. "Al-Nadeem Defiant in Face of Health Ministry Claims of Illegality," *Mada Masr*, February 25, 2016, https://www.madamasr.com/en/2016/02/25/news/u/al-nadeem-defiant-in-face-of-health-ministry-claims-of-illegality/.

20. Hossam Bahgat, "A Coup Busted?" *Mada Masr*, October 14, 2015, https://www.madamasr.com/en/2015/10/14/feature/politics/a-coup-busted/.

21. Ursula Lindsey, "Cairo: A Museum of Ghosts," *Nation*, March 2, 2016, https://www.thenation.com/article/cairo-a-museum-of-ghosts/.

22. "Culture Minister Attends Conference in Solidarity with Jailed Novelist Ahmed Naji," *Mada Masr*, February 25, 2016, https://www.madamasr.com/en/2016/02/25/news/u/culture-minister-attends-conference-in-solidarity-with-jailed-novelist-ahmed-naji/.

23. Egyptian journalist, interview, February 23, 2016.

24. Egyptian researcher, interview by author, Cairo, February 22, 2016.

25. Egyptian journalist, interview by author, Cairo, February 22, 2016.

26. Egyptian journalist, interview, February 22, 2016.

27. Egyptian journalist, interview, February 22, 2016.

28. Egyptian journalist, interview, February 22, 2016.

29. Egyptian academic, interview by author, Cairo, February 25, 2016.

30. Egyptian academic, interview.

31. Khalil and Dill, "Negotiating Statist Neoliberalism."

32. Ashraf Hussein, "Do We Really Have Big Government?" *Mada Masr*, September 10, 2015, https://www.madamasr.com/en/2015/10/09/opinion/economy/do-we-really-have-big-government/2/.

33. "Amid Mass Passing of Laws, Egypt's Parliament Rejects Civil Service Law," *Mada Masr*, January 21, 2016, https://www.madamasr.com/en/2016/01/21/news/u/amid-mass-passing-of-laws-egypts-parliament-rejects-civil-service-law/.

34. Ministry of Finance, *Financial Monthly Bulletin*, January 2016, xvi, http://www.mof.gov.eg/MOFGallerySource/English/Reports/monthly/2016/January2016/Executive-Summary.pdf.

35. "Egypt's Sisi Raises Minimum Wage to Help Assuage Economic Hardships," Reuters, March 31, 2019, https://www.reuters.com/article/us-egypt-economy-wages-idUSKCN1RB0CE.

36. The state's get out the vote campaign includes billboards that read "Participate. Say your opinion. YES for the constitutional amendments for a better future."

37. Amr Adly, interview by author, Cairo, February 25, 2016.

38. Jano Charbel, "New Wave of Public Sector Labor Strikes from Alexandria to Aswan," *Mada Masr,* March 8, 2016, https://www.madamasr.com/en/2016/03/08/feature/economy/new-wave-of-public-sector-labor-strikes-from-alexandria-to-aswan/.

39. Barayez, "More than Money."

40. Adly, interview.

41. "Prosecution Freezes Assets of *Al-Masry Al-Youm* Co-founder Salah Diab," *Mada Masr,* November 7, 2015, https://www.madamasr.com/en/2015/11/07/news/u/prosecution-freezes-assets-of-al-masry-al-youm-co-founder-salah-diab/.

42. Ketchley and El-Rayyes, "On the Breadline."

43. Mark R. Beissinger, Amaney A. Jamal, and Kevin Mazur, "Explaining Divergent Revolutionary Coalitions: Regime Strategies and the Structuring of Participation in the Tunisian and Egyptian Revolutions," *Comparative Politics* 48, no. 1 (October 2015): 1–24.

44. Jeff Goodwin, *No Other Way Out: States and Revolutionary Moments, 1945–1991* (Cambridge: Cambridge Univ. Press, 2001).

45. Kurt Weyland, "Crafting Counterrevolution: How Reactionaries Learned to Combat Change in 1848," *American Political Science Review* 110, no. 2 (May 2016): 215–31.

46. Andrea Teti, "The Middle East and the Disciplinary (Re)Production of Knowledge," in *Commitment and Complicity in Cultural Theory and Practice,* ed. Begum Ozden Firat, Sarah De Mul, and Sonja van Wichelen (London: Palgrave Macmillan, 2009), 81–101.

47. Timothy Mitchell, "The Middle East in the Past and Future of Social Science," in *The Politics of Knowledge: Area Studies and the Disciplines,* ed. David Szanton (Berkeley: Univ. of California Press, 2004), 103.

48. Ayubi, *Overstating the Arab State,* 449–50.

49. Teti and Gervasio, "Unbearable Lightness of Authoritarianism," 321–22.

50. Teti, Abbott, and Cavatorta, *Arab Uprisings,* 137.

Bibliography

Abdalla, Ahmed. "The Armed Forces and the Democratic Process in Egypt." *Third World Quarterly* 10, no. 4 (October 1988): 1452–66.

Abdelrahman, Maha. *Egypt's Long Revolution: Protest Movements and Uprisings*. London: Routledge, 2015.

———. "'With the Islamists? Sometimes. With the State—Never!': Cooperation between the Left and Islamists in Egypt." *British Journal on Middle Eastern Studies* 36, no. 1 (April 2009): 37–54.

Abou-El-Fadl, Reem. "Mohamed Morsi Mubarak: The Myth of Egypt's Democratic Transition." *Jadaliyya*, February 11, 2013. http://www.jadaliyya.com/Details/28020/Mohamed-Morsi-Mubarak-The-Myth-of-Egypt%60s-Democratic-Transition.

Abul-Magd, Zeinab. "Egypt's Coming Revolt of the Poor." *Foreign Policy*, March 31, 2017. http://foreignpolicy.com/2017/03/31/egypts-coming-revolt-of-the-poor/.

———. *Militarizing the Nation: The Army, Business, and Revolution in Egypt*. New York: Columbia Univ. Press, 2017.

Acemoglu, Daron, and James A. Robinson. *Economic Origins of Dictatorship and Democracy*. Cambridge: Cambridge Univ. Press, 2005.

Adly, Amr. *The Economics of Egypt's Rising Authoritarian Order*. Beirut: Carnegie Middle East Center, 2014. https://carnegieendowment.org/files/econ_egypt_authoritarian_order.pdf

Ahmed, Amel. *Democracy and the Politics of Electoral System Choice: Engineering Electoral Dominance*. Cambridge: Cambridge Univ. Press, 2012.

Albrecht, Holger. "Authoritarian Transformation or Transition from Authoritarianism? Insights on Regime Change in Egypt." In *Arab Spring in Egypt: Revolution and Beyond*, edited by Bahgat Korany and Rabab El-Mahdi, 251–70. Cairo: American Univ. of Cairo Press, 2012.

———. "Does Coup-Proofing Work? Political-Military Relations in Authoritarian Regimes amid the Arab Uprisings." *Mediterranean Politics* 20, no. 1 (2015): 36–54.

———. "How Can Opposition Support Authoritarianism: Lessons from Egypt." *Democratization* 12, no. 3 (2005): 378–97.

———. *Raging against the Machine: Political Opposition under Authoritarianism in Egypt*. Syracuse, NY: Syracuse Univ. Press, 2013.

Albrecht, Holger, and Dorothy Ohl. "Exit, Resistance, Loyalty: Military Behavior during Unrest in Authoritarian Regimes." *Perspectives on Politics* 14, no. 1 (March 2016): 38–52.

Ali, Amro. "Saeeds of Revolution: De-Mythologizing Khaled Saeed." *Jadaliyya*, June 5, 2012. http://www.jadaliyya.com/pages/index/5845/saeeds-of-revolution_de-mythologizing-khaled-saeed.

Allam, Nermin. *Women and the Egyptian Revolution: Engagement and Activism during the 2011 Arab Uprisings*. Cambridge: Cambridge Univ. Press, 2017.

Amar, Paul. "Why Egypt's Progressives Win." *Jadaliyya*, February 8, 2011. http://www.jadaliyya.com/pages/index/586/why-egypts-progressives-win.

Amrani, Issandr El. "Sightings of the Egyptian Deep State." *Middle East Report Online*, January 1, 2012. https://merip.org/2012/01/sightings-of-the-egyptian-deep-state/.

Arendt, Hannah. *On Violence*. New York: Harcourt, 1969.

Armbrust, Walter. "The Revolution against Neoliberalism." In *The Dawn of the Arab Uprisings: End of an Old Order?*, edited by Bassam Haddad, Rosie Bsheer, and Ziad Abu-Rish, 113–24. London: Pluto Press, 2012.

Aspinall, Edward. *Opposing Suharto: Compromise, Resistance, and Regime Change in Indonesia*. Stanford, CA: Stanford Univ. Press, 2005.

Ayubi, Nazih. *Overstating the Arab State: Politics and Society in the Middle East*. London: Tauris, 1995.

Aziz, Mohamed. "Protesting Politics in Algeria." *Middle East Report Online*, March 26, 2019. https://merip.org/2019/03/protesting-politics-in-algeria/.

Barayez, Abdel-Fattah. "More than Money on Their Minds: The Generals and the Economy in Egypt Revisited." *Jadaliyya*, July 2, 2015. http://www.jadaliyya.com/pages/index/22023/more-than-money-on-their-minds_the-generals-and-th.

———. "'This Land Is Their Land': Egypt's Military and the Economy." *Jadaliyya*, January 26, 2016. http://www.jadaliyya.com/Details/32898/"This-Land-is-their-Land"-Egypt's-Military-and-the-Economy.

Bassiouni, M. Cherif. *Chronicles of the Egyptian Revolution and Its Aftermath: 2011–2016*. Cambridge: Cambridge Univ. Press, 2016.

Bayat, Asef. *Life as Politics: How Ordinary People Change the Middle East*. 2nd ed. Stanford, CA: Stanford Univ. Press, 2013.

———. "Revolution without Movement, Movement without Revolution: Comparing Islamic Activism in Iran and Egypt." *Comparative Studies in Society and History* 40, no. 1 (January 1998): 138–69.

———. *Revolution without Revolutionaries: Making Sense of the Arab Spring*. Stanford, CA: Stanford Univ. Press, 2017.

Beblawi, Hazem (Hazim al-Bablawi). "The Rentier State in the Arab World." In *The Arab State*, edited by Giacomo Luciana, 49–62. London: Routledge, 1990.

Beinin, Joel. "Egypt's Workers Rise Up." *Nation*, February 17, 2011. https://www.thenation.com/article/egypts-workers-rise/.

———. "Revolution and Repression on the Banks of the Suez Canal." *Jadaliyya*, July 12, 2011. http://www.jadaliyya.com/pages/index/2116/revolution-and-repression-on-the-banks-of-the-suez.

———. *Workers and Thieves: Labor Movements and Popular Uprisings in Tunisia and Egypt*. Stanford, CA: Stanford Univ. Press, 2015.

———. "A Workers' Social Movement on the Margin of the Global Neoliberal Order, Egypt 2004–2009." In *Social Movements, Mobilization, and Contestation in the Middle East and North Africa*, edited by Joel Beinin and Frédéric Vairel, 181–201. Stanford, CA: Stanford Univ. Press, 2011.

Beinin, Joel, and Hossam El-Hamalawy. "Strikes in Egypt Spread from the Center of Gravity." *Middle East Report Online*, May 9, 2007. http://www.merip.org/mero/mero050907.

Beissinger, Mark R. *Nationalist Mobilization and the Collapse of the Soviet State*. Cambridge Studies in Comparative Politics. Cambridge: Cambridge Univ. Press, 2002.

———. "The Semblance of Democratic Revolution: Coalitions in Ukraine's Orange Revolution." *American Political Science Review* 107, no. 3 (August 2013): 574–92.

———. "Work in Progress: The Urban Advantage in Revolution." https://scholar.princeton.edu/mbeissinger/home.

Beissinger, Mark R., Amaney A. Jamal, and Kevin Mazur. "Explaining Divergent Revolutionary Coalitions: Regime Strategies and the Structuring of Participation in the Tunisian and Egyptian Revolutions." *Comparative Politics* 48, no. 1 (October 2015): 1–24.

Bellin, Eva. "The Robustness of Authoritarianism in the Middle East: Exceptionalism in Comparative Perspective." *Comparative Politics* 36, no. 2 (January 2004): 139–57.

Bernard-Maugiron, Nathalie. "The 2007 Constitutional Amendments in Egypt and Their Implications on the Balance of Power." *Arab Law Quarterly* 22, no. 4 (2008): 397–417.

Blaydes, Lisa. *Elections and Distributive Politics in Mubarak's Egypt*. Cambridge: Cambridge Univ. Press, 2010.

Boix, Carles, and Milan Svolik. "The Foundations of Limited Authoritarian Government: Institutions and Power-Sharing in Dictatorships." *Social Science Research Network*, September 24, 2011. https://papers.ssrn.com/sol3/papers.cfm?abstract_id=1352065.

Boudreau, Vincent. *Resisting Dictatorship: Repression and Protest in Southeast Asia*. Cambridge: Cambridge Univ. Press, 2004.

———. "State Building and Repression in Authoritarian Onset." *Southeast Asian Studies* 39, no. 4 (March 2002): 537–57.

Brooke, Steven. *Winning Hearts and Votes: Social Services and the Islamist Political Advantage*. Ithaca, NY: Cornell Univ. Press, 2019.

Brown, Nathan. "Egypt's Failed Transition." *Journal of Democracy* 24, no. 4 (October 2013): 45–58.

Brownlee, Jason. *Authoritarianism in the Age of Democratization*. Cambridge: Cambridge Univ. Press, 2007.

———. "Egypt's Incomplete Revolution: The Challenge of Post-Mubarak Authoritarianism." *Jadaliyya*, July 5, 2011. http://www.jadaliyya.com/pages/index/2059/egypts-incomplete-revolution_the-challenge-of-post.

———. "Executive Elections in the Arab World: When and How Do They Matter?" *Comparative Political Studies* 44, no. 7 (2011): 807–28.

———. "The Muslim Brothers: Egypt's Most Influential Pressure Group." *History Compass* 8, no. 5 (2010): 419–30.

Brownlee, Jason, Tarek Masoud, and Andrew Reynolds. *The Arab Spring: Pathways of Repression and Reform*. New York: Oxford Univ. Press, 2015.

Brownlee, Jason, and Joshua Stacher. "Change of Leader, Continuity of System: Nascent Liberalization in Post-Mubarak Egypt." *APSA Comparative Democratization Newsletter* 9, no. 2 (May 2011): 1, 4–9.

Bunce, Valerie. "Rethinking Recent Democratization: Lessons from the Postcommunist Experience." *World Politics* 55, no. 2 (January 2003): 167–92.

Bunce, Valerie, and Sharon Wolchik. *Defeating Authoritarian Leaders in Post-communist Countries*. Cambridge: Cambridge Univ. Press, 2011.

Cambanis, Thanassis. *Once Upon a Revolution*. New York: Simon & Schuster, 2015.

Campante, Filipe R., and Davin Chor. "Why Was the Arab World Poised for Revolution? Schooling, Economic Opportunities, and the Arab Spring." *Journal of Economic Perspectives* 26, no. 2 (Spring 2012): 167–88.

Carapico, Sheila. *Political Aid and Arab Activism: Democracy Promotion, Justice, and Representation*. Cambridge: Cambridge Univ. Press, 2013.

Carothers, Thomas. "The End of the Transition Paradigm." *Journal of Democracy* 13, no. 1 (January 2002): 5–21.

Chalcraft, John. "Horizontalism in the Egyptian Revolutionary Process." *Middle East Report* 262 (Spring 2012): 6–11.

Coll, Steve. "Mubarak and the Generals." *New Yorker*, January 28, 2011. https://www.newyorker.com/news/news-desk/mubarak-and-the-generals.

Cook, Steven A. *False Dawn: Protest, Democracy, and Violence in the New Middle East*. Oxford: Oxford Univ. Press, 2017.

Davenport, Christian. "State Repression and Political Order." *Annual Review of Political Science* 10, no. 1 (2007): 1–23.

Derpanopoulos, George, Erica Frantz, Barbara Geddes, and Joseph Wright. "Are Coups Good for Democracy?" *Research and Politics* 3, no. 1 (January–March 2016): 1–7.

Diamond, Larry. "Thinking about Hybrid Regimes." *Journal of Democracy* 13, no. 2 (April 2002): 21–35.

Droz-Vincent, Phillip. "The Military amidst Uprisings and Transitions in the Arab World." In *The New Middle East: Protest and Revolution in the Arab World*, edited by Fawaz Gerges, 180–208. Cambridge: Cambridge Univ. Press, 2014.

Earl, Jennifer. "Tanks, Tear Gas, and Taxes: Toward a Theory of Movement Repression." *Sociological Theory* 21, no. 1 (March 2003): 44–68.

Egyptian Initiative for Personal Rights. *The Weeks of Killing: State Violence, Communal Fighting, and Sectarian Attacks in the Summer of 2013*. Cairo: Egyptian Initiative for Personal Rights, 2014. https://eipr.org/sites/default/files/reports/pdf/weeks_of_killing-en.pdf.

Eskandar, Wael. "Brothers and Officers: A History of Pacts." *Jadaliyya*, January 25, 2013. http://www.jadaliyya.com/pages/index/9765/brothers-and-officers_a-history-of-pacts.

Gandhi, Jennifer. *Political Institutions under Dictatorship*. Cambridge: Cambridge Univ. Press, 2008.

Gandhi, Jennifer, and Ellen Lust-Okar. "Elections under Authoritarianism." *Annual Review of Political Science* 12 (2009): 403–22.

Gandhi, Jennifer, and Adam Przeworski. "Cooperation, Cooptation, and Rebellion under Dictatorship." *Economics and Politics* 18, no. 1 (2006): 1–26.

Ghobashy, Mona El-. "The Dynamics of Egypt's Elections." *Middle East Report Online*, September 29, 2010. http://merip.org/mero/mero092910.

———. "Egypt Looks Ahead to Portentous Year." *Middle East Report Online*, February 2, 2005. http://merip.org/mero/mero020205.

———. "Egypt's Paradoxical Elections." *Middle East Report* 238 (Spring 2006). http://merip.org/mer/mer238/egypts-paradoxical-elections.

———. "Egypt's Summer of Discontent." *Middle East Report Online*, September 18, 2013. http://merip.org/mero/mero091803.

———. "Governments and Oppositions." In *Politics and Society in the Contemporary Middle East*, edited by Michele Penner Angrist, 29–47. Boulder, CO: Lynne Rienner, 2010.

———. "The Liquidation of Egypt's Illiberal Experiment." *Middle East Report Online*, December 29, 2010. http://www.merip.org/mero/mero122910.

———. "The Metamorphosis of the Egyptian Muslim Brothers." *International Journal of Middle East Studies* 37, no. 3 (2005): 373–95.

———. "The Praxis of the Egyptian Revolution." *Middle East Report* 258 (Spring 2011): 2–13.

Goldberg, Ellis. "Mubarakism without Mubarak: Why Egypt's Military Will Not Embrace Democracy." *Foreign Affairs*, February 11, 2011. http://www.foreignaffairs.com/articles/67416/ellis-goldberg/mubarakism-without-mubarak.

———. "Sinai: War in a Distant Province." *Jadaliyya*, June 30, 2015. http://www.jadaliyya.com/Details/32327/Sinai-War-in-a-Distant-Province.

Goldstone, Jack A. *Revolutions: A Very Short Introduction*. New York: Oxford Univ. Press, 2014.

Goodwin, Jeff. *No Other Way Out: States and Revolutionary Moments, 1945–1991*. Cambridge: Cambridge Univ. Press, 2001.

Hall, Stuart, Chas Critcher, Tony Jefferson, John Clarke, and Brian Roberts. *Policing the Crisis: Mugging, the State, and Law and Order*. New York: Holmes and Meier, 1978.

Hammer, Joshua. "Is a Lack of Water to Blame for the Conflict in Syria?" *Smithsonian*, June 2013. http://www.smithsonianmag.com/innovation/is-a-lack-of-water-to-blame-for-the-conflict-in-syria-72513729/?no-ist

Hanieh, Adam. *Lineages of Revolt: Issues of Contemporary Capitalism in the Middle East*. Chicago: Haymarket, 2013.

Hawthorne, Amy, and Andrew Miller. "Worse than Mubarak." *Foreign Policy*, February 27, 2019. https://foreignpolicy.com/2019/02/27/worse-than-mubarak/.

Hellyer, H. A. *A Revolution Undone: Egypt's Road beyond Revolt*. London: Hurst, 2016.

Hessler, Peter. "Egypt's Failed Revolution." *New Yorker*, January 2, 2017. https://www.newyorker.com/magazine/2017/01/02/egypts-failed-revolution.

Hinnebusch, Raymond. *Egyptian Politics under Sadat: The Post-populist Development of an Authoritarian-Modernizing State*. Cambridge: Cambridge Univ. Press, 1985.

Holmes, Amy Austin. "Egyptians Blame Military for Failures of Transition Period." *Ahram Online*, June 28, 2012, http://english.ahram.org.eg/NewsContent/1/64/46401/Egypt/Politics-/Egyptians-blame-military-for-failures-of-transitio.aspx.

Holmes, Amy Austin, and Hussein Baoumi. "Egypt's Protests by the Numbers." *Sada*, January 29, 2016. http://carnegieendowment.org/sada/?fa=62627.

Howeidy, Amira. "Matariyya, Egypt's New Theater of Dissent." *Middle East Report Online*, June 4, 2015. http://www.merip.org/mero/mero060415.

Human Rights Watch. "All According to Plan: The Rab'a Massacre and Mass Killings of Protesters in Egypt," August 12, 2014. http://www.hrw.org/reports/2014/08/12/all-according-plan-0.

———. "Egypt Crackdown on Civil Society," February 18, 2019. https://www.hrw.org/tag/egypt-crackdown-civil-society.

———. "Egypt: Military Power Grab Creates Conditions for Abuse," June 21, 2012. https://www.hrw.org/news/2012/06/21/egypt-military-power-grab-creates-conditions-abuse.

———. "Egypt: Retry or Free 12,000 after Unfair Military Trials," September 10, 2011. https://www.hrw.org/news/2011/09/10/egypt-retry-or-free-12000-after-unfair-military-trials

———. "Egypt's Torture Epidemic," February 25, 2004. https://www.hrw.org/report/2004/02/25/egypts-torture-epidemic.

———. "Egypt: Serious Abuses in Scorpion Prison: Inmates Isolated, Beaten, Denied Food and Medicine," September 28, 2016. https://www.hrw.org/news/2016/09/28/egypt-serious-abuses-scorpion-prison.

———. "'We Do Unreasonable Things Here': Torture and National Security in al-Sisi's Egypt," September 5, 2017. https://www.hrw.org/report/2017/09/05/we-do-unreasonable-things-here/torture-and-national-security-al-sisis-egypt.

Idle, Nadia, and Alex Nunns, eds. *Tweets from Tahrir.* New York: OR Books, 2011.

International Crisis Group. "Reforming Egypt: In Search of a Strategy." *Middle East/North Africa Report* no. 46, October 4, 2005. https://d2071andvip0wj.cloudfront.net/46-reforming-egypt-in-search-of-a-strategy.pdf.

'Issa, Ibrahim. *Ladayya Aqwal Ukhra*. Cairo: Maktabat Madbuli, 2009.

Joya, Angela. "The Egyptian Revolution: Crisis of Neoliberalism and the Potential for Democratic Politics." *Review of African Political Economy* 38, no. 129 (2011): 367–86.

Kandil, Hazem. "The Muslim Brotherhood Failed in Egypt Because It Was Inept, Incompetent and Out of Touch." *The Conversation*, February 27, 2014. http://theconversation.com/the-muslim-brotherhood-failed-in-egypt-because-it-was-inept-incompetent-and-out-of-touch-23738.

———. *Soldiers, Spies, and Statesmen: Egypt's Road to Revolt.* New York: Verso, 2012.

Ketchley, Neil. *Egypt in a Time of Revolution: Contentious Politics and the Arab Spring.* Cambridge: Cambridge Univ. Press, 2017.

Ketchley, Neil, and Thoraya El-Rayyes. "On the Breadline in Sisi's Egypt." *Middle East Report Online*, March 29, 2017. https://merip.org/2017/03/on-the-breadline-in-sisis-egypt.

Khalil, Ashraf. *Liberation Square: Inside the Egyptian Revolution and the Rebirth of a Nation.* New York: St. Martin's, 2012.

Khalil, Heba, and Brian Dill. "Negotiating Statist Neoliberalism: The Political Economy of Post-revolution Egypt." *Review of African Political Economy* 48, no. 158(2019): 574–91. https://doi.org/10.1080/03056244.2018.1547187.

Khalil, Yousef. "Neoliberalism and the Failure of the Arab Spring," *New Context*, March 4, 2015. http://thenewcontext.milanoschool.org/neoliberalism-and-the-failure-of-the-arab-spring/.

Khalili, Laleh. "Thinking about Violence." *International Journal of Middle East Studies* 45, no. 4 (2013): 791–94.

Khalili, Laleh, and Jillian Schwedler, eds. *Policing and Prisons in the Middle East: Formations of Coercion*. London: Hurst, 2010.

Kienle, Eberhard. *A Grand Delusion: Democracy and Economic Reform in Egypt.* London: Tauris, 2000.

Kirkpatrick, David D. *Into the Hands of the Soldiers: Freedom and Chaos in Egypt and the Middle East.* New York: Viking, 2018.

Koehler, Kevin. "Political Militaries in Popular Uprisings: A Comparative Perspective on the Arab Spring." *International Political Science Review* 38, no. 3 (May 2016): 363–77.

Kurzman, Charles. *The Unthinkable Revolution in Iran.* Cambridge, MA: Harvard Univ. Press, 2004.

Levine, Daniel H. "Paradigm Lost: Dependency to Democracy." *World Politics* 40, no. 3 (April 1988): 377–94.

Liddle, William R. "Indonesia's Democratic Opening." *Government and Opposition* 34, no. 1 (January 1999): 94–116.

Lindberg, Staffan I., ed. *Democratization by Elections.* Baltimore: Johns Hopkins Univ. Press, 2009.

———. *Democracy and Elections in Africa.* Baltimore: Johns Hopkins Univ. Press, 2006.

Lindsey, Ursula. "Cairo: A Museum of Ghosts." *Nation,* March 2, 2016. https://www.thenation.com/article/cairo-a-museum-of-ghosts/.

Lust, Ellen. "Competitive Clientelism in the Middle East." *Journal of Democracy* 20, no. 3 (2009): 122–35.

Lust-Okar, Ellen. "Elections under Authoritarianism: Preliminary Lessons from Jordan." *Democratization* 13, no. 3 (2006): 455–70.

———. *Structuring Conflict in the Arab World.* Cambridge: Cambridge Univ. Press, 2005.

Lynch, Marc. *The Arab Uprisings: The Unfinished Revolutions of the New Middle East.* New York: Public Affairs, 2012.

Magaloni, Beatriz. *Voting for Autocracy: Hegemonic Party Survival and Its Demise in Mexico.* Cambridge: Cambridge Univ. Press, 2006.

Mahdi, Rabab El-. "Enough! Egypt's Quest for Democracy." *Comparative Political Studies* 42, no. 8 (2009): 1011–39.

Mahdi, Rabab El-, and Philip Marfleet, eds. *Egypt: The Moment of Change.* London: Zed Books, 2009.

Mahfouz, Asmaa. "Meet Asmaa Mahfouz and the Vlog that Helped Spark the Revolution (Fixed Subs)." Streamed live on February 2, 2011. YouTube video, 4:36. https://www.youtube.com/watch?v=eBg7O48vhLY.

Marshall, Shana. "The Egyptian Armed Forces and the Remaking of an Economic Empire." Carnegie Middle East Center, April 15, 2015. http://carnegie

-mec.org/2015/04/15/egyptian-armed-forces-and-remaking-of-economic-empire.

Marshall, Shana, and Joshua Stacher. "Egypt's Generals and Transnational Capital." *Middle East Report* 262 (Spring 2012): 12–18.

Masoud, Tarek. *Making Islam Count: Religion and Party Politics in the Arab World.* Cambridge: Cambridge Univ. Press, 2013.

Matthies-Boon, Vivienne. "Shattered Worlds: Political Trauma amongst Young Activists in Post-revolutionary Egypt." *Journal of North African Studies* 224, no. 4 (2017): 620–44.

Matthies-Boon, Vivienne, and Naomi Head. "Trauma as a Counter-revolutionary Colonization: Narratives from (Post) Revolutionary Egypt." *Journal of International Political Theory* 14, no. 3 (2018): 258–79.

McFaul, Michael. "The Fourth Wave of Democracy and Dictatorship: Noncooperative Transitions in the Postcommunist World." *World Politics* 54, no. 2 (2002): 212–44.

Mitchell, Timothy. "Dreamland: The Neoliberalism of Your Desires." *Middle East Report* 210 (Spring 1999): 28–33. http://www.merip.org/mer/mer210/dreamland-neoliberalism-your-desires.

———. "The Middle East in the Past and Future of Social Science." In *The Politics of Knowledge: Area Studies and the Disciplines,* edited by David Szanton, 74–118. Berkeley: Univ. of California Press, 2004.

Moore, Pete W. "The Fiscal Politics of Rebellious Grievance in the Arab World: Egypt and Jordan in Comparative Perspective." *Journal of Development Studies* 53, no. 10 (2017): 1634–49.

Nagarajan, K. V. "Egypt's Political Economy and the Downfall of the Mubarak Regime." *International Journal of Humanities and Social Science* 3, no. 10 (May 2013): 22–39.

Neep, Daniel. *Occupying Syria under the French Mandate: Insurgency, Space, and State Formation.* Cambridge: Cambridge Univ. Press, 2014.

Nixon, Rob. *Slow Violence and the Environmentalism of the Poor.* Cambridge, MA: Harvard Univ. Press, 2013.

O'Donnell, Guillermo, Phillippe C. Schmitter, and Laurence Whitehead. Vol. 4 of *Transitions from Authoritarian Rule: Tentative Conclusions about Uncertain Democracies.* Baltimore: Johns Hopkins Univ. Press, 1986.

Omar, Hussein A. H. "The Arab Spring of 1919." *LRB Blog,* April 4, 2019. https://www.lrb.co.uk/blog/2019/april/the-arab-spring-of-1919.

Owen, Roger. *The Rise and Fall of Arab Presidents for Life*. Cambridge, MA: Harvard Univ. Press, 2012.

Posusney, Marsha Pripstein. "Behind the Ballot Box: Electoral Engineering in the Arab World." *Middle East Report* 209 (Winter 1998): 12–15, 42.

———. *Labor and the State in Egypt*. New York: Columbia Univ. Press, 1997.

———. "Multi-party Elections in the Arab World: Institutional Engineering and Oppositional Strategies." *Studies in Comparative International Development* 26, no. 4 (2002): 34–62.

Pratt, Nicola, and Dina Rezk. "Securitizing the Muslim Brotherhood: State Violence and Authoritarianism in Egypt after the Arab Spring." *Security Dialogue* 50, no. 3 (2019): 239–56. https://doi.org/10.1177/0967010619830043.

Qandil, 'Abd al-Halim. *Al-Ayam al-Akhira*. Cairo: Dar al-Thaqafa al-Jadid, 2008.

Qandil, 'Abd al-Halim. *Didd al-Ra'is: Akhtar Hamlat Maqalat didd Hukm al-'A'ila*. Cairo: Dar Mirit, 2005.

Rabbani, Mouin. "Year Three." *Jadaliyya*, December 18, 2012. http://www.jadaliyya.com/pages/index/9092/year-three.

Roberts, Hugh. "The Revolution That Wasn't." *London Review of Books*, September 12, 2013, 3–9. http://www.lrb.co.uk/v35/n17/hugh-roberts/the-revolution-that-wasnt.

Robinson, William I. *Transnational Conflicts: Central America, Social Change, and Globalization*. London: Verso, 2003.

Ron, James. *Frontiers and Ghettos: State Violence in Serbia and Israel*. Berkeley: Univ. of California Press, 2003.

Rutherford, Bruce K. "Egypt's New Authoritarianism under Sisi." *Middle East Journal* 72, no. 2 (Spring 2018): 185–207.

Sadowski, Yahya. "The New Orientalism and the Democracy Debate." *Middle East Report* 183 (July–August 1993): 14–21, 40.

Sabry, Mohannad. *Sinai: Egypt's Linchpin, Gaza's Lifeline, and Israel's Nightmare*. Cairo: American Univ. in Cairo Press, 2015.

Sa'id, Muhammad Al-Sayyid. *Al-Intiqal al-Dimuqrati al-Muhtajaz*. Cairo: Dar Mirit, 2006.

Sallam, Hesham. "Egypt: Transition in the Midst of Revolution." In *Elections and Democratization in the Middle East: The Tenacious Search for Freedom, Justice, and Dignity*, edited by Mahmoud Hamad and Khalil al-Anani, 35–66. London: Palgrave Macmillan, 2014.

———. "Elections in the Midst of Revolution." *Jadaliyya*, November 28, 2011. http://www.jadaliyya.com/Details/24717/Elections-in-the-Midst-of-Revolution.

———. "Morsi Past the Point of No Return." *Jadaliyya*, December 8, 2012. http://www.jadaliyya.com/pages/index/8881/morsi-past-the-point-of-no-return.

———. "Morsy, the Coup and the Revolution: Reading between the Red Lines." *Jadaliyya*, August 15, 2012. http://www.jadaliyya.com/Details/26882.

———. "Post-Elections Egypt: Revolution or Pact?" *Jadaliyya*, February 10, 2012. http://www.jadaliyya.com/pages/index/4314/post-elections-egypt_revolution-or-pact.

———. "Striking Back at Egypt's Workers." *Middle East Report* 259 (Summer 2011): 20–25.

Sallam, Hesham, Joshua Stacher, and Chris Toensing. "Into Egypt's Uncharted Territory." *Middle East Report Online*, February 1, 2011. http://www.merip.org/mero/mero020111.

Schedler, Andreas, ed. *Electoral Authoritarianism: The Dynamics of Unfree Competition*. Boulder, CO: Lynne Rienner, 2006.

———. "Mexico's Victory: The Democratic Revelation." *Journal of Democracy* 11, no. 4 (2000): 5–19.

———. "The Nested Game of Democratization by Elections." *International Political Science Review* 23, no. 1 (2002): 103–22.

Schwedler, Jillian. *Faith in Moderation: Islamist Parties in Jordan and Yemen*. Cambridge: Cambridge Univ. Press, 2007.

Seif al-Dawla, Aida. "Torture: A State Policy." In *Egypt: Moment of Change*, edited by Rabab El-Mahdi and Philip Marfleet, 120–35. London: Zed Books, 2009.

Serrano, Francisco. "Egypt's Sisi Has Established Brutal Authority, but Not a Secure Regime." *World Politics Review*, December 27, 2018. https://www.worldpoliticsreview.com/articles/27072/egypt-s-sisi-has-established-brutal-authority-but-not-a-secure-regime.

Shahata, Dina. 'Awdat al-Siyasiyya: Al-Harakat al-Ihtijajat al-Jadida fi Misr. Cairo: Center for Political and Strategic Studies, 2010.

Shehata, Samer. "After Mubarak, Mubarak?" *Current History* 107, no. 713 (December 2008): 418–24.

———. "Dialogue of the Deaf." *Foreign Policy*, February 8, 2011. http://foreignpolicy.com/2011/02/08/dialogue-of-the-deaf-2/.

———. "Inside an Egyptian Parliamentary Campaign." In *Political Participation in the Middle East*, edited by Ellen Lust-Okar and Saloua Zerhouni, 95–12. Boulder, CO: Lynne Rienner, 2008.

Shehata, Samer, and Joshua Stacher. "Boxing in the Brothers." *Middle East Report Online*, August 8, 2007. http://merip.org/mero/mero080807.

———. "The Brotherhood Goes to Parliament." *Middle East Report* 240 (Fall 2006): 32–39.

Shenker, Jack. *The Egyptians: A Radical Story*. New York: New Press, 2016.

Shorbagy, Manar. "Understanding Kefaya: The New Politics in Egypt." *Arab Studies Quarterly* 29, no. 1 (Winter 2007): 39–60.

Siddiqa, Ayesha. *Military Inc.: Inside Pakistan's Military Economy*. London: Pluto Press, 2007.

Singerman, Diane. *Avenues of Participation: Family, Politics, and Networks in Urban Quarters of Cairo*. Princeton, NJ: Princeton Univ. Press, 1996.

———. "The Siege of Imbaba, Egypt's Internal 'Other,' and the Criminalization of Politics." In *Cairo Contested: Governance, Urban Space, and Global Modernity*, edited by Diane Singerman, 111–44. Cairo: American Univ. in Cairo Press, 2009.

Skocpol, Theda. *States and Social Revolutions: A Comparative Analysis of France, Russia, and China*. Cambridge: Cambridge Univ. Press, 1979.

Soliman, Samer. *The Autumn of the Dictatorship*. Stanford, CA: Stanford Univ. Press, 2011.

Solinger, Dorothy. "Ending One-Party Dominance: Korea, Taiwan, Mexico." *Journal of Democracy* 12, no. 1 (2001): 31–33.

Springborg, Robert. *Egypt*. Cambridge: Polity Press, 2018.

———. "Egypt's Cobra and Mongoose." *Foreign Policy*, February 27, 2012. http://foreignpolicy.com/2012/02/27/egypts-cobra-and-mongoose/.

———. "Game Over: The Chance for Democracy in Egypt Is Lost." *Foreign Policy*, February 2, 2011. http://foreignpolicy.com/2011/02/02/game-over-the-chance-for-democracy-in-egypt-is-lost/.

———. *Mubarak's Egypt: The Fragmentation of the Political Order*. Boulder, CO: Westview, 1989.

———. "The President and the Field Marshal: Civil Military Relations in Egypt Today." *Middle East Report* 147 (July–August 1987): 4–11, 14–16, 42.

Stacher, Joshua. *Adaptable Autocrats: Regime Power in Egypt and Syria*. Stanford, CA: Stanford Univ. Press, 2012.

———. "The Anatomy of Succession: Egypt's Presidential Election." *Review of African Political Economy* 35, no. 116 (2008): 301–14.

———. "Blame the SCAF for Egypt's Problems." *Foreign Policy*, October 11, 2011. http://foreignpolicy.com/2011/10/11/blame-the-scaf-for-egypts-problems/.

———. "Brotherly Intentions? Egypt's Muslim Brothers and the Politics of a Debate." *History Compass* 8, no. 4 (March 2010): 345–57.

———. *Countries at the Crossroads 2011: Egypt.* Washington, DC: Freedom House, 2011. http://www.freedomhouse.org/sites/default/files/inline_images/EgyptFinal.pdf.

———. *Countries at the Crossroads 2012: Egypt.* Washington, DC: Freedom House, 2012. https://freedomhouse.org/sites/default/files/Egypt%20-%20FINAL.pdf.

———. "Damanhour by Hook or by Crook." *Middle East Report* 238 (2006): 26–27.

———. "Egypt without Mubarak." *Middle East Report Online*, April 7, 2011. http://www.merip.org/mero/mero040711.

———. "Establishment Mursi." *Middle East Report* 265 (Winter 2012): 10–11.

———. "Parties Over: The Demise of Egypt's Opposition Parties." *British Journal of Middle Eastern Studies* 31, no. 2 (November 2004): 215–33.

———. "SCAF and the Muslim Brotherhood." Middle East Institute, April 14, 2013. http://www.mei.edu/content/scaf%C2%A0and%C2%A0the%C2%A0muslim-brotherhood.

Stacher, Joshua, and Hesham Sallam. "Egypt's Uprising: Incumbent Ejection and Opposition Politics." Unpublished manuscript, last modified December 10, 2012. Microsoft Word file.

Stepan, Alfred, and Juan J. Linz. "Democratization Theory and the 'Arab Spring.'" *Journal of Democracy* 24, no. 2 (April 2013): 12–30.

Taha, Hebatalla. "Militarisation and Security Challenges in Egypt." *Adelphi Series* 55, nos. 543–45 (2015): 177–200.

Teti, Andrea. "The Function of Violence in Egypt." *Open Democracy*, August 22, 2013. http://www.opendemocracy.net/andrea-teti/function-of-violence-in-egypt.

———. "The Middle East and the Disciplinary (Re)Production of Knowledge." In *Commitment and Complicity in Cultural Theory and Practice*, edited by Begum Ozden Firat, Sarah De Mul, and Sonja van Wichelen, 81–101. London: Palgrave Macmillan, 2009.

Teti, Andrea, Pamela Abbott, and Francesco Cavatorta. *The Arab Uprisings in Egypt, Jordan, and Tunisia: Social, Political, and Economic Transformations.* London: Palgrave Macmillan, 2018.

———. "Beyond Elections: Perceptions of Democracy in Four Arab Countries." *Democratization* 26, no. 4 (2019): 645–65.

Teti, Andrea, and Gennaro Gervasio. "After Mubarak, Before Transition: The Challenges for Egypt's Democratic Opposition." *Interface* 4, no. 1 (May 2012): 102–12.

———. "The Unbearable Lightness of Authoritarianism: Lessons from the Arab Uprisings." *Mediterranean Politics* 16, no. 2 (July 2011): 321–27.

Tilly, Charles. "Does Modernization Breed Revolution?" *Comparative Politics* 5, no. 3 (April 1973): 425–47.

———. *The Politics of Collective Violence*. Cambridge: Cambridge Univ. Press, 2003.

———. "War Making and State Making as Organized Crime." In *Bringing the State Back*, edited by Peter Evans, Dietrich Rueschemeyer, and Theda Skocpol, 167–87. Cambridge: Cambridge Univ. Press, 1985.

Trager, Eric. *Arab Fall: How the Muslim Brotherhood Won and Lost Egypt in 891 Days*. Washington, DC: Georgetown Univ. Press, 2016.

———. "Egypt's Heroic Protesters Bear Responsibility for the Mess That Followed: The Incoherence of Tahrir Square's Activists." *New Republic*, January 6, 2014. https://newrepublic.com/article/116111/square-egypts-protesters-bear-some-blame-mess-followed.

Trimberger, Ellen Kay. *Revolution from Above*. New Brunswick, NJ: Transaction Books, 1978.

Trotsky, Leon. "Five Days." In *The History of the Russian Revolution*. New York: Simon & Schuster, 1936.

Vannetzel, Marie. "The Muslim Brotherhood's 'Virtuous Society' and State Developmentalism in Egypt: The Politics of 'Goodness.'" In *Development as a Battlefield*, 220–45. International Development Policy Series 8. Geneva: Graduate Institute Publications, 2017.

Van Schaack, Beth. "A Return to Authoritarianism in Egypt." *Just Security*, November 10, 2015. https://www.justsecurity.org/27488/return-authoritarianism-egypt/.

Wedeen, Lisa. *Peripheral Visions: Publics, Power, and Performance in Yemen*. Chicago: Univ. of Chicago Press, 2008.

Weyland, Kurt. "Crafting Counterrevolution: How Reactionaries Learned to Combat Change in 1848." *American Political Science Review* 110, no. 2 (May 2016): 215–31.

Winegar, Jessica. "Taking Out the Trash." *Middle East Report* 259 (Summer 2011): 32–35.

Zartman, I. William. "Opposition as Support of the State." In *The Arab State*, edited by Giacomo Luciani, 220–46. Berkeley: Univ. of California Press, 1990.

Ziblatt, Daniel. "Of Course Generalize, But How? Returning to Middle-Range Theory in Comparative Politics." *APSA-CP Symposium* 17, no. 2 (2006): 8–11.

Index

Italic page numbers denote illustrations.

Joshua Stacher is an associate professor of political science at Kent State University. He is the author of *Adaptable Autocrats* as well as other scholarly and popular articles in outlets such as the Middle East Research and Information Project. Stacher also serves on the Middle East Studies Association's Committee for Academic Freedom. He was a fellow at the Wilson Center in 2012–13.